CHICAGO

and Suburbs

1939

WPA
Federal Writers' Project

Chicago Historical Bookworks
831 Main St.
Evanston, IL 60202

Reprinted 1991
by Chicago Historical Bookworks

0 9 8 7 6 5 4 3 2 1

ISBN: 0-924772-17-4

Cover design by Dorothy Kavka
Layout and design by Dan Heise and Rebecca Kavka

Chicago Historical Bookworks
831 Main Street
Evanston, IL 60202

Printed in the United States

Preface

It is a delight to see the Chicago-related sections of the old WPA guide to Illinois back in print. The state-by-state volumes turned out under the Federal Writers' Project during the 1930s depression era were not meant to be definitive histories. Yet their value as descriptive and historical overviews was considerable, and still is.

When originally published the guides were more or less the American Baedekers of their time, albeit without star ratings of hotels and restaurants. One suspects they got a lot of use by high school students in search of term paper material, too, for among their chief virtues were brevity and uncomplicated organization.

Today, we can still view the guides as serious references, rich lodes of trivia and—if we are old enough—as provokers of nostalgic reminiscence. Whatever your own personal interests might be, you may find it hard to put this Chicago book down after you have picked it up.

Taxis cost 20 cents for the first mile, the A Century of Progress was still vividly remembered and a swing version of "The Mikado" with an all-black cast had recently made Chicago theatrical history when the guide was first published. Nelson Algren had just published his first novel, the Palmolive Building's beacon had begun to shine and the Chicagoland Music Festival was held in Soldier Field every year on the third Saturday of August. Times were tough, but there was plenty of excitement, too.

Chicago's heroes are prominent in this book, but so are Al Capone, Sam Insull and Mayor "Big Bill" Thompson. The WPA writers and editors told it like it was. They also included some marvelous photos and mapped walking tours.

This is a history buff's delight, all right. And if reading it makes you weep over some of the things the city has lost, it may also help you better appreciate the wondrous things it has gained.

Paul Gapp,
Chicago

Contents

Introduction

The WPA Federal Writers' Project in the 1930s produced guides for the Illinois cities of Navoo, Rockford, Cairo, Hillsboro, Galena and Princeton, as well as the one for the state.

The WPA guides—now considered historical treasures—recorded time-stop pictures of Illinois and its cities with details of a fascinating time of transition: the end of the Depression. Each was well written, went far beyond the scope of guides and presented the history, culture and individuality of the locale.

Chicago, although not on the list of WPA guides, did not get shortchanged. The one for Chicago and its suburbs for more than 50 years has been buried in the pages of the Illinois guide. Chicago and its suburbs encompass more than one-third of the pages of the 700-page state guide. Perhaps, no better WPA guide book was ever written.

Chicago Historical Bookworks, 52 years later, has set out to re-focus what seemed diffused. Republishing the Chicago section of the Illinois WPA guide as a whole, is an attempt to re-create the city and its suburbs as they existed in 1939.

In reading the guide material on the Chicago area, one discovers a book on Chicago that compares in its reflection with David Lowe's *Lost Chicago*, Hugh Duncan's *Culture and Democracy* and Bessie Louise Pierce's 3-volume *A History of Chicago*.

This guide capsulizes Chicago's culture, history, and special contributions to America's thought and life-style. In so doing, it attempts—as did Lowe, Duncan and Pierce—to distill the meaning of Chicago.

The year 1939 in Chicago—unlike the years 1837, 1848, 1871 and 1893—did not see the city born, explode commercially, burn or celebrate. Rather, it noted the time when Chicago, after a century on the vine, ripened, matured and sweetened.

Chicago's braggadocio and swagger, tempered by the Depression, made way for pride. Having struggled, the city started to reflect and find its future.

In 1914, a quarter of a century earlier, Carl Sandburg had described Chicago as:

"Bareheaded
Shoveling
Wrecking
Planning
Building, breaking, rebuilding
Under the smoke, dust all over her mouth, laughing with white teeth,
Under the terrible burden of destiny laughing as the young man laughs,
Laughing even as an ignorant fighter laughs who has never lost a battle,
Bragging and laughing that under his wrist is the pulse, and under his ribs
the heart of the people,
Laughing."

In the 1930s, Chicago slowed down its building, fighting and laughing — even its bragging.

The city learned that it would not continue to grow ever bigger and stronger, as it had for 100 years, that it could lose a fight and that its destiny was not to stay forever young.

For 100 years, since the 1830s when it was incorporated, Chicago had been called "the world's youngest city" and was continually described as having the attributes of youth. Beginning in the 1930s, writers started to search for new words to describe the city on Lake Michigan.

Somehow, the name "Windy City" and Chicago's image of being boastful were becoming less relevant.

Christopher Morley, in his 1937 book *Old Loopy*, led the way, using images quite different than those of Sandburg to describe a city that he saw as still having spunk and spirit:

"I think she has less hypocrisy, less prudential qualms than some of her Eastern neighbors. She admits more freely the impulses of love, lunacy—even of anger, greed, and fear—which make up life."

Morley wrote of Chicago during those Depression days:

"She is unruly at heart; more than a little goofy; she will be one of the last to be tamed by the slow frost of correctness."

The 1930s had been a dramatic era for Chicago. They had seen Al Capone sent away to prison, Samuel Insull's utility empire crumble, the 1933 and 1934 A Century of Progress Exhibitions work, the mayor

(Anton Cermak) assassinated, the city's teachers paid with worthless script, John Dillinger gunned down on Lincoln Avenue, the Lake Shore Drive bridge dedicated by President Franklin D. Roosevelt and workers at Republic Steel massacred.

The 1930s in Chicago had witnessed the demise of Prohibition and the end of the city's infamous bootlegger era.

More so than all of these events and changes combined, Chicago during this decade experienced the Depression.

The energy that had defined Chicago for 100 years searched in vain for the kind of work that had also made Chicago what it was. The "shoveling, wrecking, planning, building" city of Sandburg's poem stood in a breadline, however.

Chicago, nonetheless, continued to do what it always has been best at: SURVIVE and CREATE.

K.J.H.

Part I

Chicago & Suburbs

CHICAGO

CHICAGO (598 alt., 3,376,438 pop.), vibrant, noisy, every inch alive, is the youngest of the world's great cities, and has the optimism, the exuberant and often rather self-assertive pride of youth. But there is more than youthful swagger—there is a legitimate sense of triumph for achievements in the past, a boundless self-confidence as it faces the future, in the challenging ring of its civic motto, I WILL!

Gargantuan alike in size and rate of growth, the New World's second largest metropolis, the seventh largest on the globe,

Stormy, husky, brawling,
City of the Big Shoulders . . .

it lies at the point where the long finger of Lake Michigan pushes deep into the continent through the North woods and touches the fertile open prairie, the granary and stock farm of the Nation. Of that contact Chicago was born.

Toward the blue waters of the lake, fringed with a green ribbon of parks, Chicago presents its most impressive front. South from Evanston to the Indiana line, in a 25-mile arc, the lake front is lined with many of its finer mansions and apartment hotels; in and around the Loop, rising high above great museums housed in vast marble piles, looms a serrated mass of towers, spires, shafts, and huge cubes, a jagged mountain range of brick, stone, steel, concrete, and glass. To the south, beyond the busy docks along the Calumet River, are great black mills, factories, and furnaces, filled with the roar and rumble of machinery, their gaunt stacks belching black clouds by day, red flames by night.

Behind this façade, for a depth of almost 10 miles, lies not so much a city as a sprawling plexus of industrial towns, local shopping districts, crowded tenement neighborhoods, green and spacious settlements, spread unevenly on 212 square miles of flat and once marshy lowland. By the North and South Branches of the Chicago River, the city is divided into three sections—the North Side, the West Side, and the South Side, each with its own characteristics. Beyond, in

3

an unbroken line of settlement, extend other cities, towns, villages, and subdivisions, with nothing but road signs to indicate where one stops and another begins.

Known to millions as the Windy City, although many American communities excel it in this respect, Chicago remains essentially a prairie town. Like every other, it is laid out in a rigid gridiron pattern, with a few diagonals. Some of its longer streets stretch straight ahead for more than 20 miles, flat gray bands tying horizon to horizon. Prairie-like, too, are the clumps of trees in occasional parks, and the raw scars of erosion in its poorer sections. But there is nothing bucolic in the roar and smoke and quick pace of its activities.

Chicago is the heart of a great arterial system of steel rails, concrete roads, waterways, and airways, radiating in all directions. No railroad line passes through the city. Freight trains are shunted around belt lines connecting the various roads, and passengers shift from one to another of the six stations that border the downtown district. A popular portage in its earliest days, Chicago remains in a sense the world's busiest portage. Only New York with its export trade transacts a larger volume of business than the Midwest Titan, "half-naked, sweating, proud to be Hog Butcher, Tool Maker, Stacker of Wheat, Player with Railroads and Freight Handler to the Nation."

But Chicago is also something more, a city of Protean shapes eluding any single formula, any simple characterization. It has sat for its portrait in more than 400 novels, in many poems and plays, but none has succeeded in catching all of its aspects and moods. Any full-length portrait would have to include State Street, with its glittering shops, and Clark Street, with its flophouses and cheap gin mills— the Stock Yards and the tower built by chewing gum—the Chicago Club and the shrill babel of "Bughouse Square"—Hull House and the bulging arsenals of the Al Capone and rival "mobs," private armies waging private war. On the canvas there would have to be room, too, for the Field Museum and the "World's Greatest Newspaper"—for Samuel Insull's "tallest opera building in the world" and the spectacular collapse of his holding-company empire—for Harriet Monroe, poet and critic of international reputation, and William Hale ("Big Bill, the Builder") Thompson, who for years has carried on a valiant and almost single-handed combat with the ghost of King George III. And no Chicagoan would admit a picture of his city to be complete without the curious horrendous charm of the old

castellated Water Tower, about which buzzes local Bohemia, or without the stately Gothic structures of the University of Chicago.
All of these reflect other basic patterns. Along no street in the world live so many different nationalities and races as along Halsted Street in its long course across the city. There is a German Chicago, and a Polish Chicago, and a Swedish, Italian, Jewish, Lithuanian, Czech, Greek, Negro, Chinese, and New England Puritan Chicago, each within rather sharply defined limits. The bawdy roisterers of James Farrell's *Studs Lonigan* and milady of the "Gold Coast" are equally at home in Chicago.

He who would reduce the city to a common denominator will perhaps approach it closest in economic functionalism, and may find Chicago's slogan of more pertinence than is expected from civic catch-phrases. A city of action, Chicago has been not only a peculiar focus for almost all of the major currents that have swirled across the continent, but also the spring from which not a few of them have welled. The figures of the city's census reports kept pace with the rapid expansion of the country. With the large scale cutting of the nation's forests and the breaking of the prairie, Chicago became the greatest grain and lumber market in the world. The spreading railroad lines of a national network converged here as nowhere else in America. The Great Fire of 1871 pointed warningly to the inflammable condition of a country filled with wooden buildings, the violence and hysteria of the Haymarket affair and the Pullman strike were the strongest expressions of the "riotous" eighties and nineties, and in the periods of mass European immigration, Chicago became the country's largest settlement for many foreign nationalities. The symbolism of the Columbian Exposition sharply revealed the imperialism of the nineties, while the first appearance of the skyscraper, the changing voice of American literature, and the inspiration of American city planning were among the significant prophecies. The scandalous political graft and antidotal reform movements around the turn of the century were indications of wide-spread corruption. The figures of Capone and Insull are, respectively, epitomes of the later period of American gangsterism and speculation.

One fourth of Chicago's heterogeneous population is foreign born. A large number of Jews is included in the three most numerous groups: 149,622 Poles, 111,366 Germans, and the 78,462 Russians. Next in order of size are the groups from Italy, Sweden, Ireland, and Czecho-

Slovakia. There are 233,903 Negroes. Among the smallest groups are the 8,766 French and French-Canadians.

In September 1673, there were seven Frenchmen here, but only for a day—Louis Jolliet, Father Jacques Marquette and five canoe-men—first white men known to have been at the site of Chicago. Returning to Mackinac after exploring the Mississippi as a possible route to the Pacific, they had ascended the Illinois and Des Plaines Rivers, portaged across a short swampy tract in the southwest section of the present city, and paddled down the South Branch and the Chicago River into Lake Michigan. They had failed of their original quest, but they had discovered something quite as important—the Chicago portage, a principal key to the continent—and they immediately appreciated the value of their find. Jolliet envisaged a canal penetrating the heart of the immense expanse of New France, reporting that it would be necessary to dig through only "half a league of prairie," to provide a continuous water route between the Great Lakes and the Mississippi Valley.

Curiously, no Indian settlement appears to have been made here until 1696 when Father Pinet, a Jesuit, established the Mission of the Guardian Angel and came periodically during the next four years to minister to the Miami, recent arrivals. The stream was known to the Indians as the Checagou, signifying anything big, strong, or powerful. But as the river was ever a small and sluggish stream, the "strong" probably referred to the pungent wild garlic that grew in profusion along its banks.

La Salle's ambitious schemes to colonize the Illinois Valley failed; hostile Indians closed the Chicago portage for long periods. When possession of the entire region passed to the British in 1763, there remained in Chicago no permanent marks of the 90 years of French rule. Twenty years later the country became part of the infant American Republic, but actual control was exercised by the British and their redskin allies until they abandoned their posts following Jay's Treaty, signed in 1794. The next year, by the Treaty of Greenville, the Indians ceded, among other territories, "a piece of Land Six Miles Square at the mouth of the Chickago River," recognized by the military authorities as a strategic point from which to command the farther reaches of the Northwest Territory, but no attempt was made to occupy it for almost a decade.

At length, in 1803, Capt. John Whistler, grandfather of the famous painter, arrived with a company of infantry from Detroit to take possession. At the point of a narrow bend in the river, which then curved sharply southward from where the Michigan Avenue bridge now stands, Whistler and his men built log blockhouses, barracks, and stores, enclosed within a strong stockade, and named the fort for Henry Dearborn, veteran of the Revolutionary War, then Secretary of War in Jefferson's Cabinet. Opposite the fort, on the north bank, stood four cabins; three were occupied by Frenchmen with their Indian or half-breed wives; the fourth, a large cabin of squared logs surrounded by numerous outbuildings, stood vacant. It had been erected about 1783 by Jean Baptiste Point Sable, an industrious and cultivated Negro of Santo Domingan origin, who had prospered in trading with the Indians and in outfitting occasional travelers using the portage, but who had suddenly vanished in 1800.

The Sable trading post was taken over in 1804 by John Kinzie, a Scotch-Canadian, the first English civilian settler, who in search of beaver pelts and shaved deerskins energetically extended his field of operation to the north and west. The settlement in the shadow of Fort Dearborn grew slowly until by 1812 it had a dozen or more small cabins sheltering some 40 persons—the Frenchmen and their families, the Kinzies, several farmers, a cattle dealer, and a few discharged soldiers with their families. The War of 1812 aroused uneasy fears in this isolated outpost, especially after the news came that the British and their Indian allies had easily captured Mackinac at the head of the lake in July 1812. General William Hull, commander of the American forces in the Northwest, reported to the Secretary of War that he was ordering the evacuation of Fort Dearborn, "provided it can be effected with a greater prospect of safety than to remain," but this conditional proviso was omitted in the order (not in Hull's handwriting) sent to Capt. Nathan Heald, Whistler's successor at the fort.

Black Partridge, a friendly Potawatomi chief, argued against removal, saying that he had been warned of trouble by "linden birds," but on the morning of August 15, 1812, the fort was evacuated, and the group, numbering approximately 100, started south along the beach on their way to Fort Wayne, led by an experienced scout, Captain William Wells. The nondescript column had not marched two miles when, with a whoop, a large band of Indians in their war paint came swarming down the dunes and fell upon the party, killing more than half—all of the dozen militiamen, twenty-six of the fifty-five regulars,

two women, and most of the children. With the exception of the
Kinzies, to whom the Indians were friendly, all survivors were taken
and held captive until they were freed by ransom or death. The next
day, the Potawatomi set fire to the fort in revenge for the many
indignities the "Long Knives" had inflicted upon them in the past.

Four years elapsed before the fort was rebuilt. Kinzie and a few
other survivors returned and some new settlers arrived. The growth
of the powerful Astor's American Fur Co. monopoly absorbed the
individual traders and led, after lobbying in Congress, to the abolition
of the government trading factory system in 1822. But the rapid decline of the fur trade in the depleted region had already set in. Although an election was held in 1826 to select state and national officers,
Chicago remained a somnolent settlement of squatters, evincing more
vigorous signs of life only when the State Canal Commissioners sur-
veyed and started the sale of a few blocks on both sides of the river as
the terminal site of the projected Illinois-Michigan Canal. The date of
the filing of the survey plat, Aug. 4, 1830, is the first in Chicago's
corporate history. The following year Chicago was designated as the
seat of Cook County.

The enormous mushroom growth of the modern city began in
1833, the year Chicago was incorporated as a town with a population
of less than 200. The surrounding area had been cleared of Indians
by the removal of the tribes following the Black Hawk War, and a
harbor was opened by cutting through the sand-bar from the bend in
the river to the lake. Glowing reports about the potential fruitfulness
of northern Illinois and southern Wisconsin were eagerly received in
the East—by farmers wearied of scratching the stony New England
fields for an existence in competition with the more productive Ohio
lands, discontented workers in the growing factories of New York
and New England, and unsettled immigrants from western Europe
in search of virgin soil on which to build new homes and an entire
new life. The way was clear—the Erie Canal through the Mohawk
pass to Buffalo, schooners and steamboats on the Lakes, and the harbor
at Chicago.

Twenty thousand swept into Chicago from Buffalo in the first
year (1833) of a wave that was years in passing. Many others came
over eastern turnpikes. All but a few went on, in wagons, into the
"plains without end."

Realizing that Chicago's marshy acres rested on economic bedrock, merchants early established the foundations for the vast trade to come. It was an era of wild speculation throughout the land-hungry country, but the fever raged nowhere more vehemently than in Chicago, climaxed in 1836 with the sale of lands along the projected Illinois and Michigan Canal. Harriet Martineau, in her *Society in America,* remarked amazement at finding in Chicago that "wild land on the banks of a canal, not yet even marked out" was selling 'for more than rich and improved lands "in the finest part of the valley of the Mohawk, on the banks of a canal which is already the medium of an almost inestimable amount of traffic."

Incorporated as a city in 1837, Chicago suffered severely in the financial panic and deflation of that year, but on his arrival by steamboat the next summer, Joseph Jefferson, destined to become one of the great actors of his day, found Chicago in a typically buoyant mood: "Off we go ashore and walk through the busy little town, busy even then, people hurrying to and fro, frame buildings going up, board sidewalks going down, new hotels, new churches, new theaters, everything new. Saw and hammer—saw, saw, bang, bang—look out for the drays!—bright and muddy streets—gaudy-colored calicos—blue and red flannels and striped ticking hanging outside the dry-goods stores—bar-rooms—real-estate offices—attorneys-at-law—oceans of them!"

And he might have noted, but for his tender years, gamblers, horse-thieves, holdup men, prostitutes, ruffians, and "rogues of every description, white, black, brown, and red," the usual riffraff of a booming frontier town. To combat sin and discourage even innocent ribaldry, the more pious organized "seasons of prayer," but with no appreciable effect.

It was the payment of eastern money for canal construction and harbor improvement that helped sustain the city until the flow of an agricultural surplus in 1841 from the rapidly developing surrounding region forced Chicago's first rooted growth. From three States in a radius of 250 miles, canvas-covered wagons, laden with wheat—200 a day by 1847—trundled prairie wealth into Chicago. Elevators rose along the river banks, holding grain until the spring arrival of dozens of steamboats and propellors "and an almost endless number of large brigs and schooners" from Buffalo. Half a million bushels in the second year of surplus (1842), 25 times as much a dozen years later, and Chicago became the world's largest grain market. Hogs and cattle were driven through prairie grass to Chicago abattoirs; barreled pork and beef reached markets as far as London.

In 1847 there were more than 450 stores, centering mainly about Lake and Clark Streets. Lumber yards, elevators, shipyards, warehouses, and factories lined the docks of the river jammed with sail and steam craft.

Industry in the main was handmaiden to the extractive economy of the period. Field and forest fed tannery and packing plant, flour and wood-work mill; fabrications of farm machine works and wagon factories helped to cultivate and garner. But a small surplus of manufactured goods produced by the more than 200 concerns began to find an eastern market.

Most of the 16,859 residents of 1847 lived in frame or "balloon" houses, painted white; successful business men built large houses, some of brick, in green squares on the North Side (now the Near North Side). Hotels and taverns housed hordes of travelers and unmarried residents and provided centers for town conviviality.

Social life was a melange of the "humbug and frippery of an eastern city" and backwoods crudities, of New England ideals of education and religion, and frontier ribaldry. Churches were established as soon as congregations could be formed. Including the newly-arrived Irish, German, and Scandinavian groups, who composed more than one-third of the population, there were 20 congregations, all but one in their own buildings and nearly all self-supporting. Methodism had the earliest start, in 1831. Catholics, Baptists, Presbyterians, formed congregations in 1833, followed the next year by Episcopalians, and by Universalists and Unitarians in 1836, Swedenborgians in 1842, and Jews in 1847. Private and semi-private schools preceded the first permanent establishment of free schools in 1841. Rush Medical College, initiated in 1837, soon had a city hospital.

Beginning in 1848, canal and railroad penetrating the fertile farmlands gushed torrents of city-building nourishment into Chicago. The city had quadrupled in size in its seven years of plenty, fed only by the comparatively trickling flow through its prairie roots, the crude wagon trails. The Illinois and Michigan Canal, opened in 1848, tapped the navigation head of the Illinois River 100 miles southwest and connected it with the Chicago River and Lake Michigan. This reversed the flow of grain and pork that had been draining southward to the Gulf of Mexico and thence to the eastern seaboard. Two years later,

New Orleans, "once the emporium and mart of the immense empire of the west" began to decline in commercial rank. By 1860 Chicago's grain receipts were nearly ten times as large as those of New Orleans. Lumber was brought down the lake by a fleet of 500 brigs, and carried into the treeless prairies by canal boat, supplying farms and towns as far as Fort Leavenworth, Kansas. Chicago became the largest lumber market in the world.

Total imports and exports quadrupled in the first year of the canal, which carried an increasing tonnage until the early eighties. But when rail replaced trail and striped the country with bands of steel, Chicago's growth rocketed to dizzy heights. A stub running a few miles to the west in 1848, then the lines of the Illinois Central and the Rock Island, and the Michigan Southern from the east in 1852, were the first of the strands that were soon tied into a knot that gripped the Middle West to Chicago.

Lake Michigan, in its dual rôle as barrier and carrier, strengthened the hold. Interposing its 307 miles of deep water between East and West, like a huge lens, it focused to a point the railroad lines between the entire Northwest and the East. Chicago became the greatest railroad center in the world. For many years interchange of cargo between waterway and railway boomed both forms of transportation. In 1869 the 13,730 arrivals at the Chicago Harbor exceeded the combined number of vessels entered at the ports of New York, Philadelphia, Baltimore, Charleston, Mobile, and San Francisco.

Local merchants had vigorously opposed the building of railroads in Chicago, arguing that trade would be ruined if farmers did not drive their produce into town and there fill up their wagons with supplies to carry home; they soon saw the transformation of their city into a vast wholesale mart, supplying entire towns and cities. Chicago's population increased six-fold between 1840 and 1850, rising from 4,470 to more than 28,000, and during the next decade vaulted to almost 100,000.

By 1856 the city embraced 18 square miles, and was trying desperately to pull itself out of the mud. Its streets had been little better than swamps—beloved by hogs, dogs, and small boys, but a terror to horses and pedestrians—and a serious menace to health, for the slops of the city were poured into these "noisome quagmires." A few streets had been paved with planking as early as 1849, and five years later the city had 27 miles of such pavement. It represented a considerable improvement, but was not without its disadvantages: laid on marshy ground only a few feet above the water level of the river, the planks rotted quickly and snapped under the weight of straining horses, or even pedestrians, and the loose ends flew up to deliver them a stunning slap in the face. Sand and then cobblestones were laid, but were immediately swallowed by the ubiquitous mud. At last, with heroic resolve, Chicago decided to raise the level of its streets 12 feet, a herculean task undertaken in 1855. Sand was dredged from the river, which accomplished the double purpose of deepening the channel and providing fill not only for the streets but for 1,200 acres of low ground between them. The new streets were huge ramps that ran level with second-story windows until people either jacked up their houses or converted their original ground floors into cellars. For years the sidewalks climbed and dipped like roller coasters. In 1859 a mile of track for horse cars was laid on State Street, which soon replaced Lake Street as the business center. A few four-story brick buildings began to replace flimsy wooden structures in the downtown section, but the Chicago of 1860 was described in its day as "one of the shabbiest and most unattractive of cities . . . . Half the town was in process of elevation above the tadpole level and a considerable part on wheels —a moving house being about the only wheeled vehicle that could get around with any comfort to the passengers."

Part of its shabbiness could be attributed to the depression that followed the panic of 1857, which struck the city a staggering blow. One-tenth of its 1,350 business establishments closed their doors; many thousands were thrown out of work to face starvation. In the midst of this distress Chicago built the Wigwam, a huge wooden shed, to accommodate the Republican National Convention, at which Lincoln was nominated for the presidency. Then came the Civil War to provide such stimulation of business as the always slightly feverish city had never known. To feed great armies in the field, farmers broke new ground and grain shipments from Chicago more than doubled in two years, rising to 65,400,000 bushels in 1862. In 1864 the mile-square Union Stock Yards were built. The McCormick and other factories were humming in their effort to satisfy the apparently insatiable demand for reapers, steel plows, agricultural implements of all kinds, harness, wagons, and a miscellany of wood and metal products.

In 1864 George Pullman built his first sleeping car, *The Pioneer*, marking the birth of another great local industry. Business transacted through the banks swelled to such a volume that the Chicago Clearing House was established in 1865. By 1870 Chicago's population numbered some 300,000, a three-fold increase within a decade. It had now outstripped Cincinnati, an old rival, and was hot on the heels of St. Louis, with whoops of joy and taunts of derision, which were repaid in kind. Chicago had to reach greedily for trade in all directions in order "to support its fast horses, faster men, falling houses, and fallen women," was the acid comment.

Times were indeed lush at the tip of the lake. Typical of the almost Hollywoodian order of things in that period was the case of the bankrupt backwoods tailor who came to Chicago, sold trousers for a few years, and built one of the largest and most celebrated hostelries of its day. Race tracks, gambling saloons, and bawdy houses multiplied. Lavish "marble" mansions went up along Michigan Avenue to 12th Street. Theaters, hotels, shops, and business buildings crowded into what is now the Loop. Coal yards, warehouses, flour mills, factories, foundries, and distilleries lined the river banks and the lake front. Scattered through the city were 170 churches—25 Catholic, 21 Methodist, 19 Presbyterian, and 5 Jewish, a partial reflection of the fact that half the Chicagoans of that day were foreign-born.

In 1867, after years of violent protest that the entire community was being poisoned by "filthy slush, miscalled water . . . a nauseous chowder" of fish and filth, which was taken from the lake into which the city poured its sewage, a sanitary water system was installed and immediately reduced the appallingly high death rate. The flow of "Garlic Creek" was reversed in 1871, and some of its foul waters were carried down the Illinois into the Mississippi, but not in sufficient quantity, so that sewage continued to pour into the river and the lake, to be thrown back at Chicago by the winds and waves.

Public high schools and evening schools, industrial and professional schools, including one of the first art schools in the country, two colleges, three theological seminaries, the Chicago Historical Society, and the Academy of Sciences were established in this period. In 1869 a ring of unimproved parks with boulevard connections surrounded the "Garden City." Beyond, in suburban subdivisions, carpenters were hammering out miles of houses that were to be swallowed in the city's growth within two decades. "More astonishing than the wildest vision of the most vagrant imagination!" visitors exclaimed, and Chicagoans agreed, although they felt that a more accurate index of the city's superiority over all others was provided when the White Stockings, its professional baseball team, defeated the Memphis nine, 157 to 1.

But, born in the haste to put wall and roof around home and business as quickly and cheaply as possible, a large part of the city's construction ran to "shams and shingles." Of the estimated 40,000 Chicago buildings in 1868, more than seven-eights were wooden. In 1871 the total increased 50 per cent, and while the 40 new stone buildings on State Street and many brick and iron-front structures elsewhere were promising improvements, solid blocks knew nothing but flimsy pine.

After months of severe drought a fire of unknown origin started in such a block, in a cow barn behind the cottage of Patrick O'Leary on DeKoven Street, Sunday night, October 8th, 1871. It soon spread beyond the control of the firemen, who were wearied by fighting and celebrating the defeat of a blaze that burned four blocks the previous day. A powerful wind swept flames to the north and northeast and hurled brands in advance of the roaring columns of fire, which destroyed the notorious "Conley's Patch" and practically everything north of Van Buren Street in the areas now designated as the Downtown District and the Near North Side. So intense were the flames that hot blasts were felt in Holland, Michigan, 100 miles across the lake. Tapering to a point near the lake at Fullerton Avenue, the boundary with the then suburban Lake View, the fire stopped after consuming 17,450 buildings in 27 hours. At least 250 persons perished. Homes of one-third the population, about 1,600 stores, 60 manufacturing establishments and 28 hotels, railroad structures, government and other public buildings, and bridges became three and one-third square miles of ashes and debris. Thousands were penniless, stripped of their last possession.

The embers were scarcely cool before rebuilding began. Generous contributions of money and supplies came from the entire country and from Europe. Thousands of temporary structures provided for immediate needs while more than 100,000 artisans were reconstructing the city under stricter construction codes, although the latter were frequently violated. Extensions of credit and payment of about half of the $88,634,022 insurance on the $192,000,000 loss helped rebuild the business district within a year. In another two, scarcely a scar of the fire remained anywhere. Many buildings, particularly hotels and depots, were replaced by far costlier structures. Fashion took over Michigan Avenue south of 12th Street, and Prairie Avenue, and brought in granite and brownstone. Chicago dumped its debris within the lake breakwater, forming subsoil for a future park, and went about its increasing business. Local manufactures doubled between 1870 and 1873; Chicago banks, alone of those in the larger cities, continued steadily to pay out current funds during the acute financial panic of 1873.

The germ of American industrialism found the Chicago of the middle seventies an ideal medium. A circle of 500 miles contained the principal ingredients. Around western Lake Superior lay one-fifth of the world's richest iron-ore reserve, yielding at the slightest scratch, easily loaded on lake 'freighters after a short land haul, and carried away by the most economical form of transportation on the continent. In Illinois, Indiana, Kentucky, West Virginia, and Pennsylvania, Chicago's railroads clutched at a trillion tons of coal. Blast furnaces and large factories forged tremendous wealth that filled Prairie Avenue and spread into Lake Shore Drive.

Nationwide labor unrest, following the wave of western settlement that had "broken against the arid plains" became particularly acute here. The line between wealth and poverty, cutting sharply into a single generation of workmen with rapidity unequalled elsewhere, drew Chicago into the forefront of "radical" cities. In 1877, led by Albert R. Parsons, workers in the factories and on the railroads struck for increased wages and the 8-hour day. Federal troops broke the strike, but without removing the causes of discontent. Industrial warfare over wages and hours grew increasingly bitter and culminated in the Haymarket bombing of 1886. Although no adequate evidence was produced that they had thrown the bomb, Parsons and three other labor leaders were hanged for the crime. Two others escaped death by having their sentences commuted to life imprisonment, and a third received a sentence of 15 years in prison. These three were pardoned seven years later by Governor John P. Altgeld, ". . . eagle 'forgotten" in Vachel Lindsay's phrase, who denounced the trials as unfair and illegal and was himself denounced as little better than a criminal for daring to doubt highly questionable evidence. Again large strikes broke out in the depression years that followed 1893, notably that which began in the local Pullman shops and spread to the railroads; once more Federal troops broke the strike.

Meantime, as one result of the Haymarket tragedy, the Civic Federation was founded by Lyman C. Gage, a banker, to provide free and open discussion of controversial questions. In 1889 Jane Addams opened Hull House in the worst slum district on the West Side. By 1890 Chicago had more than 1,000,000 people, having added 200,000 the previous year by the annexation of several surrounding municipalities. The Newberry Library, and The Public Library, had been founded, and in 1892 the University of Chicago began with the most auspicious program in university history. Theodore Thomas had organized the Chicago Orchestral Association and had long been presenting the popular concert series that brought the city renown as a musical center. W. L. B. Jenny, Daniel H. Burnham, John W. Root, William Holabird, and other architects were constructing huge new buildings on steel frames and evolving a new architectural form. In Maitland's *Dictionary of American Slang*, published in 1891, the new term "skyscraper" was defined as "a very tall building such as are now being built in Chicago."

Commerce, manufacture, labor, and these new cultural developments united to bring the city one of its great triumphs, the World's Columbian Exposition of 1893, in celebration of the 400th anniversary of the discovery of America. Jackson Park was developed out of swamp land on the South Side and here were built the great white buildings of the Fair in accordance with a master plan drawn by Daniel H. Burnham. The "White City," as it was soon known on five continents, was hailed as the miracle of the day, the "miniature of an ideal city . . . built as a unit on a single architectural plan . . . a symbol of regeneration." Millions crowded into the Fair to stare at and be equally impressed with "the most beautiful building since the Parthenon," a knight on horseback made of California prunes, cannons by Krupp, the Tower of Light, and the Parliament of Religions—the whole providing "matter of study to fill 100 years."

Remembrance of the genuine triumph of the Fair helped buoy up the spirit of Chicago during the hungry winters that followed, when thousands of unemployed walked the streets, hungry and homeless. The city joined the farmers of the Midwest in the Populist campaign against monopolies and the high finance of Wall Street, cheering William Jennings Bryan to the echo when he delivered his "Cross of Gold" speech here during the Democratic National Convention of 1896. George E. Cole organized the Municipal Voters League and launched a frontal attack on the brazen corruption in the City Hall, on the organized vice and violence in the almost ducal kingdoms ruled

LOOP NIGHT SCENE

CERES OVER LA SALLE STREET

OUTER DRIVE BRIDGE

GOLD COAST

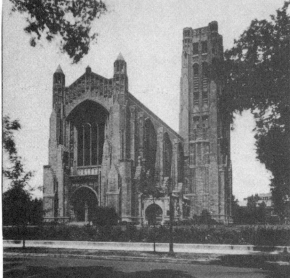

JOHN D. ROCKEFELLE

MEMORIAL CHAPE

UNIVERSITY OF CHICAG

SHEDD AQUARIUM

THE MUSEUM

OF SCIENCE

AND INDUSTRY

ART INSTITUTE

OF CHICAGO

STANLEY FIELD HALL

CHICAGO NATURAL

HISTORY MUSEUM

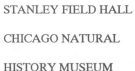

ADLER

PLANETARIUM

MERCHANDISE MART

DAILY NEWS BUILDING

PALMOLIVE BUILDING

WRIGLEY BUILDING

MEDINAH CLUB

TRIBUNE TOWER

MICHIGAN AVENUE IN THE NINETIES

VIEW OF MODERN MICHIGAN AVENUE

by such potentates as "Bath House John" Coughlin and "Hinky Dink" Kenna, and on the local traction king, "Yerkes the Boodler." A determined and finally successful effort was made to solve, once and for all, the distressing sewage problem; in 1900 the Sanitary and Ship Canal was opened, a wide channel some 28 miles long, and 20 feet deep. The Drainage Canal, as popularly known, served a triple purpose; it entirely reversed the polluting flow of the Chicago River, served as a link on the Lakes-to-Gulf Waterway, and by a generating plant built at Lockport, provided electricity to light the city's streets and parks.

By 1900, Chicago, which already had more Scandinavians and Dutch than any other city in the United States, became the Nation's largest Polish, Lithuanian, Bohemian, Croatian, and Greek settlement.

After a long battle the first Juvenile Court in the country was established, and it was soon adopted as a model by other cities. New parks and playgrounds were laid out to bring breathing space into crowded tenement areas. A comprehensive plan for the physical and cultural development of the city was drawn up by Daniel H. Burnham and presented to the city by the Commercial Club. Although much of it was characterized by what Lewis Mumford later called "municipal cosmetic," it was accepted by the city, and the Chicago Plan Commission, an advisory body formed in 1909, has used it with important modifications, to guide civic improvements since that time. Streets were widened and bridges were built to facilitate movement in the city, which had been growing at a rate of more than 500,000 each decade since 1880.

The World War found Chicago somewhat divided in counsel, for Mayor William Hale Thompson was vigorously opposed to American intervention. When the die was finally cast, however, Chicago contributed more than her quota to the armies in the field. The war greatly stimulated production in almost all local plants, particularly in the food-processing and metal industries, and incidentally created a grave new problem. Thousands of workers were drawn from the factories to the military training camps, and with immigration from Europe cut off, 65,000 Negroes poured in from the South to fill the demand for labor. Sporadic clashes occurred as the newcomers rapidly filled up the constricted Negro areas and spilled over into neighborhoods in which they "did not belong." In July 1919, an incident on a South Side beach precipitated five days of rioting which took a death toll of 22 Negroes and 16 whites; more than 500 persons were more or less seriously injured. A voluminous study of the psychological, social, and economic causes of the outbreak was made, but no effective steps were taken to improve conditions, which grew more acute as Negroes continued to move into the already overcrowded Black Belt.

During the fantastic 1920's Chicago boomed as never before. By 1930 it had passed the 3,000,000 mark in population, and it was manufacturing or processing $4,000,000,000 of goods a year—meat and meat products, books and printed matter of all kinds, machinery, clothing, and steel leading among thousands of products. Within three years it expended $1,000,000,000 on new buildings, erecting more than 90 miles of them in one year. Field Museum, a massive marble pile, and the great oval of Soldier Field took form in Grant Park, extended and improved as "Chicago's front yard." On the fringes of the city the chain of forest preserves expanded to approximately 30,000 acres of recreational areas. Downtown streets became deep canyons with sheer limestone walls as skyscrapers, one more aspiring than the other, shot up toward the heavens. The financial structures of the buildings and other enterprises soared to even dizzier heights, reaching an apogee in the huge inverted pyramid of public utility holdings assembled by Samuel Insull.

But with the lavish abandon of a booming frontier touched with a kind of Continental *laissez faire*, Chicagoans on the whole cared not about the financial soundness of these structures, nor about how the city was run. The traction muddle, the wasteful multiplicity of governmental units, the archaic taxing system—for each of these and other pressing problems solutions were offered, but were turned down by the electorate.

The chauvinistic clowning of Mayor William Hale Thompson (1915-23 and 1927-31) was climaxed by the emergence of the "wide open town." The enormous trade in alcohol and beer, gambling and prostitution, and the various "rackets" preying on legitimate businesses moved smoothly; the conviction of a gangster was extremely rare. The blazing sub-machine guns and sawed-off shotguns that were heard around the world were employed by rival gangs in the battle for control of the business whose sales ran into scores of millions annually. Of the several combines resulting from this warfare, Alphonse Capone's was the largest.

Although its effects were not immediately apparent, the knell of this gawdy period sounded with the stock market crash of 1929.

Prices of commodities in which Chicago had a vital interest tumbled disastrously; the Insull utilities empire and other elaborate financial edifices collapsed with a roar, while the "underground" empire shriveled to a remnant after the removal of Capone for income tax evasion, and later, the repeal of the eighteenth amendment. Unemployment spread in ever widening circles; teachers and other city employees endured long periods of payless pay days.

In the midst of the world-wide depression, Chicago courageously proceeded with plans for A Century of Progress Exposition, which opened in 1933 in a striking group of modern, plainly geometrical structures erected in newly-made Burnham Park and Northerly Island. Its central theme was applied science, and its exposition at the fair was guided by data furnished by the National Research Council. Hard times accounted in large part for the fact that the exposition was a financial disappointment in its first year, but Sally Rand and her fan dancers accomplished what applied science had failed to do, and the exposition closed in 1934 with a net profit, which was donated to participating cultural institutions, excluding Sally Rand.

Although its mood was somewhat sobered by the depression, Chicago still retains the tremendous vital energy that enabled it to grow from an isolated frontier post to a giant metropolis within a century. In its boisterous youth it was not inclined to stop for self-appraisal, but now, more mature, it is beginning to turn a critical eye upon itself and its problems. In the Midwest Titan's I WILL! is the assurance that these problems, too, will be solved, as those in the past.

The Loop and Vicinity

The Loop, the crowded rectangle between Wabash Avenue and Lake, Wells, and Van Buren Streets, is bound round with a steel band of elevated tracks, upon which converge trains from all parts of Chicago. The commercial center of the city since the beginning, it received its name in 1897 when the elevated lines were linked and routed to "loop" the district. At the present time the term is used loosely to designate the bustling commercial section that lies around as well as within the steel frame of tracks.

The cluster of towers at the Loop is the expression of Chicago as Big Town, with all the attributes of Big Town: the roar of traffic, on the street and overhead; sidewalks crowded with restless throngs;

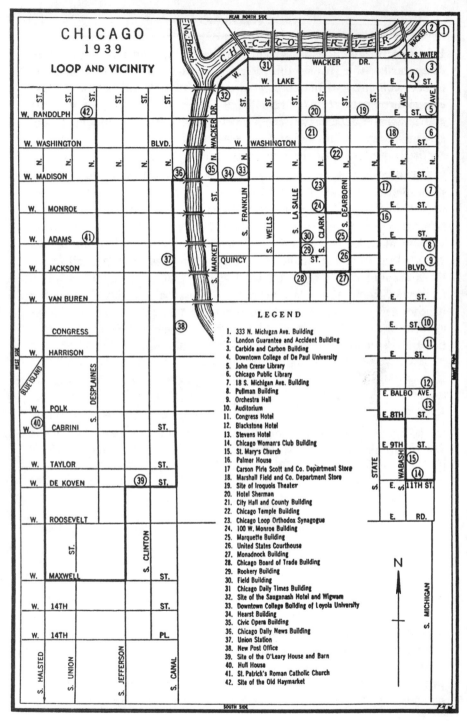

CHICAGO
1939
LOOP AND VICINITY

LEGEND

1. 333 N. Michigan Ave. Building
2. London Guarantee and Accident Building
3. Carbide and Carbon Building
4. Downtown College of De Paul University
5. John Crerar Library
6. Chicago Public Library
7. 18 S. Michigan Ave. Building
8. Pullman Building
9. Orchestra Hall
10. Auditorium
11. Congress Hotel
12. Blackstone Hotel
13. Stevens Hotel
14. Chicago Woman's Club Building
15. St. Mary's Church
16. Palmer House
17. Carson Pirie Scott and Co. Department Store
18. Marshall Field and Co. Department Store
19. Site of Iroquois Theater
20. Hotel Sherman
21. City Hall and County Building
22. Chicago Temple Building
23. Chicago Loop Orthodox Synagogue
24. 100 W. Monroe Building
25. Marquette Building
26. United States Courthouse
27. Monadnock Building
28. Chicago Board of Trade Building
29. Rookery Building
30. Field Building
31. Chicago Daily Times Building
32. Site of the Sauganash Hotel and Wigwam
33. Downtown College Building of Loyola University
34. Hearst Building
35. Civic Opera Building
36. Chicago Daily News Building
37. Union Station
38. New Post Office
39. Site of the O'Leary House and Barn
40. Hull House
41. St. Patrick's Roman Catholic Church
42. Site of the Old Haymarket

N

great movie palaces, and vast department stores. But in the Loop stands a reminder that its economic roots are in the prairie, its primary source of wealth: crowning the Board of Trade Building, the highest elevation in the city, stands a gigantic statue of Ceres, goddess of grain, whose cornucopia of plenty symbolically pours a golden shower of wheat and corn on the city.

In the buildings of the Loop can be clearly traced the architectural evolution of Metropolis. Within its bounds stand great masonry buildings, in their day among the tallest in the world; some of the first structures built with steel framework; many buildings plainly revealing the painful struggle of architects to adapt old styles to new structural forms; and many newer buildings of simple modern functional design, unadorned and starkly vertical, with no strivings to disguise them as Greek temples, French chateaux, or Chinese pagodas.

Chicago lies on land easily dug for subways but unsuited for heavy building construction, but, paradoxically, it was the first to build skyscrapers and the last of the large cities to tunnel passenger subways. With bedrock in places more than 100 feet below the soft and marshy surface, engineers had to erect the first large buildings on "floating" foundations; caissons were sunk to bedrock to provide footing for modern towers. After many years of planning and public clamor, construction of a subway began in 1938. For more than 30 years, however, Chicago's traffic congestion has been considerably relieved by an unusual system of freight tunnels. Some 60 miles of narrow gauge track have been laid 40 feet under downtown streets and carry a large part of coal and other heavy shipments between the freight terminals and downtown buildings.

TOUR 1 — 5 m.

S. from the Chicago River on Michigan Ave.

MICHIGAN AVENUE, from the river to Randolph Street, is a wide thoroughfare between towering buildings. South of Randolph Street the lake side of the avenue opens on Grant Park, but on the west side the line of buildings continues unbroken in the "Splendid Mile," best known part of the Chicago skyline. Here, in sharp contrast, are spread many of Chicago's finest buildings, the old, for the most part, in the southern portion, the new northward, near the river. Bordered with smart shops, fine hotels, and office buildings, Michigan Avenue is somewhat reminiscent of Gotham's Fifth Avenue, but has a vigorous, breezy character all its own.

1. The 333 N. MICHIGAN AVE. BUILDING commands the northern approach to downtown Michigan Avenue. Designed by Holabird and Root (before 1928 Holabird and Roche), its slender mass, seen edgewise from the bridge, soars to a height of 435 feet in clean unbroken lines.

2. The LONDON GUARANTEE AND ACCIDENT BUILDING, SW. corner of Michigan Ave. and Wacker Drive, was erected in 1923 on the approximate site of Fort Dearborn, a fact commemorated in a bronze relief over the entrance. Designed by Alfred S. Alschuler, the 21-story building has a concave façade, in the center of which the imposing entrance resembles a Roman triumphal arch. Surmounting the building is an adaptation of the Athenian Choragic Monument.

3. The CARBIDE AND CARBON BUILDING, 230 N. Michigan Ave., a 40-story tower completed in 1929, presents a striking color scheme with its black marble base, dark green terra cotta walls, gilded trim, and green-eyed campanile.

R. from Michigan Ave. on Lake St.

4. The DOWNTOWN COLLEGE OF DE PAUL UNIVERSITY, 64 E. Lake St., consists of the university's Colleges of Commerce and Law, School of Music, Secretarial School, Department of Drama, and Graduate School. Here, too, are held the late afternoon, evening, and Saturday classes of the College of Liberal Arts and Sciences.

Retrace Lake St.: R. on Michigan Ave. R. on Randolph St.

5. The JOHN CRERAR LIBRARY (*open 9-6 weekdays, non-circulating*), 86 E. Randolph St., an internationally known scientific library, occupies ten of the fifteen floors of a building that outwardly resembles a dignified office block. The library was established in 1894 with a bequest of $2,500,000 by John Crerar, Chicago railway magnate. Until 1920, it was housed in the Marshall Field store building. Its many valuable collections include 600,000 volumes and more than 225,000 pamphlets, as well as thousands of periodical publications. Especially noteworthy are the Senn Medical Collection (12th floor), the DuBois Raymond Collection on comparative physiology, the Martin Collection on physiology, the Lane Collection on histology, the Gradle Collection

on ophthalmology, the Baum Collection on historical medicine, the Huntington Jackson Collection on constitutional law, and the Chanute Collection of aeronautics.

In addition to these, definitive collections in other fields of study attract thousands of general readers and many scholars doing advanced research work in the various sciences.

Adjoining Crerar on the west, and reached from the fourth floor, is the LIBRARY OF INTERNATIONAL RELATIONS (*open* 9-5:30 *weekdays*), a separate organization founded in 1932. The library contains a specialized open-shelf collection of source material on current international affairs.

6. The CHICAGO PUBLIC LIBRARY (*open* 9 *a.m.*-10 *p.m. weekdays;* 1-6 *Sun.*), Randolph St. between Michigan Ave. and Garland Ct., and extending to Washington St., a massive structure of Bedford limestone designed by Shepley, Rutan, and Coolidge, and completed in 1897 at a cost of $2,000,000, combines Renaissance and Neo-Greek features. The Washington Street side of the interior is decorated with favrile glass mosaics and marble, executed by Tiffany of New York. They are seen at their best in the curved surface of the pendentives supporting the glass dome of the delivery room.

After the fire of 1871 a movement was fostered in London by Thomas Hughes, a member of Parliament and author of *Tom Brown at Rugby,* to provide bookless Chicago with the nucleus of a library. Several thousand volumes, donated by Queen Victoria, Darwin, Huxley, Carlyle, Disraeli, Tennyson, Browning, Ruskin, and others, arrived in 1872. The first library quarters were in an iron water tank which had escaped the flames. The present collection of some 1,750,000 books and 400,000 pamphlets forms the core of a city-wide library system of 45 branches, with numerous sub-branches and deposit stations.

On the first floor are the newspaper room, the A. W. Swayne collection of 80,000 lantern slides, and a library for the blind that includes books phonographically recorded and some 20,000 volumes in Braille and Moontype. On the second floor are the offices of the Illinois department of the G. A. R., a Memorial Hall housing Civil War relics, and an assembly hall. The delivery room on the third floor is flanked by the open shelves and the foreign book section. On the fourth floor are the reference and general reading rooms, the children's department, the periodical department, and the Civics Room. The Music Room, containing 22,000 volumes and an extensive file of sheet music, and the Arts and Crafts Room, are on the fifth floor.

Retrace Randolph St. R. on Michigan Ave.

7. The 18 S. MICHIGAN AVE. BUILDING houses on its upper floors the University College of the University of Chicago, where afternoon and evening courses are conducted by members of the university faculty. The exquisitely modeled ornament on the front of the building was designed by Louis Sullivan.

R. from Michigan Ave. on Adams St.

8. The PULLMAN BUILDING, 79 E. Adams St., built in 1884, typifies the Victorian brownstone period of architecture, in which medieval details were combined in restless, fantastic patterns. S. S. Beman was the architect. Formerly housing "highly respectable bachelors" in its upper six floors, the building became known as an "Eveless Eden." Now the Pullman Company uses all nine floors, but with its arrangement of rooms, cherry woodwork, and four small elevators, the interior retains its early charm.

Retrace Adams St. R. on Michigan Ave.

9. ORCHESTRA HALL, 216 S. Michigan Ave., is a dignified brick and limestone building in the French Renaissance style. It was designed by Daniel H. Burnham and completed in 1904 at a cost of $1,000,000. Approximately one half was underwritten by the music-loving public as an expression of its regard for Theodore Thomas, founder and first conductor of the orchestra now known as the Chicago Symphony Orchestra. After Thomas's death in 1905, the baton passed to his violinist, Frederick Stock, who is its present conductor (1939). The auditorium seats 2,600; in addition to its use during the regular concert series and for special musical events, is the meeting place of the non-sectarian Sunday Evening Club, and the Central Church. The church was founded by the Reverend David Swing in 1875, after his noted heresy trial before the Presbyterian Synod.

R. from Michigan Ave. on Congress St.

10. The AUDITORIUM, Congress St. between Michigan and Wabash Aves., in its day "the most famous building on the American

continent," houses a great theater, and also incorporates a hotel and offices, income from which was intended to aid in the support of a grand opera company.

This is perhaps the best known of Louis Sullivan's buildings. Begun in 1887 and completed three years later, it is of masonry construction. Although Sullivan denied that he was influenced by H. H. Richardson, the Romanesque style is evident in the exterior, and Sullivan's partner, Dankmar Adler, admitted that alterations in the original plans were inspired in part by the Auditorium directors' admiration for Richardson's newly completed Marshall Field Wholesale Building. The Auditorium is an excellent example of Sullivan's ambivalent theory of design. The massive and rather simple exterior illustrates his tenet that form should follow function, but throughout the interior examples of his intricate and graceful surface decorations abound. The main dining room, the bar, and the lobby are enriched with plaster reliefs in foliage designs; ornamentation is especially rich in the great series of arches in the auditorium proper. Of these, Hugh Morrison wrote in his biography of Sullivan:

Even the borders of the arched panels are enriched by relief bands and an inner lace-like pattern delicately stencilled in gold. Rarely has there been such a wedding of large and majestic simplicity with refined and subtle detail. The effect is superb.

Both the structural plans of the building and the complex acoustical design were drawn by Dankmar Adler. His solution of the construction problem posed by the massive tower was particularly ingenious. The foundation of the building is not on bedrock, and Adler feared that the imposition of the heavy tower might cause uneven settling that would crack the masonry. By loading pig iron and bricks equal to the weight of the finished tower on the lower floors, he obtained an even settling before the masons had finished the body of the building and begun to erect the huge tower.

On the opening night, Dec. 9, 1889, 5,000 of Chicago's elite crowded into the Auditorium to hear Adeline Patti sing. Governor Fifer of Illinois and President Harrison, accompanied by a large party, sat in special boxes. In following seasons, the theater rang with the voices of the operatic great. In 1929, the Chicago Civic Opera Company, an outgrowth of Chicago's first permanent opera company, moved to the new Civic Opera House. But the Auditorium, its acoustics unsurpassed, is still used for leading musical events.

Retrace Congress St. R. on Michigan Ave.

11. The CONGRESS HOTEL, Michigan Ave. between Congress and Harrison Sts., built as an annex to the Auditorium Hotel, now functions separately. Designed by Holabird and Roche, it dates from the Columbian Exposition of 1893, and has been the headquarters of the Democratic and Republican parties during all national conventions held in Chicago.

12. The BLACKSTONE HOTEL, Michigan Ave. at Balbo Ave., completed in 1910, was designed by Benjamin Marshall, who received the gold medal of the American Institute of Architects for his plans. One of the swankiest Chicago hotels, it has frequently housed visiting royalty. Its red and white shaft, crowned with a green mansard roof, is a prominent landmark on the lake front.

13. The STEVENS HOTEL, Michigan Ave. between Balbo Ave. and 8th St., is the largest hotel in the world, having 3,000 rooms. French Renaissance in decoration, it was designed by Holabird and Roche, and completed in 1927. Part of the third floor corridor is used as a permanent gallery by the All Illinois Society of the Fine Arts.

R. from Michigan Ave. on 11th St.

14. The CHICAGO WOMAN'S CLUB BUILDING (*apply two days in advance for club room tour*), 72 E. 11th St., was designed by Holabird and Root and completed in 1928. Graceful ornament in a sophisticated modern style gives the building a distinctly feminine character. Notable features of the interior are the little theater, and the Tudor Gallery (*open 9-5 weekdays*), used for one-man shows by Chicago artists. A limited-membership organization, the club has done notable pioneer work 'for compulsory education legislation, birth control, social hygiene, and other progressive social measures.

R. from 11th St. on Wabash Ave.

15. ST. MARY'S CHURCH, 9th St. and Wabash Ave., erected in 1865, one of the few churches antedating the Great Fire, is the center

of worship for the oldest Roman Catholic parish in Chicago, organized in 1833. The three o'clock mass is popular with late Loop crowds.

L. from Wabash Ave. on 8th St. R. on State St.

STATE STREET, between 8th and Van Buren Streets, is a short stretch of cheap taverns, men's hotels, lady barber shops, pawnshops, dime burlesque and peep shows, tattoo parlors, and penny arcades. As the street passes under the elevated at Van Buren, it undergoes a remarkable transformation. Northward, to Lake Street, it is the shopping center of Chicago, lined with huge department stores and small retail shops. Most metropolitan of Chicago's streets, State Street is the heart of the Loop, said to be the most brilliantly lighted in the world; the corner at State and Madison Streets is one of the world's busiest intersections.

16. The PALMER HOUSE, State and Monroe Sts., completed in 1925, succeeded the hostelry that enjoyed an international reputation for its splendor. When Lake Street was the principal business thoroughfare, Potter Palmer (1826-1902) bought a mile of State Street frontage and pioneered its commercial development.

17. The CARSON PIRIE SCOTT AND CO. DEPARTMENT STORE, SE. corner of State and Madison Sts., is housed in a building designed by Adler and Sullivan and erected in 1899. Unusually large windows light the store well while expressing naturally the steel frame. On the lower stories the lacy ornament which Sullivan intended to be "a rich frame for a rich picture" seems too ornate for present tastes.

18. The MARSHALL FIELD AND CO. DEPARTMENT STORE (*tours arranged at the Information Bureau, third floor*), covers the entire block bounded by State, Washington, Randolph Sts., and Wabash Ave., with an annex occupying the northeast quarter of the block to the south. It is one of the largest and best known retail stores in the world. Marshall Field, born in 1834 near Conway, Massachusetts, began his business career in Chicago in 1856 as a dry goods clerk. In 1865, together with Levi Z. Leiter, he bought an interest in Potter Palmer's Lake Street dry goods store. In 1881, after the retirement of Field's partners, the present firm name was adopted. Marshall Field developed many new practices and policies in department store management and invested heavily in Chicago real estate. At his death in 1906 he had accumulated a fortune which has since become one of the largest in the world.

L. from State St. on Randolph St.

RANDOLPH STREET in the Loop is the Rialto of Chicago, ablaze at night with theater, night club, hotel, and cafe signs. In the four blocks between State and Wells Streets, and at short distances on intersecting streets, are most of the first-run movie and legitimate theaters in Chicago.

19. The SITE OF THE IROQUOIS THEATER, N. side of Randolph St. between State and Dearborn Sts., is occupied in part by the modern, fireproof Oriental Theater. At the newly completed Iroquois, on December 30, 1903, occurred one of the most horrible disasters in the nation's history. While a matinee performance of *Mr. Bluebeard* was playing to a crowded house, the stage curtain caught fire, probably from an incompletely enclosed electric arc floodlight. The elaborate stage sets went up in flames, and a draft from the opened stage door swept a gale of fire over the audience. In a few minutes the locked gallery exits were further barred by piles of trampled bodies. When the flames were finally curbed, 596 persons were dead or dying—more than twice the toll of the Great Fire of 1871. The investigation disclosed the guilt of responsible persons and led to drastic reforms in theater regulations, both here and abroad. Annually, on the anniversary of the disaster, memorial services are held in the City Council Chamber.

20. The HOTEL SHERMAN, NW. corner of Randolph and Clark Sts., was completed in 1925, the latest of a succession of hotels that have occupied this site since 1837. The noted Tony Sarg cartographic ceiling in the Old Town Room depicts Chicago in 1852.

L. from Randolph St. on Clark St.

21. The CITY HALL AND COUNTY BUILDING, Clark St., between Randolph and Washington Sts., and extending to La Salle St., is actually two buildings, uniform in style; the section facing Clark was erected as the County Building in 1907; the west half, the city section, was added in 1910. Simple in design and ponderous in size, it represents a compromise between functional and classic styles; its long rows of huge columns, which support nothing but the cornice, are insufficient to make a temple out of what is obviously a city hall. The City Council Chamber, on the second floor, is an impressive oak-paneled room with murals by Frederick Clay Bartlett.

The Municipal Reference Library (*open* 9-5 *Mon.-Fri.; 9-12 Sat.*), on the 10th floor, contains over 150,000 books and pamphlets, including reports, proceedings, and treatises on the government of Chicago and other cities.

22. The CHICAGO TEMPLE BUILDING, SE. corner of Clark and Washington Sts., houses commercial offices and the First Methodist Episcopal Church, an outgrowth of Chicago's first church society, organized in 1831. For 100 years, with the exception of a short period after the Chicago Fire, the site has been occupied continuously by the various churches of the congregation. The present building, Gothic in detail, designed by Holabird and Roche and completed in 1923, rises 568 feet above the street. The delicately illuminated cross-tipped spire is a soaring note of beauty in the night sky. The tubular carillon, one of the largest in the world, sounds on the quarter hour, and in season fills the air with holiday tunes.

23. The CHICAGO LOOP ORTHODOX SYNAGOGUE, 16 S. Clark St., has walls decorated with murals, each symbolizing one of the Ten Commandments. Symbols were employed by the artist, Raymond Katz, because of the traditional Jewish ban on the depiction of figures in art.

R. from Clark St. on Monroe St.

24. The 100 W. MONROE BUILDING contains, of all things, a cowpath. Ten feet wide, 18 feet high, and 177 feet deep, it opens on Monroe Street at the west end of the building, and leads nowhere. The functionless path is maintained in accordance with deeds drawn by Willard Jones, original owner of the land. When the growing city forbade cows and pigs to use the streets in the 1840's, Jones provided in the sale of his property for a perpetual 10-foot easement whereby his cows could plod to and from their pasture, which lay where the Board of Trade Building now stands. When the present building was erected in 1926, a reputed $350,000 was sacrificed because of the unusual cantilever construction and loss of rentable property.

Retrace Monroe St. R. on Dearborn St.

25. The MARQUETTE BUILDING, 140 S. Dearborn St., an office building notable for its decorations representing early historic figures and events, has bronze reliefs over the entrance depicting Father Mar-

quette's journey, and bronze medallion portraits of other explorers and of several Indian chiefs in the rotunda, the work of Hermon A. MacNeil. Martin Roche designed the mosaics around the mezzanine balcony to illustrate scenes from the journeys of discovery of Jolliet and others in this region.

26. The UNITED STATES COURTHOUSE, Dearborn St. between Adams St. and Jackson Blvd. and extending to Clark St., which served until 1934 as the main post office, now houses a large branch post office, a number of local Federal offices, and United State District Courts. The courtrooms, adorned by William B. Van Ingen's murals depicting the development of Law, have been the scene of many famous trials. It was here that the Standard Oil Company was fined $29,000,000, and Al Capone was sentenced. The Weather Bureau (*open 9-4 weekdays*), on the fourteenth floor, has a display of instruments used in its work, and a library of climatological data for the entire country. The cross-shaped building surmounted with an octagonal dome derives a certain grim splendor from its ornate design in the Roman Corinthian style. It was planned by Henry Ives Cobb and completed in 1905. In 1851, part of the site was occupied by the first Jewish house of worship built in Illinois.

R. from Dearborn St. on Jackson Blvd.

27. The MONADNOCK BUILDING, 53 W. Jackson Blvd., was studied and highly praised by European critics during the Columbian Exposition. Last and largest of the old type masonry buildings, it has walls 15 feet thick at the base. Its lines are as pleasing now as in 1892 when John Root erected the building. Not only is it devoid of ornament, but all the angles are rounded in a manner that would be called "streamlined" today. This is especially noticeable in the flaring base, the lower parts of the soaring bay windows, and the subtle swelling at the top that replaces the usual heavy cornice of the period.

28. The CHICAGO BOARD OF TRADE BUILDING (*observatory, 10-9 daily, 25c*), Jackson Blvd. and La Salle St., the tallest building in Chicago, has also the most dramatic location. Typifying the Board of Trade's importance in Chicago's economy, it stands as a climax to La Salle Street, at the apparent end of its long gorge. Designed by Holabird and Root and completed in 1930, the building towers in huge set-back masses to a statue of Ceres, goddess of grain,

a 31-foot aluminum figure by John Storrs. Ornament throughout the building contains symbols of the harvest.

Organized in 1848, the Board of Trade, with a present membership of more than 1,500, is by far the largest grain exchange in the world. More than 85 per cent of the United States trade in grain futures and approximately one-half of the world total, is transacted here.

On the trading floor of the immense Exchange Hall (*visitor's gallery on 5th floor open* 9:30-1:15 *Mon.-Fri.,* 9:30-12 *Sat.*), are the grain pits, bordered with batteries of telephones and telegraph instruments, and the small sections for trading in cotton, provisions, and stocks. Quotation boards cover three walls; at the north side of the hall nine huge windows open on La Salle Street. The tables at the windows contain samples of cash grain, each bag representing a carload on hand and available for immediate delivery. Trading in futures constitutes the principal function of the Exchange. Shouting, gesticulating traders crowd the grain pits, as messengers scurry back and forth between the wire desks and the pits. Trading usually opens briskly and closes in a brief frenzy. The gong that marks these periods was used for many years in the old Board of Trade, the scene of Frank Norris' *The Pit.* A free pamphlet, available at the gallery entrance, explains the intricate system governing the apparent bedlam. In Room 740 are exhibited working models of grain elevators and handling equipment.

R. from Jackson Blvd. on La Salle St.

LA SALLE STREET, north of the Board of Trade Building, is the most canyon-like of the city's streets, a stone-walled gorge cut through Chicago's richest stratum of finance.

29. The ROOKERY, SE. corner of La Salle and Adams Sts., maintains the name and occupies the site of the ramshackle structure that served as a temporary city hall after the Fire. The name was inspired, it is said, by the hundreds of pigeons that roosted on the eaves of the old building. Designed by Burnham and Root and erected in 1885, the Rookery reflects the Romanesque vogue of the period, but its profuse ornamentation is of Hindoo inspiration. It has been commended as the first tall building to solve intelligently the problems of grouping and lighting a large number of offices.

30. The FIELD BUILDING, NE. corner of La Salle and Adams St., newest of Chicago's skyscrapers, was designed by Graham, Anderson,

Probst, and White, and completed in 1934. Its clean soaring masses ascend to a height of 535 feet. The building stands on the site of the Home Life Insurance Building, erected in 1883, the first in the world of steel skeleton construction.

L. from La Salle St. on Wacker Drive

WACKER DRIVE, a wide double-decked boulevard of architectural beauty, follows the south bank of the Chicago River, where Chicago's earliest development took place. One of the chief units of the Chicago Plan, the drive was named for Charles H. Wacker, late chairman of the Chicago Plan Commission. The massive driveway, resting on 598 caissons sunk to hardpan, is a distributive artery for eight north-south streets, and has an express highway for freight traffic on the lower level. The construction of Wacker Drive, completed in 1926, displaced the fascinatingly chaotic South Water Street Market, which cluttered the Loop for many years with a creaking confusion of wagons.

31. The CHICAGO DAILY TIMES BUILDING, 211 W. Wacker Drive, designed by Holabird and Roche, was completed in 1928 for the old Chicago *Evening Post,* which sold it to the tabloid *Times* four years later.

32. The SITE OF THE SAUGANASH HOTEL AND THE WIGWAM, is at the SE. corner of Wacker Drive and Lake St. Here, in the early 1830's, convivial Mark Beaubien kept one of the first hotels in Chicago, a political and entertainment center of the pioneer community. The inn burned in 1851; later the Wigwam, a large wooden structure, was erected in its place to accommodate the second national convention of the Republican Party, at which Abraham Lincoln was nominated for the Presidency.

L. from Wacker Drive on Lake St.; R. on Franklin St.

33. The DOWNTOWN COLLEGE BUILDING OF LOYOLA UNIVERSITY, 28 N. Franklin St., houses the Loop departments of the Jesuit university: the Graduate School, the University College, and the Schools of Law, Social Work, and Commerce.

R. from Franklin St. on Madison St.

34. The HEARST BUILDING (*tours by arrangement*), 326 W. Madison St., houses the two Chicago newspapers of William Randolph

Hearst, the Chicago *Herald and Examiner,* a morning tabloid, and the Chicago *American,* an evening journal. The newspapers maintain separate editorial offices, but share the same press and composing rooms. The building also houses the International News Service and other affiliated Hearst corporations.

R. from Madison St. on Wacker Drive

35. The CIVIC OPERA BUILDING, 20 W. Wacker Drive, was designed by Graham, Anderson, Probst, and White, and completed in 1929 to house the Chicago Civic Opera Company and offices for the support of opera. The building, 555 feet in height, is best viewed from the plaza of the *Daily News* building across the river. From that point it appears to be a huge throne, which won it the newspaper soubriquet of "Insull's Armchair." The late Samuel Insull, who occupied a penthouse suite in the building, was the chief promoter in the erection of the immense opera house. The gilded auditorium, seating 3,800 persons, with an immense stage 13 stories in height, departs from the usual opera house design in that it replaces the "Golden Horseshoe" with 31 boxes arranged in a barely perceptible curve.

TOUR 2 — 3.5 m.

W. from the river on Madison St.

36. The CHICAGO DAILY NEWS BUILDING (*tours by arrangement*) 400 W. Madison St., houses the plant and offices of the Chicago *Daily News.* A $10,000,000 Indiana limestone structure, designed by Holabird and Root and completed in 1929, it was one of the first Chicago buildings constructed in a large measure over a railroad right-of-way and the first to develop the river front aesthetically as well as commercially. The vast plane of its block-long façade rises from a balustraded plaza. Exterior stone panels depict the evolution of printing; murals by John W. Norton, on the ceiling of the main floor concourse, illustrate the gathering, printing, and distributing of news.

The Chicago *Daily News,* noted for the many authors developed on its staff, was published by the late Victor Lawson from 1876 to 1925. Control has been in the hands of Col. Frank Knox since 1931.

L. from Madison St. on Canal St.

37. The UNION STATION, on both sides of Canal St. between Adams St. and Jackson Blvd., is composed of two large units con-

nected below street level. Although the exterior is treated in Roman Doric and the monumental waiting room is distinguished in its ornamental detail, the concourse is frankly functional in its deliberately unconcealed steel girders. The vast station, designed by Graham, Anderson, Probst, and White, and opened in 1926, serves four large railroad systems.

38. The NEW POST OFFICE (*tours by arrangement*), Van Buren St. from Canal St. to the river and extending to Harrison St., is the largest post office building in the world, a bulky Indiana limestone structure designed by Graham, Anderson, Probst, and White, and completed in 1934 at a cost of $21,500,000. The building is constructed over railroad tracks which permits the direct handling of one-third of the daily mail. On May 15, 1938, an autogyro landed on the roof of the two-block long structure, with mail from the Municipal Airport, in a test flight of transfer service. In addition to the postal plant, the building houses the regional offices of several Federal Departments.

R. from Canal St. on DeKoven St.

39. The SITE OF THE O'LEARY HOUSE AND BARN, 558 DeKoven St., is occupied by a three-story flat-building. Here, as the inscription on the stone front indicates, began the Chicago Fire of 1871. Legend ascribes the cause of the fire to a lantern shattered by Mrs. O'Leary's cow.

L. from DeKoven St. on Jefferson St. R. on Maxwell St.

The MAXWELL STREET MARKET, frequently called the Ghetto, centering at Halsted and Maxwell Sts., is a confusion of wagons, stalls, pushcarts, and boxes, a littered jungle of used umbrellas, festoons of shoes, high-piled vegetables, and wind-swung underwear. The sidewalks run between a solid line of stalls and stores, along which salesmen solicit the custom of passers-by. Few of the stores have fixed prices; extended bargaining is the rule. The crescendo is reached on Sunday mornings, when Poles and others of European extraction come to bargain with the Jewish merchants for their incredibly varied stores of goods.

R. from Maxwell St. on Halsted St.

HALSTED STREET, between the Maxwell Street and the Randolph Street markets, is a cosmopolitan mile, a shabby commercial corridor through the old settlements of several foreign-language groups. Large numbers of Mexicans, Italians, and Greeks inhabit other parts of the city, but nowhere is there such a concentration of stores displaying the native goods of these people. Gypsies winter here in scattered stores along the street, gaining a livelihood ostensibly by fortune telling.

LITTLE ITALY, largest of the settlements, spreads westward from Halsted St. near Taylor St. Here, in stores marked by curbside pyramids of tinned olive oil, are displayed deviously wrought spaghetti and macaroni, Romane and Provolone cheeses, many varieties of olives, spices, fish, and sausages. Some of the larger stores are wholesale establishments, catering to outlying districts. In other shop windows are bundles of spindly black cigars, paper-backed novels, "art" calendars, and huge wedding cakes. The residents of Little Italy hold street festivals in spring and summer at nearby churches.

LITTLE MEXICO centers on Hull House, Halsted St. at Polk St., where shops sell native handicrafts, particularly pottery, and restaurants serve *tacos, enchiladas, tostadas,* and tender vinegar-soaked cactus.

40. HULL HOUSE (*open* 11-8 *daily; other hours by arrangement*), 800 S. Halsted St., one of the first settlement houses in America, has become one of the most 'famed institutions of its kind in the world. About the original plant, the old Charles J. Hull residence, built in 1856, are clustered a dozen buildings. Some of the buildings provide living quarters for the large resident staff, most of whom engage in self-sustaining occupations, devoting their leisure time to the House programs. Activities include classes in English for foreigners, group discussions and investigations of social problems, instruction in the manual and fine arts, and gymnasium classes. Among the exhibits at Hull House are the Labor Museum, displaying various spinning and weaving devices formerly found in the homes of the foreign groups living in the surrounding area; the Benedict Art Gallery; and the Octagon Room, Jane Addams' study, furnished as it was during her lifetime, and containing memorabilia of her achievements. In the House are the offices of such co-operating organizations as the Juvenile Protective Association, Immigrants' Protective League, Visiting Nurse Association, United Charities, and Infant Welfare Society.

Hull House won its fame as a social center largely through the devoted and indefatigable efforts of Jane Addams, who, together with her Rockford College classmate, Ellen Gates Starr, founded the institution in 1889. Miss Addams remained head resident until her death in 1935. A visit to Toynbee Hall, the London settlement house, and a study of London slums, were the immediate inspiration for her pioneering work in Chicago.

Immigrants constituted about half of Chicago's population when Hull House was chartered "to provide a center for a higher civic and social life, to institute and maintain educational and philanthropic enterprises, and to investigate and improve the conditions in the industrial districts of Chicago." The splendid accomplishments of Hull House are modestly revealed by Miss Addams in her *Twenty Years at Hull House* (1912) and *The Second Twenty Years at Hull House* (1930), and in James Weber Linn's *Jane Addams* (1935).

LITTLE GREECE is bounded by the delta formed by Halsted and Polk Sts. and Blue Island Ave. The colony has dwindled sharply in recent years, but it retains much of its color. At the approach of the Greek Orthodox Easter the store fronts are gayly decorated with banners. The Good Friday procession, the Funeral of Christ, draws thousands of participants, many of them carrying lighted candles. Market fronts are filled with live lambs; on Easter Sunday they are barbecued in a vacant lot on Polk Street, with much dancing and drinking of sweet wines and *mastika*.

R. from Halsted St. on Adams St.

41. ST. PATRICK'S ROMAN CATHOLIC CHURCH, Adams and Desplaines Sts., dedicated in 1856, is the oldest church building in use in Chicago. The interior is notable 'for its windows of colored glass, designed in 1912 by Thomas O'Shaughnessy. The window patterns follow fifth century precepts formulated by St. Bride (St. Bridget), and employ symbolism used in the ancient Book of Kells. Save for the faces of the saints, the windows are of pot-metal glass, some pieces of which are one-thousandth of an inch thick. The main window, composed of 250,000 pieces, is valued at $100,000.

L. from Adams St. on Desplaines St. to Madison St.

WEST MADISON STREET, for several blocks on either side of Desplaines Street, is a sordid "Skid Row," lined with missions, pawnshops, flop houses, saloons, dime movies, and cheap lunch rooms. From the railroad yards come the transient worker, the bum, the veteran cadger, the down-and-outer. Here, for half a century, a ragged army has shuffled in bewildered frustration, moving into breadlines at dawn, kneeling in missions during rain, wandering in and out of "cake flops," where the price of a pallet includes a lump of stale pastry.

L. from Desplaines St. on Randolph St.

The RANDOLPH FARMERS' MARKET, Randolph St. between Desplaines and Sangamon Sts., expands westward to Union Park during the harvest season. Large numbers of farmers and truck gardeners from northern Illinois gather in the wide street to sell their fruits and vegetables. One block is utilized by flower growers.

42. The SITE OF THE OLD HAYMARKET, the scene of the tragic bombing of May 4, 1886 (*see Labor*), is at Desplaines and Randolph Sts.

Grant Park

Central link of Chicago's chain of lake front parks, Grant Park lies between the most imposing section of Michigan Avenue and the inner basin of the Chicago Harbor. Known as the Front Yard of Chicago, it contains many of Chicago's finest museums and monuments, and its 303 acres provide the mile-long Loop with an open view of the lake.

Practically all of the land in the park has been reclaimed from the lake; in 1852 the Illinois Central tracks, only 100 yards east of Michigan Avenue, were laid on trestles in the water. Subsequent filling created new land on both sides of the Illinois Central, which raised the grade around the tracks, so that the railroad right-of-way is now hidden some 20 feet below the level of the park.

Before the Columbian Exposition in 1893, many attempts were made to secure the embryo park for private use. Largely through the persistent efforts of A. Montgomery Ward, the "Watchdog of the Lake Front," it was kept free of buildings, except for the Art Institute. Later, Field Museum and Shedd Aquarium were built on a southeast extension of Grant Park, beyond the Loop area.

The pattern of the park, broken by the railroad right-of-way, the two major boulevards, and the connecting extensions of several downtown streets, is essentially formal. But the park is not merely a formal showpiece. On warm days students pore over books in the shadow of the peristyle, where passers-by feed the great flocks of pigeons. After

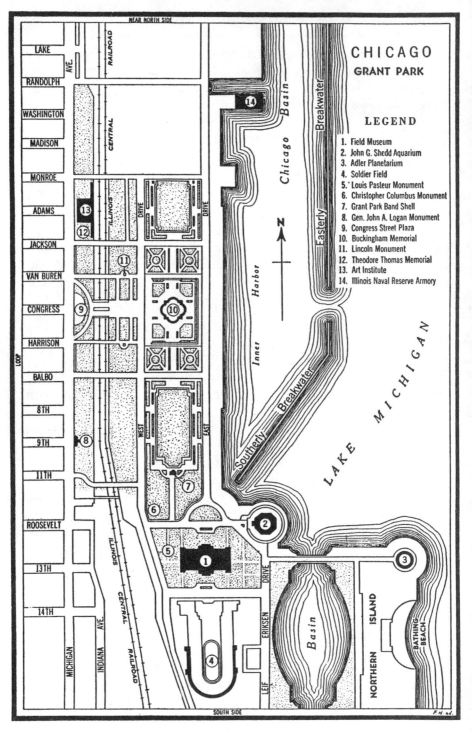

CHICAGO
GRANT PARK

LEGEND

1. Field Museum
2. John G. Shedd Aquarium
3. Adler Planetarium
4. Soldier Field
5. Louis Pasteur Monument
6. Christopher Columbus Monument
7. Grant Park Band Shell
8. Gen. John A. Logan Monument
9. Congress Street Plaza
10. Buckingham Memorial
11. Lincoln Monument
12. Theodore Thomas Memorial
13. Art Institute
14. Illinois Naval Reserve Armory

working hours in summer months, the ball fields and tennis courts are crowded with players and spectators from Loop offices. At dusk, dense throngs converge on the band shell for the open air concerts, and always, the year round, visitors cross the viaducts to view the exhibits in the museums.

Facing Roosevelt Road, overlooking the entire length of Grant Park, is the broad façade of (1) the FIELD MUSEUM OF NAT-URAL HISTORY. (*Open 9-4 Nov.-Feb.; 9-5 Mar., Apr., Sept., and Oct.; 9-6 May-Aug. Children, students, and teachers free; others free, Thurs., Sat., and Sun.; other days, 25c. Tours 3 p.m., Mon.-Fri., also 11 a.m. July-Aug., and by arrangement at other times. Cafeteria, ground floor; guidebooks and other publications for sale at main entrance. Wheel chairs, 25c per hour; visitor must furnish attendant. Free parking*).

The Field Museum, one of the renowned scientific museums in the world, houses a vast and constantly growing collection of exhibits on anthropology, zoology, botany, and geology. Founded in 1893 after the Columbian Exposition, it was endowed by a number of prominent citizens, chief among whom was the late Marshall Field, Chicago merchant. To his initial gift of $1,000,000 he added more than $400,000 during his life, and at his death in 1906 bequeathed $8,000,000. Until 1921, when the present building was opened, the Museum was housed in the Palace of Fine Arts in Jackson Park. Nucleus collections were exhibits transferred from the Exposition, purchases, and private gifts, notably an anthropological collection by Edward E. Ayer.

Most of the objects have been collected by expeditions, of which the Museum has had as many as eighteen at work in one year. Their scientific reports, as well as the findings of the local research staff, are published and circulated internationally by the Museum. The vast research collections are open to scholars, on application. New acquisitions, improvements in the permanent exhibits, and the extensive lecture activities create recurring interest in many of the 1,000,000 annual visitors to the Museum.

The massive white Georgia marble building, one of the largest marble structures in the world, was designed by Daniel H. Burnham, but the work was completed after his death by Graham, Anderson, Probst, and White. Its architecture is pure Greek Ionic, with some of its details following the Erechtheum in Athens. A great flight of steps leads to the majestic pedimented portico, two rows of columns in depth. This is flanked by long wings, four stories high, that are decorated with Ionic colonnades ending in transverse halls.

The main hall, known as Stanley Field Hall, rises unbroken to the roof. The heart of the Museum, it contains exhibits, frequently changed, drawn from the various divisions of the Museum. Two African elephants mounted in fighting pose, and bronze groups of African natives in the act of spearing lions, all the work of the late Carl Akeley, are permanent exhibits. Sculptor, author, and naturalist, Akeley became chief taxidermist in 1896, and for fourteen years his research, exploration, and taxidermy brought renown to him and to the Museum.

The Department of Anthropology occupies the first floor of the east wing, most of the exhibition space on the ground floor, and the five second-floor halls around the nave. Its exhibits include, in Hall 3, east of the entrance, Malvina Hoffman's widely known *Races of Mankind,* 101 statues and busts based on six years of research among the races of the world. A bronze group of a white, a yellow, and a black man, indicates that humanity is a single species; statues and busts of various racial types surround this central composition. South of this exhibit are seven halls devoted to the anthropology of American races, with an extensive exhibit of the works of North American Indians and Eskimos, past and present. Collections in Halls D and E, on the ground floor, illustrate the ethnology of Africa and include the only Madagascar collection of importance in the United States. Polynesia, Micronesia, Malaysia, and the Philippine Islands are represented in Halls F, G and H; Hall A contains the most comprehensive Melanesian collection in America.

The Egyptian collection, in Hall J, includes reproductions of the Rosetta Stone and papyri, but most of the articles are originals, including a funeral barge 3,800 years old. One of the rare items is the body of a woman preserved in sand for more than 6,000 years. It antedates the period when bodies were mummified. Hall C, devoted to Stone Age relics, contains dioramas of prehistoric scenes, with life-size figures. Adjacent to each diorama are authentic artifacts, and animal and human remains of the period, including the Cap Blanc skeleton.

The H. N. Higinbotham Hall of gems and jewels, west of the main stairway on the second floor, contains examples of almost every known gem, including the famous Sun God opal and the De Vrees engraved diamond. Most of the other exhibits on this floor are devoted to China and Tibet, with a fine jade collection in Hall 30.

The Department of Botany occupies the second floor of the east wing. Few other general natural history museums have attempted to cover this subject. The Hall of Plant Life offers a general view of the entire range from the lowest orders, such as bacteria and fungi, up through the many varieties of flowering plants. Two halls are devoted to general economic botany—food products, palms, and plant raw materials. Nearby are halls showing varieties of wood from all over the world. Many of the botanical exhibits, skillfully processed in wax, glass, and celluloid in the museum's laboratory, cannot be distinguished from natural specimens.

The Department of Geology occupies the second floor of the west wing. Crystals, meteorites, and a systematic display of minerals are in Hall 34; the meteorites, with specimens from more than two-thirds of the known meteorite falls, includes one weighing 3,336 pounds. In the Ernest R. Graham Hall of Historical Geology is traced the development of life from earliest times to the present. A huge skeleton of a dinosaur of the species *Apatosaurus,* surrounded by other fossil reptiles, as well as mammals and birds, forms one of the exhibits. A series of murals by Charles R. Knight around the hall depicts various prehistoric animals as they probably appeared in life. There are also several life-size three-dimensional restorations by the sculptor Frederick Blaschke. Exhibits in Hall 35 illustrate geologic processes. Relief maps in the corridor represent the Chicago area in various stages following the glacial period. Specimens and models in Hall 36 and 37 illustrate the occurrence, processing, and utilization of petroleum, coal, clay, and various ores.

The first floor of the west wing and Hall N are occupied by the Department of Zoology's systematic and habitat groupings of animals. The sculptural methods of taxidermy, principally devised by Akeley, account for the life-like appearance of the specimens. Hall 22, which includes some of Akeley's best work, contains all major African species of mammals. Several series of habitat groups, in many respects more spectacular than the African series because of their more elaborate scenic backgrounds, include the groups of American mammals in Hall 16, the Asiatic group in Hall 17, and the birds in Hall 20. In the Hall of Domestic Mammals, west of the main stairway, is an

unusual exhibit of quarter-sized statues, modeled by Herbert Hasel-
tine 'from prize-winning livestock.

The Museum library (*open weekdays; closed Sat. at 12*) contains
more than 100,000 scientific books and pamphlets. There are many
rare volumes, as well as current scientific periodicals and publications
of institutions throughout the world.

The Department of the N. W. Harris Public School Extension
circulates 1,200 special exhibit cases among 500,000 school children
to stimulate their interest in local natural history. Through the James
Nelson and Anna Louise Raymond Foundation for Public School
and Children's Lectures, lectures and pictures are presented in the
schools, and in the James Simpson Theatre of the Museum on Saturday mornings in spring and autumn. On Saturday afternoons during
these seasons, illustrated lectures are given here for adults by eminent
naturalists and explorers.

At the east end of Field Museum a pedestrian subway leads under
Lief Eriksen Drive to (2) the JOHN G. SHEDD AQUARIUM
(*open 10-5 daily; children free, adults free Thurs., Sat., and Sun.,
other days, 25c. Guidebooks at information desk, 50c*).

The Aquarium was endowed in 1924 with a gift of more than
$3,000,000 by the late John G. Shedd, a Marshall Field executive.
The displays of live fish and aquatic animals attracted 4,700,000
visitors in 1931, the first year after the aquarium was completed.

The many-sided white Georgia marble building, of simple Doric
design, is effectively set in a terrace at the water's edge. The architects,
Graham, Anderson, Probst, and White, used marine symbols throughout the decorations. Outside, this is seen in the wave-like cresting
and the trident of Neptune on the pyramidal roof. Inside, a marble
wainscoting has markings that give a wave effect and the clock in
the foyer, which substitutes aquatic figures 'for numerals, is typical
of the imaginative use of water symbols. In the center of the rotunda
is a rockery with a swamp pool, in which carp wind in and out among
tree stumps that serve as resting places for turtles and frogs.

Six main galleries radiate from the rotunda. The symbols that
identify the majority of the exhibits are coded with the comprehensive guidebook; the numbers indicate the family and species of
the fish; the colored oblong denotes the kind of water from which it
was taken. Special attention is given to reproducing the appearance
and conditions found in the natural habitats of the specimens. As

many of them cannot live long in captivity, there is constant fluctuation in the number and kinds of fish exhibited, but there are always many varieties of gorgeously colored and curiously shaped specimens from the warmer waters, American game fish, and the odd rays, eels, sharks, lungfish, and sea horses. Such invertebrates as shrimps, star fish, and sea anemones, are usually represented.

The balanced aquariums, in which the water is oxygenated by growing plants, occupy a separate room to the left of the entrance foyer. The room, in colorful Japanese style, is illuminated with lanterns on bamboo poles, and contains many small tropical fishes, including those commonly kept in homes.

Southeast of the Aquarium over a causeway is Northerly Island, officially a separate park of 91 "made" acres; on its northeast corner stands (3) the ADLER PLANETARIUM AND ASTRONOMICAL MUSEUM. (*Open* 10-5 *Mon., Wed., Thurs., and Sat., demonstrations at* 11 *and* 3; 10-9 *Tues. and Fri., demonstrations at* 11, 3, *and* 8; 2-5 *Sun., demonstrations at* 2:30 *and* 3:30. *Free Wed., Sat., and Sun.;* 25c *other days; children free every morning. Descriptive booklets at entrance,* 20c.)

The approach to the building is along a broad esplanade, which has a series of twelve cascading pools in the center. On the bottom of each pool is the zodiacal symbol of one of the twelve months. The building, designed by Ernest Grunsfeld, Jr., follows no historical style but achieves a monumental effect by its mass and its plain surfaces of rich rainbow granite. It is in the form of a regular dodecagon, topped with a circular dome of green copper. Bronze plaques of the twelve signs of the zodiac by Alfonso Iannelli are inset at the exterior corners. The gift of Max Adler, Chicago merchant-executive, the Planetarium was dedicated in 1930, the first in the western hemisphere. It is operated by the commissioners of the Park District.

In the planetarium chamber are reproduced the intricate phenomena of the heavens. Chairs arranged in concentric circles provide a comfortable view. The projection instrument, a fantastic and highly complex machine weighing more than two tons, was manufactured by the Carl Zeiss Company of Germany. More than 100 lenses stud its exterior and cast images of all visible heavenly bodies on a linen screen shaped in the form of a dome. The motor-driven projector, moving on its various axes, enables the lecturer to show four types of apparent celestial motion: the change of latitude; the diurnal motion; the interlocked motion of the sun, moon, and planets; and the precessional cycle. Thus the heavens can be viewed as they appear from any spot on earth, at any time. The day, year, and even the precessional cycle can be shortened to seconds by means of controls on the lecturer's desk.

For sheer drama and realism the demonstrations are superb. As the lecture begins, the chamber lights are slowly dimmed until the dome assumes the lambency of twilight. On the apparent horizon— the base of the dome—the silhouette of Chicago's skyline enables spectators to orient themselves. The light fades lower, the hum of the great stilted projector is heard, and gradually the first and brightest stars appear. When the room is black as night, the illusion is complete. At the end of the lecture, when the lights come on slowly to reveal the prosaic domed screen, spectators invariably blink for a moment in astonishment. The demonstrations are changed monthly, and include the Calendar, the Seasons, the Annual Journey of the Sun, the Winter and the Summer Constellations.

Seventy-two large transparencies from negatives made by the world's largest telescopes are mounted in niches along the walls of the corridors. Here, also, is displayed the fine collection of old instruments gathered by the Strozzi family of Florence, Italy; nocturnals, armillae, globes, sundials, and telescopes dating from 1479 to 1800. On the lower floor are modern astronomical instruments and exhibits to illustrate their use.

Directly behind the Field Museum in Burnham Park is (4) SOLDIER FIELD, begun in 1922 and named in tribute to Chicago's fallen soldiers. Seating approximately 80,000, with provisions for adding many thousands of temporary seats, it has been the scene of such events as the 28th Eucharistic Congress in 1926, and the second Dempsey-Tunney fight in 1927. Enclosing the north end of the horseshoe stadium is the Chicago Park District Administration Building, completed in 1939.

West of Field Museum is (5) the LOUIS PASTEUR MONUMENT, a bronze bust of the great scientist by Leon Hermant.

To the north stands (6) the CHRISTOPHER COLUMBUS MONUMENT by Carlo Brioschi, presented by citizens of Italian ancestry.

(7) The GRANT PARK BAND SHELL faces the entrance of the Field Museum (*concerts 8 p.m. nightly, except Tues., 7:30 p.m.,*

July 1-Labor Day.) The Park District and the Chicago Federation of Musicians sponsor concerts by various bands and orchestras.

West of the Band Shell, on Michigan Ave., at the foot of Ninth St., is (8) the GENERAL JOHN A. LOGAN MONUMENT, an equestrian work by Augustus Saint-Gaudens. The small grassy mound supporting the statue is often humorously referred to as the only hill in Chicago.

Northward is (9) the CONGRESS STREET PLAZA, formal entrance to the park. The broad concourse is marked by stone pylons, bronze eagles by Frederick C. Hibbard, and two immense symbolic equestrian Indian monuments, the work of Ivan Mestrovic.

At the end of the concourse stands (10) the BUCKINGHAM MEMORIAL FOUNTAIN (*operated May-Sept.*), formally landscaped as the "centerpiece of Grant Park." Dedicated in 1927, the pink Georgia marble fountain is the gift of the late Miss Kate Buckingham, in memory of her brother, Clarence Buckingham, a former trustee of the Art Institute. The main pool, 300 feet in diameter, contains four pairs of sea horses, dedicated to and facing each of the four states bordering Lake Michigan. For creating these fine large figures, N. Marcel Loyau won the *Prix National.* In the center of the pool three concentric basins rise to a height of 25 feet, and from their outer rims spouts a series of diminishing water domes. A central column of water rises almost 100 feet above the apex of the highest dome. At night, hidden lights of 45 million candlepower concentrate a blaze of color, constantly shifting in pattern, on the cascades of spray. The intricate control mechanism is housed in an underground room. During displays the fountain shoots 15,500 gallons of water per minute from its 134 jets. It is twice the size of the Latona Fountain at Versailles, which in a measure inspired its design. The architects were Bennett, Parsons, and Frost, with Clarence Farrier and J. H. Lambert as associates.

In an imposing architectural setting is (11) the SEATED LINCOLN MONUMENT, across Columbus Drive at the pedestrian extension of Van Buren St. One of the last of Augustus Saint-Gaudens' statues, it was completed in 1907, but was not placed until nineteen years later.

On Michigan Ave., just south of the Art Institute, is (12) the THEODORE THOMAS MEMORIAL, half-draped figure in bronze symbolizing Music. Behind it a long granite seat bears a bas-relief of an orchestra grouped around a profile of Chicago's great conductor. The memorial was designed by Albin Polasek and unveiled in 1924.

(13) The ART INSTITUTE OF CHICAGO faces Michigan Ave., at the foot of Adams Street. (*Open weekdays 9-5; Sun. and holidays 12-5. Free Wed., Sat., Sun., and holidays; other days 25c; children under 14 always free. Libraries open weekdays 9-5 and Mon., Tues., and Fri., 6-9:30. Guidebooks and catalogues for sale in the Department of Reproductions. Guides by appointment. Cafeteria on ground floor. See Calendar of Events for lecture series and annual exhibitions.*) This building, with its warm smoky-toned patina, has long been the Mecca of artists in the Middle West. Designed by Shepley, Rutan, and Coolidge in the Italian Renaissance style, it is notable for its delicate and fine proportions. Broad steps guarded by Edward Kemeys' bronze lions lead from the avenue to the main entrance, above which is a deep loggia sheltering statues of Minerva, Mercury, and Augustus Caesar. The bareness of the second story gallery walls is relieved by sections of the Parthenon frieze and on the north and south façades by a fine Palladian arcade. Lorado Taft's *Fountain of the Great Lakes,* at the south terrace, is composed of five female figures, the topmost symbolizing Lake Superior. From the shell in her hand water spills to the figures representing the other Great Lakes. The fountain memorializes Benjamin Franklin Ferguson, donor of a $1,000,000 trust fund, the income from which is used by the Institute trustees to erect and maintain monuments throughout Chicago. One of the eleven monuments already constructed by this fund, a replica of Jean Antoine Houdon's bronze of George Washington in regimental dress, stands at the entrance doors.

The Institute, incorporated in 1879 as the Chicago Academy of Fine Arts, is an outgrowth of one of the first art schools in the country, the Chicago Academy of Design, founded in 1866. The organization received its present name in 1882 and a few years later achieved international recognition when it purchased the Demidoff Collection of fifteen old Dutch Masters. At this time the Columbian Exposition authorities, instead of building a temporary structure to house the Parliament of Religions, cooperated financially with the Institute trustees in erecting the present permanent building. The Institute has since used the building and constructed large additions, notably Gunsaulus Hall spanning the Illinois Central right-of-way, and Hutchinson Wing, east of the tracks.

The Institute is supported largely by endowment and trust funds, together with Park District tax funds, membership dues, and entrance fees. For the past three decades there has been an annual average of one million visitors. Approximately seventy exhibitions held every year, ranging from international to one-man shows, make the Institute a constant source of fresh interest.

In the chronologically arranged galleries on the second floor of the main building are works by masters of almost every great school of painting from the thirteenth century to the present. But the Institute is richest in French paintings of the late nineteenth and early twentieth centuries. Many of the exhibits were gifts from Chicagoans. Earliest of these was the Henry Field collection, forty-one canvasses representing some of the best work of the Barbizon School and including Breton's popular *Song of the Lark.* Other notable collections include the Palmer French Impressionists; the Kimball British and Dutch paintings; the Ryerson loan group of Monets and Renoirs, primitives, and eighteenth and nineteenth century works; the Birch-Bartlett Post-Impressionists; the Butler Innesses; the Munger nineteenth century paintings, and the De Wolf and Schulze American canvasses. El Greco's *Assumption of the Virgin,* Rembrandt's *Young Girl at an Open Half-Door,* Seurat's *Sunday on the Island of Grand Jatte,* Constable's *Stoke-by-Nayland,* Manet's *Jesus Mocked,* and Renoir's *Two Little Circus Girls,* were selected by Robert S. Harshe, director of the Institute from 1921 until his death in January 1938, as perhaps the most valued of all the canvasses.

American and European drawings, water colors, and sculptures line the corridor galleries in the center of the second floor. The entrance hall, on the first floor, is devoted to modern sculpture, and is flanked by galleries of Egyptian and classical arts. The north half of the floor contains Fullerton Hall, the center of the extensive lecture activities of the Institute, and the print galleries. In these galleries exhibits are frequently arranged from the Institute's collection of 25,000 European and American prints; the important International print exhibitions are also held here. The Print Department Library is a general collection of 1,200 works on prints and drawings, and portfolios of reproductions of drawings.

In the south half of the first floor are the Children's Museum, filled with objects of interest to children, and the main libraries. Ryerson Library contains more than 35,000 volumes on the fine and decorative arts, including many monographs on individual painters and sculptors, and an exceptional series of Japanese and Chinese illustrated books. In addition, it receives 200 magazines and museum bulletins in English and other languages, even the Oriental. The 7,700 volumes and the 45 current issues of magazines in Burnham Library embrace the fields of architecture, town planning, housing, and landscape architecture. The unusually complete files of bound periodicals in both libraries make them especially valuable for research. The Photograph and Slide Department has 80,000 photographs and color prints, and 34,000 lantern slides, loaned free to educational and religious institutions in Chicago, and for a nominal fee to individual Chicagoans and to institutions outside the city.

Blackstone Hall, extending to the ground floor in the rear of the main building, houses interior architectural casts and the imposing cathedral fronts exhibited by the French government at the Columbian Exposition.

Some of the decorative arts collections are found in lower Gunsaulus Hall. Here the galleries are bright with English and Continental glass, pewter, American pottery, porcelain, wallpaper, and printed cottons. The fine collection of English lustreware includes rare specimens of "resist" and "stencil" processes.

The Alexander McKinlock, Jr. Memorial Court, in the center of the Hutchinson Wing, surrounds Carl Milles' *Triton Fountain,* a bronze group of 'four mythological figures returning from the sea with marine trophies. The south half of the wing, together with the most recent addition, the Allerton Wing, is given over mostly to European period rooms, furniture and rugs, metal and wood work, and textiles from the Coptic Period to the present. Rotating exhibitions are drawn from extensive groups of woven fabrics, lace, and needlework.

The north half houses the Oriental collection, one of the finest in America. The ceremonial bronze vessels, chiefly of the Chou and Han dynasties, are among the oldest existing works of Chinese art; other treasures are rare Cambodian sculptures, fine ceramics of various dynasties, and Mohammedan art objects. The history of Japanese prints is illustrated in the Buckingham collection, one of the most complete in existence. Frequently changed exhibits from it are shown in the Japanese gallery.

The School of the Art Institute, progenitor of the entire institution and one of the largest art schools in America, occupies part of the ground floor of the main building. Enrolling some 3,000 students, it awards degrees in fine arts, art education, and dramatic art.

In 1925 a School of Drama, offering a 3-year course of professional training in all branches of theater work, was added to the Schools of Fine Arts and Industrial Art. Connected with Hutchinson Wing is the KENNETH SAWYER GOODMAN MEMORIAL THEATER. Designed by Howard Van Doren Shaw, the theater is largely below surface level; for this reason it has no loft, and sets are wheeled into place. The arrangement of the main auditorium, seating 800, is an adaptation of the Continental type; the rows of seats, reached by longitudinal aisles on either side, stretch unbroken in their full width. Several productions are given for the public by the Goodman Theater players during the year.

The CHICAGO HARBOR is formed by inner and outer breakwaters extending the length of Grant Park to a point a mile north of the mouth of the river. In the second half of the nineteenth century, the Chicago River·was one of the busiest ports in the world, constantly crowded in the shipping season with grain and lumber boats. Breakwaters were first built in 1874 to protect the mouth of the river and provide basins for boats waiting to enter it. Today, except for an occasional tramp steamer from Norway or a few barges, there is little shipping to be seen in the river. The large tonnage still registered for Chicago is handled mainly near the southern limits at Calumet Harbor, which receives iron ore, coal, and limestone, and exports grain. The inner basin of the Chicago Harbor is now an important part of the city's recreational facilities, providing free anchorage for hundreds of boats, ranging from tiny sail boats to sleek yachts. Some of the boat owners are members of the Chicago and Columbia yacht clubs, which have clubhouses at the piers north of Monroe Street.

The pier at the north end of Grant Park is occupied by (14) the ILLINOIS NAVAL RESERVE ARMORY. The training ship *Wilmette,* usually tied up alongside, is, as few Chicagoans know, the remodeled excursion steamer, *Eastland,* on which occurred Chicago's most appalling disaster. On July 24, 1915, loaded with a holiday crowd, the *Eastland* capsized as it was about to leave the dock at the Clark Street bridge, drowning 812 persons.

The Near North Side

The Near North Side, the birthplace of Chicago, lies almost within the shadows of the Loop. Within its two square miles, which extend from the Chicago River to North Avenue, from Lake Michigan to the North Branch of the Chicago River, is a jumble of the diverse elements of Chicago life. A spearhead of smart shops and office buildings thrusts up Michigan Avenue past the old Water Tower, the center of Towertown, the "Gold Coast" of the late nineteenth century; here, in old mansions and converted coach houses, live many of Chicago's artists, and a number of young professional and business people who prefer high ceilings, old fireplaces, and "atmosphere" to modern conveniences. Farther north is the present "Gold Coast," with its mansions and apartments along the lake front. A few blocks inland lie the desolate tenements and shacks of Italians and Negroes, bounded by factories and warehouses along the river. Moody Bible Institute neighbors on "Bughouse Square"; the sombre, mansard-roofed mansions on lower Rush Street end abruptly at the towering Wrigley Building; the chili parlors and cheap saloons on Clark Street are a few steps from swank restaurants and cocktail lounges; from a corner of the Seminary that he founded, Archbishop James Edward Quigley fixes a stony gaze on two elaborate night clubs across the street.

A century ago the great bulge of land south of Oak Street and east of Michigan Avenue did not exist. In 1886 a small craft, manned by Capt. George Wellington Streeter, grounded on a shoal off the foot of Superior Street. Unable to float the boat, Streeter decided to make his home on it. The shoal gradually filled in; eventually Streeter's boat stood on solid ground; to the amazement of Chicago, the Captain claimed it for himself as the District of Lake Michigan, renouncing allegiance to the State of Illinois. In his *Captain Streeter, Pioneer,* Everett Guy Ballard describes the long series of battles, legal and physical, between the Captain and city authorities in their efforts to evict him. Title to the land was eventually cleared, and the valuable section, now the site of some of Chicago's finest apartment buildings and hotels, remembers the Captain only in its name, Streeterville.

TOUR 1 — 1.2 m.

N. from the Chicago River on Michigan Ave.

1. The MICHIGAN AVENUE BRIDGE, a massive double-decked

bascule structure, spans the Chicago River between the sites of Chicago's earliest settlements—that of Fort Dearborn on the South bank and of its first houses, four log cabins, on the north bank. Until the bridge was built in 1920, Michigan Avenue north of the river was a narrow lane lined with old-fashioned mansions. All but one of the old houses on the west side of the Avenue were removed when it was widened; a few remain on the east side, overshadowed by modern buildings. The bridge replaced the old Rush Street span, and until the Outer Drive bridge was opened in 1937, carried the major traffic stream between the North Side and the downtown district.

Bas reliefs adorn the four bridge pylons. *The Pioneers* and *The Discoverers,* at the north end, are by J. E. Fraser; at the south end are *Defense* and *Regeneration,* symbolizing Chicago's recovery from the Great Fire, by Henry Hering. At the memorial services commemorating the 300th birthday of Father Marquette in May, 1937, nine years after the erection of *The Discoverers,* it was noted that the figure of Marquette, a Jesuit, was wearing Franciscan robes.

2. The WRIGLEY BUILDING (*observatory 9-5 daily, 25c includes a package of gum and use of telescopes*), NW. plaza of Michigan Avenue bridge, a terra-cotta office building designed by Graham, Anderson, Probst and White, French Renaissance in style, is visible for miles, immaculately white by day and incandescent at night. From the south its oblique façade resembles a partly opened gate, inviting entrance to the modernized north section of Michigan Avenue, the development of which it pioneered. From a certain angle across the street the building appears to flatten into an elaborate stage prop. Its four-faced tower clock furnishes small talk for Chicagoans who know that its figures are really not Roman numerals but simply single keystone strips of tile, 3½ feet high. The Arts Club of Chicago maintains clubrooms and galleries on the second floor; at intervals, exhibitions by well-known artists are shown here.

3. The TRIBUNE TOWER (*open; tours* 2:30, 3:30, 4:30, *and* 8:00 *Mon.-Fri.; reservations for evening tour; observatory 9-5 daily, 25c*), 435 N. Michigan Ave., contains the plant and offices of the Chicago *Tribune.* Cathedral-like, its vertical shaft of soft-toned Indiana limestone terminates in a crown reminiscent of the Butter Tower in Rouen. At the 25th floor a setback provides a promenade enclosed within a Gothic cloister of delicate tracery, above which soaring arches simulate flying buttresses.

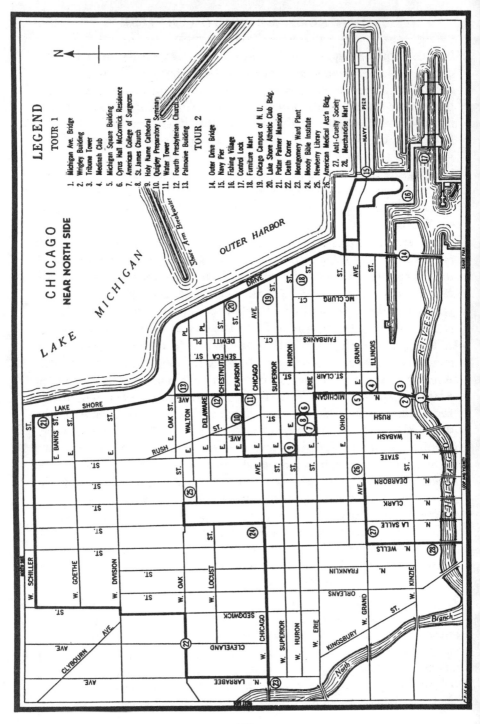

LEGEND

CHICAGO
NEAR NORTH SIDE

TOUR 1

1. Michigan Ave. Bridge
2. Wrigley Building
3. Tribune Tower
4. Medinah Club
5. Michigan Square Building
6. Cyrus Hall McCormick Residence
7. American College of Surgeons
8. St. James Church
9. Holy Name Cathedral
10. Quigley Preparatory Seminary
11. Water Tower
12. Fourth Presbyterian Church
13. Palmolive Building

TOUR 2

14. Outer Drive Bridge
15. Navy Pier
16. Fishing Village
17. Control Lock
18. Furniture Mart
19. Chicago Campus of N. U.
20. Lake Shore Athletic Club Bldg.
21. Potter Palmer Mansion
22. Death Corner
23. Montgomery Ward Plant
24. Moody Bible Institute
25. Newberry Library
26. American Medical Ass'n Bldg.
27. Anti-Cruelty Society
28. Merchandise Mart

Flanked by built-in stone fragments from celebrated buildings, the richly carved entrance arch is three stories high; light enters the lobby through a pierced stone screen of fanciful design. Entwined in foliage are figures from Æsop's fables and facetious representations of the architects—a howling dog for John Mead Howells, a figure of Robin Hood for Raymond M. Hood—whose design won the $50,000 award in the world-wide competition held by the *Tribune* in 1921 for "the most beautiful and distinctive office building in the world." The second prize was won by the Finnish architect, Eliel Saarinen, whose severely vertical design has had a more profound and extensive influence on skyscraper architecture.

On the travertine walls of the spacious lobby are quotations on the freedom of the press, a mural depicting man's struggle for freedom of speech, letters written by Abraham Lincoln to Joseph Medill, founder of the *Tribune,* and several weather recording devices.

The Chicago *Tribune,* occupying a large part of the building, was established in 1847. Oldest and most widely circulated newspaper in Chicago, it is one of the most profitable publishing enterprises in the world. Col. Robert R. McCormick, grandson of Joseph Medill, has been editor and publisher since 1925. Tours of the plant take visitors through the news room, engraving and composing rooms, and other offices associated with the production and distribution of the newspaper, including the great press room. Here, in the lower levels of the building, some of the largest and fastest presses in the world roar out 2,500 miles of newsprint daily. Adjoining the tower is WGN RADIO STATION (*tours* 10-4:30 *weekdays;* 11-4:30 *Sun.*), with rich portals and decorations in flamboyant Gothic style.

4. The MEDINAH CLUB OF CHICAGO (*observatory* 10-10 *daily,* 25c), distinguished by its exotic Moorish dome and minaret, is a residential club, formerly for Shriners but now unrestricted. The 42-story structure, designed by Walter W. Alschlager, incorporates a miscellany of architectural styles and was completed in 1928 at a cost of $10,000,000.

5. The MICHIGAN SQUARE BUILDING, 540 N. Michigan Ave., within a severe exterior, contains a striking blend of commerce and art. Holabird and Root turned the disadvantages of an uneven lot into an architectural triumph by planning a number of small shops on different levels. Concentric semi-circular floors and flying stairways radiate from the Fountain of Diana. Sculptured by Carl Milles in a

technique resembling archaic Greek, the central statue and secondary figures of the fountain reveal strength and movement rather than grace, creating an impression of wild forest life. The illusion is furthered by the details of the court, the lighting of which suggests a forest glade; massive striped pillars symbolize tree trunks.

L. from Michigan Ave. on Erie St. R. on Rush St.

RUSH STREET became a dead-end street when its old bridge was superseded by the Michigan Avenue bridge. The first building erected on new Michigan Avenue, the Wrigley, turned its back on Rush Street with its line of mansard-roofed mansions south of Chicago Avenue. Rush Street's brownstone gentility has been further invaded by restaurants and modernistic night clubs.

6. The CYRUS HALL McCORMICK RESIDENCE (*private*), 675 Rush St., a Victorian mansion designed by Cudell and Blumenthal, was built in 1879 for the inventor of the reaper, and is owned by his son, Harold Fowler McCormick. An iron-railed mansard roof and tower crown the three-story brownstone structure.

The McCormick Historical Association Library (*open to research workers on application*), in the former coach house, contains more than 1,500 printed and 1,500,000 manuscript items concerned with the activities and interests of the McCormick family: the history of agriculture, the evolution of farm machinery, early Virginiana, the development of the Presbyterian church in the Midwest, and records of the McCormick reaper companies.

Retrace to Erie St. R. on Erie St.

7. The AMERICAN COLLEGE OF SURGEONS (*open* 9-4:30 *Mon.-Fri.*, 9-1 *Sat.*), 40 E. Erie St., is the national headquarters of a fellowship of 12,000 surgeons. The gray stone building, formerly the mansion of S. M. Nickerson, a banker, was completed in 1883; the great entrance hall is entirely of marble; carved alabaster openwork graces the stair-rail.

An enclosed passageway leads to the JOHN B. MURPHY MEMORIAL, 50 E. Erie St., an auditorium dedicated to the memory of one of the great surgeons of the early twentieth century. From the street the colonnaded façade appears to be wedged between the adjoining buildings. Panels in the imposing bronze entrance doors picture epoch-making discoveries in the history of medicine.

R. from Erie St. on Wabash Ave.

8. ST. JAMES CHURCH, Wabash Ave. at Huron St., was rebuilt around parts of the tower and rough stone walls that withstood the flames of 1871. The Episcopal Parish of St. James, established in 1834, built the original Gothic structure in 1857. At the north end of the church is the Chapel of St. Andrew, a beautiful bit of Gothic architecture, designed in 1913 by Bertram Goodhue; the chapel commemorates James L. Houghteling, founder of the Brotherhood of St. Andrew.

L. from Wabash Ave. on Superior St.

9. HOLY NAME CATHEDRAL, Superior and State Sts., a Victorian Gothic structure of limestone, dominates six diocesan and parish buildings. Containing the cathedra of the archbishop of the diocese, it is the center of Roman Catholic worship in metropolitan Chicago. At the Sunday noon high mass the Cardinal's cathedral choristers sing; the Cardinal himself celebrates the Pontifical high masses. The music of the cathedral is in authentic liturgical form. In the library (*private*) are the complete works of Palestrina, said to be one of only two such collections in the United States.

R. from Superior St. on State St. R. from State St. on Pearson St.

10. The QUIGLEY PREPARATORY SEMINARY, Pearson and Rush Sts., prepares some 900 youths for the Roman Catholic priesthood. Regarded by some as the most picturesque Gothic group in Chicago, the seminary buildings, designed by Zachary Davis, surround a quadrangle court. The Chapel of St. James is reminiscent of Sainte Chapelle, Paris, in the delicacy of its design. Its windows, designed by Robert Giles, are composed of many thousands of pieces of antique English glass with fused pigments; the rose window was patterned on that in Notre Dame de Paris.

11. The WATER TOWER (*closed*), Michigan Ave., between Chicago Ave. and Pearson St., was one of very few Near North Side buildings that survived the Chicago Fire. It again escaped destruction when streets were widened in 1928 because it had endeared itself to Chicagoans as a favorite landmark. Built in 1869, it performed an important function in the water system for many years. An ornamented standpipe, the tower absorbed the pulsations caused by the old style

pumps in the station across the street, steadying the water flow in the city mains. The 186-foot tower of rough-hewn Lemont limestone is now a buffer between the old and the new in Chicago. In style it is "goldfish castle" Gothic, striking an anachronistic note in the midst of trim modern buildings. The tower stands like a hoop-skirted matron in a garden, majestically deflecting the surging flow of Michigan Avenue traffic; at night it is bathed in the amber glow of concealed lights.

The WATER WORKS (*open 8 a.m.-9 p.m. daily*), opposite the tower, is the oldest link in the chain of twelve stations pumping Chicago's water supply. In 1842 the first station was built at Lake Street and Michigan Avenue to pump water through hollowed cedar logs. The first municipally owned plant was built on Chicago Avenue in 1854. Of the plant that replaced it in 1867, the Chicago Fire left only the walls, which were used in the present building.

The tank-like structures in the lake, about two miles offshore north of Chicago Avenue, are two of the six cribs, or intakes, where approximately a billion gallons of water per day enter tunnels under the bed of the lake and flow to the pumping stations for distribution through the mains. The system was designed by E. S. Chesborough in 1864.

L. from Pearson St. on Michigan Ave.

12. The FOURTH PRESBYTERIAN CHURCH, Michigan Ave. and Delaware Pl., designed by Ralph Adams Cram, is a fine example of English Gothic in beautifully carved Bedford stone. With the parish house and manse adjoining, it encloses a grass plot on three sides. The fourth side of the rectangle is an arcade through which passers-by glimpse the cloister garth and fountain. The church is a massive edifice with pinnacled gables, slender spire, and generous buttresses. The beautiful stained-glass windows were designed and executed by Charles Connick. For many years the Fourth Presbyterian has been a focal point of Chicago's fashionable Easter Sunday parade.

13. The PALMOLIVE BUILDING, 919 N. Michigan Ave., an impressive modern office structure designed by Holabird and Root, faces the Gold Coast on one side and the downtown district on the other. Rising 37 stories in a series of setbacks, the building is topped with a slender aluminum tower supporting the Palmolive Beacon, formerly known as the Lindbergh Beacon. Flood lights on the setback terraces project interesting patterns on the smooth limestone walls.

The beacon, the most powerful in the world, a high-intensity arc of two billion candlepower, rotates twice a minute. At an altitude of 45,000 feet it can be seen 500 miles; the average visibility is 250 miles. Newspapers have been read by its light in planes 27 miles away. Below it, a directional light of 11,500,000 candlepower points to the Municipal Airport.

TOUR 2 — 6.5 m.

N. from mouth of the river on Lake Shore Drive

14. The OUTER DRIVE BRIDGE, at the mouth of the Chicago River, together with the smaller bridge immediately north over Ogden Slip, connects the express highway systems between the north and the south lake shore, diverting through traffic from the downtown area and providing another artery between the Loop and the North Side. The largest bascule bridge in the world, it was dedicated October 5, 1937 by President Franklin D. Roosevelt in a memorable address castigating aggressor nations.

R. from Lake Shore Drive on Ohio St. leading into Grand Ave.

15. NAVY PIER, at the foot of Grand Avenue, extends 1,000 yards into the lake as a terminal for freight and pleasure craft, and as a summer playground. Recreational facilities at the east end include picnic and dining pavilions, children's playground, dance hall, auditorium, excursion landing, and promenades. Garden clubs and others use the long sheds for periodic displays. From the far end of the pier is an excellent view of Chicago's skyline.

16. The FISHING VILLAGE, SW. of the Navy Pier, is one of the two commercial fishing centers of Chicago. Shacks, with store fronts, house the fishermen and provide a market for their catch, principally perch and lake herring. Smokehouses process chubs and other fishes shipped in from northern points. Linen gill nets, wound on reels, dry in the sun along the wharf, to which gasoline launches are tied. Early each morning the fishermen first set miles of nets on the lake bottom several miles offshore and then reel in the nets set the previous day.

17. The CONTROL LOCK, SE. of the village, forms an anteroom to the mouth of the river through which all boats passing between the lake and the river must go. It was built in 1938 to prevent the possibility of the river flowing into the lake, as it did before the Drainage

Canal reversed the flow in 1900. The Supreme Court ordered a reduction in the diversion of lake water from a maximum of 10,000 cubic feet per second to 1,500, beginning January 1, 1939. It was feared that this reduced withdrawal might at times be insufficient to maintain the delicately balanced westward flow of the river, which would then back its polluting waters into the lake. At such times, the lock will hold the river back until the control gates at Lockport, which regulate the rate of diversion, are opened wide.

Retrace Ohio St. R. on Lake Shore Drive

18. The AMERICAN FURNITURE MART (*open to wholesale trade only*), 666 Lake Shore Dr., reflects the current merchandising trend toward centralized wholesale markets. The largest building in the world at the time of construction in 1924, its huge utilitarian bulk is the most massive structure on the lake front. Gothic entrances and ornamentation, as well as a blue campanile tower, somewhat mitigate the heaviness of this great block of pressed brick, 28,000,000 cubic feet in volume. Housing the national showrooms of the country's leading manufacturers of home furnishings, it provides a convenient year-round market for buyers, and semi-annually makes Chicago the greatest wholesale furniture market in the United States. The building was designed by Henry Raeder and associates, N. Max Dunning and George C. Nimmons.

WCFL Broadcasting Station (*open 9 a.m.-10 p.m. daily*), on the 20th floor of the Mart tower, is the largest independent radio broadcasting unit devoted to the interests of organized labor in the United States. It is owned and operated by the Chicago Federation of Labor.

19. The CHICAGO CAMPUS OF NORTHWESTERN UNIVERSITY, formerly McKinlock Memorial Campus, Lake Shore Drive at Chicago Ave., is the Chicago group of professional and part-time schools under the general administration of Northwestern University in suburban Evanston. The cluster of six Tudor Gothic structures, designed by James Gamble Rogers, with Frank A. Childs and William J. Smith as associates, stands on a 14-acre landscaped tract, secured in 1920. The schools enroll about 1,300 full-time and 9,000 part-time students.

The Montgomery Ward Memorial Building, tallest of the group, gift of Mrs. Elizabeth J. Ward in memory of her husband, houses the medical school on its lower floors and the dental school above. The medical college was the first in the United States to establish a certain standard of preliminary education as a prerequisite to enrollment. Its list of alumni includes such illustrious names as Mayo, Billings, and De Lee. The Frederick Robert Zeit Museum of Pathology (*open* 9-5 *Mon.-Fri.; 9-12 Sat.; apply room 694 for guide*), one of the finest of its kind in the country, contains approximately 3,000 labeled specimens showing changes produced by disease in the various organs of the human body. The William Bebb Library and Museum (*open* 9-5 *Mon.-Fri., 9-12 Sat.*), on the 10th floor, contains rare and comic prints and etchings of dental practice, busts and biographical placques of famous dentists, old instruments, and pathological and normal animal and human dentures.

East of the Ward building is WIEBOLDT HALL, in which are held the evening classes of the School of Commerce, the second largest in the United States, and of the Medill School of Journalism. Clubrooms and a large commerce library serve the largest group of students on the campus.

LEVY MAYER HALL and the ELBERT H. GARY LIBRARY BUILDING, east of Wieboldt Hall, are used by the Law School, established in 1859, oldest in Chicago. A cloistered garden between the ivy-covered buildings is enclosed within an arched wall connecting the wings. Hundreds of illustrations of the history, customs, and leaders of the legal profession, and facsimiles of historically interesting documents line the corridors.

THORNE HALL, on Lake Shore Drive, contains an auditorium and a social room. The Alexander McKinlock Memorial Gate, at the south entrance, is a high and massive archway of ornamental bronze and wrought iron, with two beautifully designed gates.

20. The LAKE SHORE ATHLETIC CLUB BUILDING (*private; apply for permission to view murals*), 850 N. Lake Shore Drive, is a dignified 18-story building of buff brick. The fifty panels on the walls of the five private dining rooms on the second floor were designed by Otto E. Hake, and depict Chicago scenes and historical events from Indian days to the present.

21. The POTTER PALMER MANSION (*closed*), Lake Shore Drive between Banks and Schiller Sts., designed by Henry Ives Cobb, was completed in 1885, first of the Drive's imposing houses. Battlemented turrets and towers, brown sandstone walls trimmed with gray

granite, and a stone balcony, create the impression of a feudal castle. The mansion was the scene of many brilliant social events.

L. from Lake Shore Drive on Schiller St.
L. on Sedgwick St. R. on Oak St.

22. DEATH CORNER, Oak St. and Cleveland Ave., in the heart of the crowded Italian slum area, was the scene of more slayings during the prohibition era than any other point in the city. The numerous shootings and stabbings of men engaged in the "alky" trade, were invariably "unwitnessed," although many occurred in broad daylight.

L. from Oak St. on Larrabee St. R. on Chicago Ave.

23. The MONTGOMERY WARD AND CO. PLANT (*tours by arrangement*), sprawls along the North Branch at Chicago Ave. The three huge eight-story buildings, each a block long and half as wide, are a far cry from the 12- by 14-foot room, at 825 N. Clark Street nearby, in which A. Montgomery Ward and George R. Thorne started the first mail-order house in the world in 1872. The present catalogue issues, grown from a few 8- by 12-inch single sheets to millions of voluminous books, are familiar throughout the country.

The company, the second largest mail-order house in the world, maintains eight other plants and approximately 500 retail stores in the United States. The building on the south side of Chicago Avenue, surmounted with the symbol of the institution, a figure of the *Spirit of Progress,* houses the general administrative offices and a large department store. In the north buildings, mail orders are speedily assembled and shipped, as many as 200,000 a day.

Working out of St. Louis as a traveling salesman in the late 1860's, Montgomery Ward recognized the merchandising limitations of the small stores in rural areas. When he conceived the idea of mail order selling, he came to Chicago, and initiated the business with a capital of less than $2,500.

Retrace Chicago Ave. L. from Chicago Ave. on La Salle St.

24. MOODY BIBLE INSTITUTE (*open* 8:30-5 *Mon.-Fri.,* 8:30-12:30 *Sat., evenings by arrangement*), La Salle St. at Chicago Ave., is a coeducational, interdenominational, Christian training school sup-

ported largely by contributions from friends throughout the world. Twenty-eight buildings serve the needs of 2,700 resident and evening students, prospective teachers, and preachers of the Gospel. The curriculum emphasizes Biblical doctrine and the ministry of music. The activities of Dwight L. Moody gradually expanded from his Sunday School class, his North Market Mission, and the Illinois Street Church, to this "West Point of Christian Service," founded in 1886.

The ADMINISTRATIVE BUILDING, 812 N. La Salle Street, a 12-story Gothic structure of red brick and Bedford stone, was designed by Thielbar and Fugard and completed in 1938. In the tower of the building is the Institute's radio station, WMBI, devoted entirely to religious programs. The MOODY EXHIBIT, 830 N. La Salle Street, contains various Bibles and relics from Moody's home and office.

R. from La Salle St. on Oak St. R. on Clark St.

BUGHOUSE SQUARE, Walton St. between Dearborn and Clark Sts., separates Newberry Library from Washington Square, the oldest park in the city. This is the outdoor forum of garrulous hobohemia. On summer nights local and visiting intellectual hoboes and hobophiles expound unorthodoxy, socio-political and sexual. Tourists in the many sight-seeing buses that tarry in the square frequently find themselves the target of a verbal barrage.

25. The NEWBERRY LIBRARY (main reading and genealogy rooms open 9 a.m.-10 p.m. weekdays; Edward E. Ayer, John M. Wing and rare book collections, 9-5; non-circulating), Clark, Walton and Dearborn Sts., was named for Walter Loomis Newberry, pioneer Chicago merchant and financier, whose bequest forms the principal part of its endowment. Established in 1887, it contains more than 500,000 books, bound pamphlets, and manuscripts on Americana, British history, English and American literature, typography, genealogy, music, and comparative philology.

The library is notable for its rare books and source material. It contains some 1,700 books issued before 1500, many of them superb examples of early printing, such as the *Hypnerotomachia Poliphili*, Venice, 1499, regarded as the most beautiful of early illustrated books. Its collection of European and Oriental manuscripts contains examples dating from the ninth century. The music collection, one of the best in the country, contains autographed scores by Richard Wagner, Edward MacDowell, Robert Schumann, Franz Schubert, and Johann Sebastian

Bach. The philological library, assembled by Prince Louis Lucien Bonaparte and acquired in 1900, ranks as one of the finest collections on linguistics in the world. The Edward E. Ayer Collection is particularly rich in materials on the archaeology and ethnology of the North American Indian, the native races of Mexico, and the Hawaiian and Philippine Islanders. The collection is increased from year to year, with emphasis on South American archaeology, ethnology, and colonial history, and the general subject of cartography. Another distinctive collection, provided by the John M. Wing Foundation, is devoted to typography and provides a comprehensive view of the history of book-making.

The Library holds periodic exhibitions of its rare books, prints, maps, and manuscripts. There is a regular annual exhibition of the fifty books of the year, under the auspices of the American Institute of Graphic Arts, and of Chicago fine printing, under the joint auspices of the Library and the Society of Typographic Arts.

The five-story building constructed of Connecticut granite in Spanish-Romanesque style, designed by Henry Ives Cobb, occupies the site of the Mahlon Ogden residence, the only Near North Side house saved during the Chicago Fire. About the various rooms and corridors hang thirty-four portraits, painted and presented to the library by G. P. A. Healy.

CLARK STREET, for a few blocks on either side of Grand Ave., provides a night life section for the down-at-the-heeler. Taverns, five and six to a block, advertise whisky and gin for 5 and 10 cents a shot, and incredibly large schooners of beer for a dime. Conveniently interspersed between the taverns are pawnshops. The street is lined with ornate red brick buildings, once pretentious family hotels. Some still function as hotels but serve a much less moneyed clientele.

North from Chicago Avenue, Clark Street was formerly the center of the "Nort Seit" of early German immigrants. The celebrated Turner Hall was recently demolished, but on and near North Avenue, at Clark Street, remain a number of German restaurants and food shops, and the old Germania Club.

L. from Clark St. on Grand Ave.

26. The AMERICAN MEDICAL ASSOCIATION BUILDING (*open* 8:30-4:30 *Mon.-Fri.*, 8:30-12 *Sat.*), NE. corner of Grand Ave. and Dearborn St., is the headquarters of the co-ordinating organiza-

tion of some 100,000 doctors whose delegate sessions shape the policies of the medical profession. The eight-story building contains laboratories, libraries, assembly rooms, and the editorial and production rooms of *Hygeia,* the *American Medical Directory,* and the *Journal of the American Medical Association.*

Retrace Grand Ave.

27. The ANTI-CRUELTY SOCIETY (9-5 *Mon.-Fri.,* 9-1 *Sat.*), 153 W. Grand Ave., maintains an establishment that would delight the most ardent zoophile. For the unfortunate among the animals of Chicago, the Society provides in its beautiful limestone building and grounds such modern comforts and conveniences as a clinic with X-ray equipment, and an exercise yard with trees and running water. Ambulances pick up stray, crippled, and unwanted animals at all hours. The placement service and free counsel by veterinarians are widely used.

L. from Grand Ave. on Wells St. R. on North Bank Drive

28. The MERCHANDISE MART (*commercial exhibits open to wholesale trade only*), 222 N. Bank Dr., is the largest building in the world. An enterprise of Marshall Field and Company, it was completed in 1930 as a wholesale market; more than 5,600 lines of department and general store goods are displayed here by wholesalers, manufacturers, and importers from all parts of the country. Built in part over the Chicago and North Western tracks, the $30,000,000 structure, designed by Graham, Anderson, Probst, and White, covers two city blocks. Six and one-half miles of store front corridors give access to 93 acres of floor space, an area almost two-thirds as large as the Chicago Loop. This concentrated commercial city houses a working population of 25,000, and has its own "L" station, bank, post office, telegraph and railroad ticket offices, large restaurants, and retail shops.

Set back from the river bank along a wide private street, its southern façade is visible for blocks, an example of dignified beauty in modern business architecture. Concealed lighting of the massive symmetrical structure forms a beautiful composition of light and shadow in the Chicago night scene. Fifteen murals by Jules Guerin depicting market scenes in foreign countries decorate the lobby walls. In the Home Building Exhibit (*open 9-5 Mon.-Fri.,* 9-1 *Sat.*), on the seventh floor, are model homes and a great variety of building materials.

The National Broadcasting Company studios and offices, and stations WMAQ and WENR (*open 9-5 daily; after 5 by appointment or by special ticket to a specific broadcast*), occupy the 19th and 20th floors of the Mart. There are eleven studios and five public observation rooms; Studio A is one of the largest in the world. The operations in the main control room include the amplification of programs for transmission to network stations, over some 45,000 miles of special telephone lines.

Lincoln Park

Along the lake shore between North and Foster Avenues stretches Lincoln Park, more than a thousand acres of rolling woodlands, bridle paths, quiet lagoons, yacht basins, grassy playgrounds, golf courses, and gardens, dotted with monuments and museums. For diversity of use the park is unequalled in Chicago. Originally a 120-acre city cemetery, the tract was designated as a park in 1864, and most of the graves were moved to outlying cemeteries. Adjacent lands were acquired, but the largest part of the park was created with sand from the lake in the present century.

At the south end of the park, commanding the Dearborn Parkway entrance, is (1) the STATUE OF ABRAHAM LINCOLN, by Augustus Saint-Gaudens, unveiled on October 22, 1887, regarded by many as the noblest portrait statue in the country. It captures in bronze the mood of the Gettysburg address. The simple base and the spacious exedra, backed by the foliage of the park, are the work of Stanford White.

West of the statue is (2) the CHICAGO HISTORICAL SOCIETY MUSEUM (*open 9:30-5 weekdays, 1-6 Sun.; children, students, and teachers free; adults free, Mon., Wed., Fri., other days, 25c; handbooks, 25c; guide service by arrangement*). Georgian in style the red brick building with limestone trim has two stories and a basement (which on the west is at ground level) and a flat balustraded roof; a broad flight of steps sweeps down from the Doric portico. Opened in 1932, the museum is the fourth home of the society, founded in 1856 to collect and preserve materials pertaining to the history of the United States, particularly those relating to Chicago and the Northwest Territory.

On the main floor, (east entrance) adjoining the foyer, which is patterned after that of Independence Hall, are the Marine Room, illustrative of the merchant marine and the Navy, and the Chicago Diorama Gallery, with eight scenes from the city's history.

The dozen period rooms on the main floor pictorialize the story of America from the days of Columbus through the World War; several reproduce famous old rooms. Objects range from anchors used by Columbus to messages sent by carrier pigeon from the "Lost Battalion" in the Argonne Forest. The George Washington collection includes several noteworthy paintings of Washington, the velvet suit he wore at his inauguration, and other personal effects. In the Chicago rooms are women's costumes of various periods, illustrations of the Chicago Fire, and miscellaneous relics.

On the top floors are other period rooms more specifically Illinoisan; among others, the Pioneer Room, containing a reproduction of the Lincoln log cabin and three store buildings of the 1840's and 1850's. The Illinois Room has a mask of Stephen A. Douglas and some of his effects, a first edition of the Book of Mormon, and part of the Lovejoy press. Lincoln Hall, lined with portraits and sculptures of the martyred President, contains his blanket shawl, the penholder with which he signed the Emancipation Proclamation, and the clothes he wore at the time of his assassination. His deathbed is preserved in a room that reproduces the one in which he died. The Lincoln Parlor, a reproduction of that in his Springfield house, has the original furniture.

In an adjoining large room portraits and busts of men and women prominent in the history of the city gaze down upon a huge model of contemporary Chicago. Constructed of balsa wood on a scale of one inch to 300 feet, the model accurately reproduces Chicago's 445,000 buildings as seen from an altitude of 8,000 feet. The work was done as a WPA project under the direction of Col. M. O. Kasson. Also on the top floor is the Gilpin Reference Library (*for research only; closed Sun.*), containing 75,000 volumes, and files of maps, newspapers, and documents pertaining largely to Chicago.

In the foyer of the ground floor (west entrance) is the dynamic *Massacre Monument,* by Carl Rohl-Smith. Behind it are logs from the second Fort Dearborn and various relics of pioneer days. The Carriage Room contains a Conestoga wagon and other early types of vehicles. Also on the ground floor is the Pike collection of American city prints, and the Auditorium, where lectures on Chicago history are

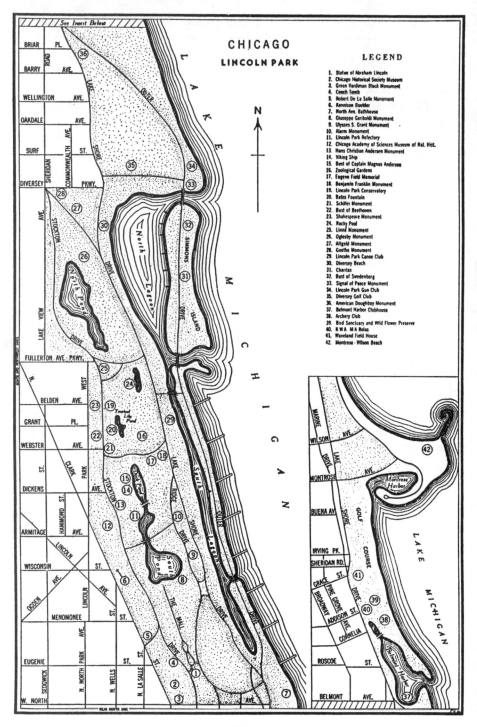

given Saturdays (10:30 *a.m.*) for school children and popular movies of historical background are shown on Sundays (3 *p.m.*), except during the summer months.

The Thorne Miniature Rooms (*adm. 25c, children, 10c on museum free days; otherwise no charge; lectures 3 pm. Mon., Wed., Fri.*), designed by Mrs. James Ward Thorne of Chicago, are architectural models of various rooms in American, Italian, Spanish, French, and English homes of different periods. Most of the miniature objects were collected in European shops or made by wood-carvers and iron-workers. Scaled one inch to the foot, they are so exact in detail that tiny books can be read with the aid of a magnifying glass.

South of the Historical Museum is (3) the GREEN VARDI-MAN BLACK MONUMENT, a memorial to the "Father of Modern Dentistry," by Frederick C. Hibbard (1918). North of the building, a dense growth of shrubbery screens (4) the COUCH TOMB. Many legends concerning this incongruous remnant of the old cemetery exist; actually, it escaped removal by order of the Illinois Supreme Court, because the stone blocks, fastened with copper rivets, could not be taken apart without completely demolishing the mausoleum. Ira Couch, owner of the old Tremont House, several members of his family, and a stranger who died in the old hostelry, are interred at this spot. (5) The ROBERT DE LA SALLE MONUMENT, by Count Jacque de la Laing (1889), faces the street that bears the explorer's name. (6) The KENNISON BOULDER, at the foot of Wisconsin Street marks the approximate location of the only other known grave in the park. Here lies David Kennison (1736-1852), veteran of the Revolutionary War, and last survivor of the Boston Tea Party.

Lake Shore Drive, which throughout most of its length marks the former shore line of Lake Michigan, enters the park east of the Lincoln statue and the adjoining play fields. In 1938-39 sand was pumped in between North and Fullerton Avenues to form a beach a mile long. The NORTH AVENUE BATHHOUSE (7) stands in the southeast corner of the park.

North of the Lincoln statue, the Mall runs through the heart of the old park. It divides into paths to skirt South Pond and continues north to the Zoo. At the southeast corner of the pond is (8) the GUISEPPE GARIBALDI MONUMENT, a memorial (1901) to the Italian patriot, by Victor Gherardi. Between Ridge and Lake Shore Drives,

(9) the ULYSSES S. GRANT MONUMENT, a heroic equestrian bronze, stands on a massive stone arch. The work of Louis Rebisso, it was erected by popular subscription and unveiled with elaborate ceremony on October 7, 1891. Northward, along Ridge Drive, is (10) the ALARM MONUMENT, a memorial (1884) to the Ottawa Indians, the work of John Boyle. (11) LINCOLN PARK RE-FECTORY, at the northwest corner of South Pond, contains the Cafe Brauer (*open summer only*) and a rowboat concession.

West of the refectory, at Clark St. and Armitage Ave., is (12) the CHICAGO ACADEMY OF SCIENCES MUSEUM OF NATURAL HISTORY (*open weekdays* 9-5, *Sun.* 1-5), which por-trays the natural history of the Chicago region. The ivy-mantled building, designed by Patton and Fisher in Italian Renaissance style, was made possible by a gift from Matthew Laflin. Gov. John P. Alt-geld laid the cornerstone in 1893. Collections include plants and ani-mals of Chicago's dune and marsh regions, arranged with large tinted photographs of their habitats as backgrounds. Geological and paleonto-logical specimens, systematic exhibits of flora and fauna—some once common but no longer found in the Chicago area—are labeled with cards bearing interpretive data. Collectors of edible fungi frequently use the mushroom case to check doubtful specimens.

The Academy of Sciences, founded in 1857, is one of the oldest scientific bodies in Chicago. The original collections, later destroyed by fire, were secured by the first director, Robert Kennicott, on the Western Union survey for a telegraph-line route between Alaska and Russia in 1865. The Academy, supported by endowments, gifts, and memberships, not only maintains the museum and a library, but en-gages in field studies, extension work, and laboratory research. The vast study collections, particularly rich in invertebrates, are open to qualified students. Illustrated talks on natural history, travel, and exploration are given in the lecture hall (3 *p.m. Sun., Oct.-Mar.*). The Academy publishes scientific bulletins and the *Chicago Naturalist,* a quarterly; it also distributes gratis a map of the Chicago region of interest to naturalists.

Eastward, across Stockton Drive, is (13) the HANS CHRIS-TIAN ANDERSEN MONUMENT, a bronze by Johannes Gelert (1896) to the memory of the Danish author of fairy tales. (14) The VIKING SHIP, northeast of the monument, is a reproduction of the vessels used by the Norse in crossing the North Atlantic 1,000 years ago. In this ship Captain Magnus Andersen and a crew of eleven crossed the Atlantic for the Columbian Exposition in 1893. (15) The BUST OF CAPTAIN MAGNUS ANDERSEN, at the prow of the ship, is the work of Carl Paulsen (1936).

(16) The ZOOLOGICAL GARDENS, frequently visited by 100,000 people a day, occupy 25 acres between Stockton and Lake Shore Drives, and center upon a group of five animal houses (*open 9-5 daily; feeding hours 1 :30-4*). In the LION HOUSE are lions, tigers, jaguars, and leopards; to the south is the REPTILE HOUSE, formerly the Aquarium. Eastward, in the SMALL ANIMAL HOUSE, are the primates; the trained chimpanzees and Bushman, a gorilla acquired in 1930 when two years of age, attract large crowds. Across the parkway is the BIRD HOUSE, riotous in color and sound, and the ELEPHANT HOUSE, sheltering Deed-a-day, an Indian pachyderm donated by the Boy Scouts of Chicago. In the outdoor pens, cages, and shelters are bears, foxes, camels, llamas, zebras, buffaloes, and animals from all over the world.

Near the center of the Zoo buildings is (17) the EUGENE FIELD MEMORIAL, by Edward McCartan (1922). Depicted in bronze are the Dream Lady with two drowsy children, and inscribed on the granite base below are the poems of "Wynken, Blinken, and Nod" and the "Sugar Plum Tree in the Garden of Shut-Eye Town." End panels represent "The Fly Away Horse" and "Seein' Things." Northeastward is (18) the BENJAMIN FRANKLIN MONUMENT, by Richard Parks (1896).

West of the Zoo rise the glass buildings of (19) the LINCOLN PARK CONSERVATORY (*open 8-6 daily; 8 a.m.-10 p.m. July-Aug. and show periods; see Annual Events for show dates*). The Palm Room and Fern Room are lush with tropical foliage; exotic plants fill the Stove Room. The Show Room, brilliant with flowers at all times, are at their best during the four annual major shows, when thousands of blossoms are arranged in symphonies of color and form. About 650,000 persons visit the Conservatory annually.

In the Main Garden in front of the conservatory is (20) the BATES FOUNTAIN, designed by Saint-Gaudens and MacMonnies (1887). Nearby is (21) the SCHILLER MONUMENT, a memorial to the German poet and dramatist, by Ernst Raus (1886). Across Stockton Drive, in a planting of old-fashioned perennials known as Grandmother's Garden, are (22) a BUST OF BEETHOVEN, the work of Johannes Gelert (1897), and (23) a SHAKESPEARE MONUMENT, by William Ordway Partridge (1894). Northeast of the Conservatory is (24) the new ROCKY POOL, resembling a small limestone canyon, around which grow native wild flowers, hawthorns and willows. Overlooking the Conservatory from the north is (25) the LINNE MONUMENT, an impressive bronze memorial to the Swedish botanist, Karl Von Linne (Linnaeus), by C. Dyfverman (1891), with four allegorical figures surrounding the pedestal.

North Pond, with a casting pool at one end, lies across the parkway from the monument. On a wooded eminence at the northeast corner of the pond is (26) the OGLESBY MONUMENT, dedicated to the memory of Richard James Oglesby, three times elected governor of Illinois (1865, 1872, 1885) ; it is the work of Leonard Crunelle (1919). To the north, across the drive, is (27) the ALTGELD MONU-MENT, by Gutzon Borglum (1915), a memorial to Gov. John Peter Altgeld (1892-96) ; opposite the Elks Memorial (*see North and Northwest Sides*) is (28) the GOETHE MONUMENT, the work of Herman Hahn.

Eastward in this section of the park are the North and South Lagoons, between Lake Shore and Outer Drives. On South Lagoon is (29) the LINCOLN PARK CANOE CLUB (*private*) ; on North Lagoon is (30) DIVERSEY BEACH. On Simmons Island, east of North Lagoon, is (31) CHARITAS, a statue by Ida McClelland Stout (1922), symbolizing the humanitarian work of the Chicago Daily News Fresh Air Sanitarium, which for years occupied the adjoining building. At the north end of the island is (32) a BUST OF SWEDENBORG, the Swedish religious leader, by Adolph Jonsson (1924).

Across the bridge is (33) a SIGNAL OF PEACE MONU-MENT, depicting a mounted Indian with upraised hand, by Cyrus Dallin (1894). On the lake shore is the whitewashed concrete block building of (34) the LINCOLN PARK GUN CLUB, members of which practice trap and skeet shooting on the adjoining ranges (*range open to public; rates slightly higher than for members*). Northward stretches (35) the DIVERSEY GOLF COURSE (9-*hole*) ; at its northwestern end, on Lake Shore Drive, is (36) the AMERICAN DOUGHBOY MONUMENT, by E. M. Viquesney (1927), enclosed within a barbed wire fence.

To the north, on Belmont Harbor, a 53-acre basin, is (37) the

BELMONT HARBOR CLUBHOUSE, the two-story houseboat of the Chicago Yacht Club. The harbormaster's office and slips for power boats line the east bank. This harbor is the starting point for the Chicago to Mackinac race, the longest fresh-water course in the world (*see Annual Events*). North of the harbor, beyond the range of (38) the ARCHERY CLUB, is (39) a BIRD SANCTUARY AND WILD FLOWER PRESERVE; 'facing Addison St. is (40) the KWA MA ROLAS, Haidan Indian totem pole from the Queen Charlotte Islands. Beyond is (41) the WAVELAND FIELD-HOUSE, with the Wolford chimes which announce the quarter-hours. Athletic fields and tennis courts adjoin the building, and a 9-hole golf course lies to the north.

Into the lake, north of Montrose Avenue, juts a huge peninsula, from the end of which is a fine view of the entire Chicago skyline and part of the North Shore. A hook of land on the south shore shelters Montrose Harbor for pleasure craft; on the north side spreads (42) the MONTROSE-WILSON BEACH; one of the largest in the world made by man. To the north the drives through the park turn abruptly westward on Foster Avenue to Sheridan Road, but some day may continue as 'far as Evanston over land yet to be made.

North and Northwest Sides

Coursing southeasterly into Chicago, the North branch of the Chicago River divides the section north of North Avenue into the North Side and the larger Northwest Side. Together they contain more than a quarter of the area and the population of Chicago. Up to the nineties this section was made up of farmlands, truck gardens, hamlets and villages, subdivisions, and suburban towns. The settlements were focused along the railroads and along the former plankroads now followed in general by Clark Street and Milwaukee Avenue.

Only a small corner of the present area was a part of Chicago until the contiguous City of Lakeview (pop. 46,164) and the Town of Jefferson (pop. 11,600) were annexed in 1889. Jefferson consisted of many hamlets scattered about what is now the Northwest Side. Around the borders, the former villages of Rogers Park, West Ridge, Edison Park, and Norwood Park, annexed to the city at later dates, comprise most of the rest of the section.

Least industrialized of the principal divisions of Chicago, the North

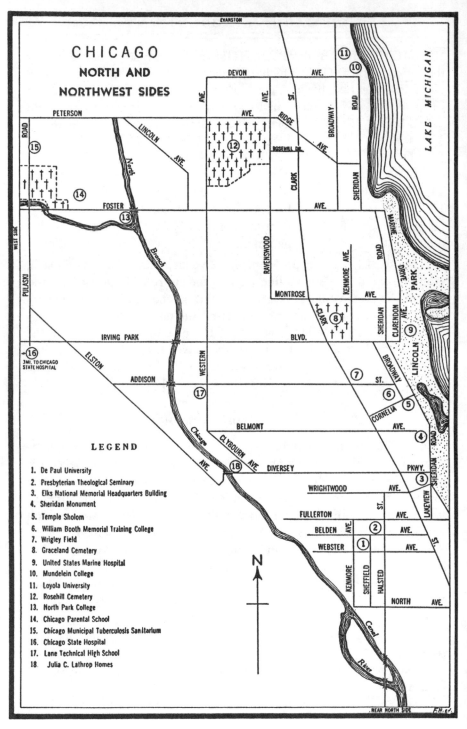

CHICAGO
NORTH AND
NORTHWEST SIDES

LEGEND

1. De Paul University
2. Presbyterian Theological Seminary
3. Elks National Memorial Headquarters Building
4. Sheridan Monument
5. Temple Sholom
6. William Booth Memorial Training College
7. Wrigley Field
8. Graceland Cemetery
9. United States Marine Hospital
10. Mundelein College
11. Loyola University
12. Rosehill Cemetery
13. North Park College
14. Chicago Parental School
15. Chicago Municipal Tuberculosis Sanitarium
16. Chicago State Hospital
17. Lane Technical High School
18. Julia C. Lathrop Homes

N

and Northwest Sides contain the full range of types of residences, with few blighted areas and more cemeteries and institutions, such as colleges and hospitals, than any other part of Chicago. The line of large homes, apartments, and hotels opposite Lincoln Park, which borders two-thirds of the North Side lake shore, is continued along the lake through Rogers Park to the city limits. The developments along the river provide typical cross-sections of the entire inland district. The lower half of the river is improved for navigation and heavily industrialized on both banks. To the east are small houses in the old German and Swedish settlements, and several Polish groups live westward. Beyond Addison Street the river winds past many small parks, and, above the entrance of the North Shore Channel at Argyle Street, becomes a small stream in open subdivisions and forest preserves, passing the city border near the still village-like Norwood Park and Edison Park.

POINTS OF INTEREST

1. DE PAUL UNIVERSITY, occupying the block formed by Kenmore, Belden, Sheffield, and Webster Aves., was founded in 1898 as St. Vincent's College by the Fathers of the Congregation of the Mission. The coeducational institution enrolls approximately 400 students. The Downtown College Building houses professional and evening classes for 7,000. North of the new HALL OF SCIENCE, Kenmore and Belden Aves., is the COLLEGE OF LIBERAL ARTS AND SCIENCE BUILDING, a four-story modern Gothic structure. The ADMINISTRATION BUILDING, 2235 Sheffield Ave., contains the 25,000 volumes of the Liberal Arts Library. On the domed ceiling of the UNIVERSITY AUDITORIUM, south of the Administration Building, are murals illustrating the history of education. The university church, ST. VINCENT'S, 1010 Webster Ave., a massive Romanesque stone structure, stands next to DE PAUL UNIVERSITY ACADEMY.

2. The PRESBYTERIAN THEOLOGICAL SEMINARY, Halsted St., between Belden and Fullerton Aves., and extending to Sheffield Ave., was founded in 1829 at Hanover, Indiana, and established here in 1859 when endowed by Cyrus H. McCormick. About 130 students are enrolled for the three year course leading to the Bachelor of Divinity degree. On the west half of the large campus are the English Gothic limestone GYMNASIUM and the COMMONS. Long rows of dormered red brick residences face on Belden and on Fuller-

ton Avenues. Between them, opening on a square, are the faculty residences. At the east end stands a group of age-scarred dormitory and classroom buildings. Ewing Hall, erected in 1863, contains a small museum of Palestinian archeology. The Virginia Library, a classical structure of Indiana limestone, has more than 70,000 volumes and a museum of objects from various mission fields.

3. The ELKS NATIONAL MEMORIAL HEADQUARTERS BUILDING (*open* 10-5 *daily: guide at entrance*), Lakeview Ave. at Diversey Parkway, a shrine to the 70,000 Elks who served in the World War, designed by Egerton Swartwout and completed in 1926, consists of a domed rotunda surrounded by a Roman Doric colonnade above a high base; narrow wings connect the rotunda with end pavilions and house the national offices. The symbols of the order, a pair of reclining elk, by Laura Gardin Fraser, flank the entrance stairway. The frieze under the colonnade illustrates the theme, "The Triumphs of Peace Endure—The Triumphs of War Perish." The frieze and *Patriotism* and *Fraternity,* symbolic groups by Adolph Weinman, fill niches in the ends of the wings.

The impressive marble Memorial Hall is decorated with murals by Eugene Savage, inspired mainly by the Beatitudes, and with statues by James E. Fraser and panels by Edwin Blashfield. Peace is the theme of the panels, also by Savage, in the Grand Reception Room.

4. The SHERIDAN MONUMENT, Sheridan Road, Belmont Ave., and Lake Shore Drive, a dynamic bronze designed by Gutzon Borglum, represents Gen. Philip Sheridan mounted on his galloping stallion.

5. TEMPLE SHOLOM, Lake Shore Drive at Cornelia Ave., an impressive modern Romanesque structure of ancient-looking Lannon stone, designed by Coolidge and Hodgdon, with Loebl, Schlossman, and Donnuth as associate architects, was built in 1930 for the North Chicago Hebrew Congregation, a reform Jewish congregation organized in 1867. The temple has a seating capacity of 1,500, which can be doubled on holidays by moving a huge sliding partition separating it from the Frankenstein Memorial Center.

6. The WILLIAM BOOTH MEMORIAL TRAINING COLLEGE (*open by arrangement*), Brompton Ave. at Broadway, occupies the 'former Joseph E. Tilt mansion, built in 1914. One of the four colleges of the Salvation Army in the United States, it trains young men and women to be officers in all branches of the service; the

seventy students are taught orders and regulations, doctrine and Bible.

Designed by Holabird and Roche, the Tudor Gothic structure, with pitched roof and buttressed chimneys, stands in grounds enclosed within a 7-foot wall and has the air of a secluded English country home. The block-long servants' quarters have been converted into a men's dormitory.

7. WRIGLEY FIELD, Clark and Addison Sts., home of the Cubs, Chicago's National League baseball club, seats approximately 45,000 people.

8. GRACELAND CEMETERY (*open* 8-5 *daily*), Clark St. and Irving Park Blvd., organized in 1861, contains many re-interments from the old city cemetery, now part of Lincoln Park. John Kinzie, Chicago's first white civilian settler, is buried here. Within the 119 landscaped acres are a crematory, and many family tracts and imposing mausoleums, particularly around the artificial lake near the east border. The Carrie Getty and the Martin Ryerson tombs are among Louis Sullivan's finest works.

9. The UNITED STATES MARINE HOSPITAL (*not open to the public*), 4141 Clarendon Ave., operated by the U. S. Public Health Service, provides hospitalization (300 beds) and clinical treatment mainly for men in the merchant marine, coast guard, and lighthouse services. Constructed in 1873, the long Lemont limestone building is a distinctive Lakeview district landmark. Several new buildings house the hospital staff.

10. MUNDELEIN COLLEGE (*tours* 2-5 *Sun. except last Sun. of month*), 6363 Sheridan Road, was founded in 1930 by the Sisters of Charity of the Blessed Virgin Mary on the initiative of George, Cardinal Mundelein, as a center of the higher education for Catholic young women. The student body of 500 is instructed by nuns, and lay and clerical professors. The student publications of the college are well known. The bi-weekly *Skyscraper*, a news sheet, has won All-American Collegiate Press Association honors. *Mundelein College Review*, a literary magazine, is a quarterly; *Quest*, an anthology of verse, is published annually.

Designed by Joe W. McCarthy and Nairne Fisher, the college building, striking in the long sweeping lines of its Indiana limestone walls, rises fourteen floors above the lake shore campus. Setbacks provide terraces used as recreation courts and roof gardens.

The LIBRARY, a white Italian marble building with a wide carved porch, contains 35,000 volumes, including many vellum-bound volumes of early church history, and early Aldines, Elzevirs, Bodinis, and other rare editions.

11. LOYOLA UNIVERSITY, 6625 Sheridan Road, grew from Saint Ignatius College, which, founded by the Jesuit Fathers in 1870, became the College of Arts and Sciences of Loyola University in 1909, and was removed to the present 23-acre shore campus in 1922. Six hundred of the 6,000 Loyola students attend classes on this campus. Others receive instruction in the Downtown College Building, and at the medical, dental, and nursing schools in the West Side Medical Center.

The ELIZABETH M. CUDAHY MEMORIAL LIBRARY (*open* 8:30-5, *Mon.-Fri.;* 8:30-12 *Sat.*) designed by A. N. Rebori in modern Romanesque style, is a finely modeled structure of Indiana limestone. The interior is lined with pink-striped Mankato stone. The mural on the west wall, by John Norton, depicts cartographically the activities of the Jesuit missionaries in the Great Lakes and upper Mississippi Valley regions. Among the 71,000 volumes are incunabula, rare editions, and an extensive collection of Jesuitica. The MADONNA DELLA STRADA CHAPEL, constructed in 1939, harmonizes with the library building. Between them stands the ADMINISTRATION BUILDING, which houses the Jesuit members of the faculty.

To the west are CUDAHY SCIENCE HALL, with classrooms, laboratories, and a seismographic observatory; DUMBACH HALL, housing the Loyola Academy; and the ALUMNI GYMNASIUM, in which the national Catholic high school basketball tournament is held annually.

12. ROSEHILL CEMETERY (*open* 9-5 *daily*), Ravenswood Ave. at Rosehill Drive, the largest in Chicago, was developed privately after the city closed its cemetery. Beyond the castellated Gothic entrance are 331 park-like acres containing more than 110,000 graves, including many of Chicago's great of the past century. An immense marble and granite mausoleum (*not open to the public*) stands at the west end of the cemetery.

13. NORTH PARK COLLEGE, Foster and Kedzie Aves., has the appearance of a small town college, with its seven modest buildings clustered on an 8-acre campus in a quiet residential section on the North Branch of the Chicago River. The Evangelical Mission Covenant of America, organized in 1885, controls the college, which had

its beginnings in Minneapolis and moved to Chicago in 1894. Offering 2-year courses in liberal arts and commerce, North Park, one of the largest privately owned junior colleges, has an enrollment of more than 500 students. With the exception of the Theological Seminary, the institution is non-sectarian and coeducational. The Music School offers a four-year course leading to the senior diploma.

14. The CHICAGO PARENTAL SCHOOL (*grounds always open; tours by arrangement*), 3600 Foster Ave., trains boys and girls of school age committed to its charge for truancy by the Juvenile Court. Organized in 1902 and conducted by the Chicago Board of Education, the school attempts to provide normal home conditions by use of the cottage plan. Its red brick buildings are clustered on a 75-acre tract, partly landscaped, partly used as a farm, and seem far removed from the Chicago scene.

15. The CHICAGO MUNICIPAL TUBERCULOSIS SANI-TARIUM (*open 2-4 Mon., Wed., Fri., Sat.*), 5601 N. Pulaski Road, has contributed much to Chicago's fight against the "White Plague." Since the erection in 1915 of the first red brick buildings here on the 160-acre grounds, the city's tuberculosis mortality rate has dropped from 170.6 to 55.7 per 100,000. Although more than 1,200 patients are admitted annually, there remains a long waiting list. Eight dispensaries throughout the city treat thousands of additional cases. The institution has won renown for its pioneer work in the field of home pneumothorax.

16. The CHICAGO STATE HOSPITAL (*open 9:30 and 1:30 Mon.-Fri.*), 6500 Irving Park Road, an insane asylum commonly known as Dunning, was founded as a county institution in 1869. Its various buildings house 5,100 inmates and employees.

17. LANE TECHNICAL HIGH SCHOOL, Western Ave. at Addison St., one of the largest school buildings in the world, accommodates approximately 9,000 students. The modified Tudor Gothic structure of red brick, designed by Paul Gerhardt, spreads like a double-barred H on a 31-acre tract. The murals in the cafeteria and at the auditorium entrance are by the Federal Art Project.

18. The JULIA C. LATHROP HOMES, Diversey Parkway at Damen and Clybourn Aves., named in honor of the revered social worker, provide low cost modern housing for 925 families of limited income. The 29 reinforced concrete and brick buildings were constructed by the Public Works Administration in units of 2 to 5 rooms.

Central conveniences include a laundry and ample storage space; seven large social rooms and as many recreation rooms are the center of community activities. The grounds were laid out by Jens Jensen and occupy more than three-quarters of the 37-acre site, which embraces gardens, lawns, and playgrounds.

The West Side

The West Side lies between the two branches of the Chicago River, but it is commonly limited on the north by North Avenue. Chicago has grown and flowered most conspicuously along the lake front, with the result that the "inland" West Side is sometimes called the city's neglected back yard. But from this soil has sprung much of the vitality and color for which Chicago is known, for here have come thousands of persons from foreign lands, year after year. Scandinavians and Germans and Irish, no longer found in the West Side in great number, had their roots here; still flourishing are the later arrivals, the great colonies of Poles and Jews, Italians and Czecho-Slovakians and many others. But the West Side is more than a nursery in which various groups have established themselves and then been transplanted to other sections of the city. Although the east half of the district is spotted with slums and the whole is streaked with rail lines and grey manufacturing zones, there is a belt of fine parks and boulevards in the center from north to south, and farther west, such sections as Austin, a village annexed in 1899, resemble the adjoining prosperous suburbs.

The West Side, like the North and the South Sides, had its rows of expensive houses close to the downtown district. Brownstones and mansard-roofed mansions line the streets leading west from the Loop for about two miles, and the streets intersecting them. Although the mansions spared demolition have been cubicled into rooming houses, their exteriors are reminders of nineteenth century magnificence.

POINTS OF INTEREST

1. CHICAGO COMMONS (*open* 8 *a.m.*-10 *p.m. daily*), Grand Ave. at Morgan St., a social settlement in an Italian and Polish neighborhood, was founded in 1894 by Graham Taylor, widely known for his civic work. The many outgrowths of its work are revealed in his publications, *Pioneering on Social Frontiers* (1930) and *Chicago Commons Through Forty Years* (1936). A monthly leaflet first published

by the institution later became the nationally known social service magazine, *The Survey*.

2. NORTHWESTERN UNIVERSITY SETTLEMENT (*open 9 a.m.-10 p.m. daily*), 1400 Augusta Blvd., was founded in 1891 by Charles Zueblin and Mrs. Henry Rogers. The neighborhood, largely Polish, is one of the most densely settled in the city.

3. HUMBOLDT PARK, Augusta Blvd. at Sacramento Ave., with its lagoons, islands, hills, and large variety of trees, is a 207-acre tract containing some of the most beautiful park landscapes in the city. Near Division Street is the STABLE, a park maintenance building erected in 1896 from plans drawn by Emil H. Frommann and Ernst Jebsen. The building rambles near a stream and rustic bridge. In style it resembles a German hunting lodge, with a foundation of rock boulders, half-timbered walls of red brick, and a tile roof, romantically gabled. Little known, even to Chicagoans, the charming building is markedly appropriate in its park setting.

North of Division Street, bronze bison by Edward Kemeys flank the entrance to the ROSE GARDENS. Fountain figures by Leonard Crunelle rise from the four corners of the garden pool. Opposite the entrance is a STATUE OF FRITZ REUTER, German poet, by Frederick Engelmann. HOME, a modest little sculpture of a miner and his child, at the east end of the park, is by Charles J. Mulligan. A STATUE OF ALEXANDER VON HUMBOLDT, German naturalist, by Felix Gorling, stands in the center of the park beside the old boathouse. Westward, near the garish Refectory Building, is the LEIF ERIKSEN MONUMENT by Sigvald Asbjornsen. The equestrian STATUE OF THADDEUS KOSCIUSKO, Polish hero of the American Revolution, by Casimir Chodinski, at the north entrance, is the center of the Polish Constitution Day celebration on the Sunday nearest May 3, when thousands of neighboring Poles parade to the park.

4. In GARFIELD PARK, Central Park Ave. at Lake St., is an immense CONSERVATORY (*open 8-4:30 daily, 8-6 summer, 8 a.m.-10 p.m. special show periods; tours by arrangement*). Erected in 1907, it has 8 exhibition halls for the display of more than 5,000 varieties of plants. At the entrance to the Palm House is a shadowy pool flanked with marble figures, *Pastoral* and *Idyl*, by Lorado Taft, and displays of orchids and other exotics. Opposite the pool lies a sunken garden of tropical ferns, with delicate fronds of tree-ferns and cycads arching over tufa rock formations and ponds. In the cool dry Succulent House,

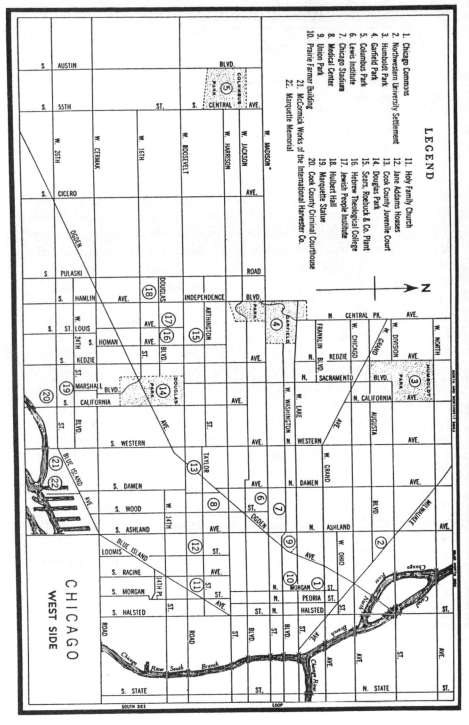

LEGEND

1. Chicago Commons
2. Northwestern University Settlement
3. Humboldt Park
4. Garfield Park
5. Columbus Park
6. Lewis Institute
7. Chicago Stadium
8. Medical Center
9. Union Park
10. Prairie Farmer Building

11. Holy Family Church
12. Jane Addams Houses
13. Cook County Juvenile Court
14. Douglas Park
15. Sears, Roebuck & Co. Plant
16. Hebrew Theological College
17. Jewish People Institute
18. Hulbert Hall
19. Marquette Statue
20. Cook County Criminal Courthouse
21. McCormick Works of the International Harvester Co.
22. Marquette Memorial

CHICAGO
WEST SIDE

DIANA COURT, MICHIGAN SQUARE BUILDING

LONGSHOREMEN

STOCK YAR

ALONG THE "L"

STATE STREET

CORNER OF MILWAUKEE AND CHICAGO AVENUES

CONTRAST, NEAR NORTH SIDE

HULL HOUSE

BRONZEVILLE SL

XWELL STREET

JANE ADDAMS HOUSES

NAVY PIER

MANSIONS—ON

cacti extend their spiny arms in weird postures. The Warm House and the Aeroid House, high in temperature and humidity, contain colored and variegated foliage plants, and vines that curtain the hall with their long, free-hanging aeroid roots. Another hall is devoted to economically useful plants, each labeled with pertinent information. The Easter, Mid-summer, Chrysanthemum, and Christmas Flower Shows fill the Show House and Horticulture Hall with thousands of blooms raised in adjoining propagating houses, and attract a large part of the 500,000 people who visit the conservatory each year.

The ADMINISTRATION BUILDING stands on a knoll between two lagoons south of the conservatory, a gold-domed Spanish Renaissance structure with a rotunda containing casts of classical statuary. Immediately south is the bronze MONUMENT OF LINCOLN, THE RAIL SPLITTER, by Charles J. Mulligan; a few yards west stands the bronze ROBERT BURNS MONUMENT, by W. Grant Stevens, a replica of the monument in Edinburgh, with bas-reliefs on the pedestal depicting scenes from Burns' poems. Formal flower gardens surround the tropical WATER-LILY POOLS, at Madison Street.

5. COLUMBUS PARK, Jackson Blvd. at Central Ave., newest of the large West Side parks, is a tract of 144 acres landscaped by Jens Jensen in his naturalistic style. The prairie motif is carried out in the long horizontal sweep of meadow threaded by running streams. Subtly adorned with sun-loving flowers, accented by thickets of hawthorn and other native trees and shrubs, the park is particularly charming in the autumn. Additional attractions are the waterfalls near the Refectory, and a 9-hole golf course.

6. LEWIS INSTITUTE, Madison St. at Damen Ave., endowed by Allen C. Lewis, was opened in 1896 as an academy and junior college. Now a four-year college, housed in two 6-story buildings, it is known principally for its engineering, home economics, and pre-professional courses. About two-thirds of the 3,000 students attend evening classes. The Psychological Museum (*tours by arrangement*), opened in 1937, contains psychological testing devices of all kinds.

7. The CHICAGO STADIUM, Madison St. at Honore St., an indoor amphitheater seating more than 25,000 persons, was erected in 1928 as a center for sports, circuses, and conventions. Here Franklin D. Roosevelt was nominated for President of the United States in 1932.

8. The MEDICAL CENTER (*arrangements for inspection must be made with each institution*), extends south from Congress St. to Tay-

lor St., and west from Wood St. to Wolcott Ave. Some 30 buildings, old and new, form Chicago's largest grouping of public and private hospitals; medical, dental, pharmacy, and nursing schools; research institutes and nurses' homes. Dominating the group is COOK COUNTY HOSPITAL, founded in 1866 to provide medical aid for the poor of the county, now one of the largest in the world, capable of caring for more than 3,000 patients. In addition to the florid white terra cotta and brick GENERAL BUILDING facing Harrison Street at Honore Street, the County group includes the MORGUE; the CHILDREN'S DENTAL CLINIC; the PSYCHOPATHIC, and TUBERCULOSIS, CONTAGIOUS, and MEN'S HOSPITALS; and the CHILDREN'S HOSPITAL, widely known for its Mothers' Milk Bureau. The County Hospital is known, too, for its Blood Bank, in which the four types of blood are stored for emergency use in transfusions.

LOYOLA UNIVERSITY SCHOOL OF MEDICINE, 706 S. Wolcott Ave., has a collection of human embryos and foetuses in various stages of development, and a comprehensive series of sections of the human body. The school enrolls more than 300 students.

The COOK COUNTY SCHOOL OF NURSING, 1910 Polk St., an imposing 17-story brick structure, was completed in 1935. The school succeeded the Illinois Training School for Nurses, founded in 1880, first institution of its kind west of the Alleghenies.

In the block south of the County group are the new medical buildings of the University of Illinois and the State Department of Public Welfare. The College of Medicine, enrolling more than 600 students, and the College of Dentistry, both started as proprietary schools, are housed in the MEDICAL AND DENTAL COLLEGE LABORATORIES BUILDING, fronting on Polk St. The medical unit was occupied in 1931; the dental unit, with its commanding 15-story tower on the Wood Street corner, in 1937. On the south, the parallel ILLINOIS RESEARCH and EDUCATIONAL HOSPITALS are joined to form a rectangle, from which extend in series to the south, the PSYCHIATRIC, ORTHOPAEDIC, and JUVENILE RESEARCH INSTITUTES. Designed in the collegiate Gothic style by Schmidt, Garden and Erikson, associated with Granger and Bollenbacher, the Illinois buildings are constructed of red brick trimmed with limestone. Artists of the Works Progress Administration Federal Art Project have decorated them with frescoes, stained glass windows, sculptures, mosaics, and canvases.

Rush Medical College, Harrison St. and Wood St., Chicago's first medical school, was founded in 1837 by Dr. Daniel Brainard and. named for Dr. Benjamin Rush, eminent Philadelphia physician. In 1923, Dr. Arthur Bevan, a Rush professor, performed the first operation in which ethylene-oxygen was used as an anaesthetic. In 1924, Rush became part of the University of Chicago. Offering the last two years of the regular medical course, the school enrolls more than 200 students.

9. UNION PARK, Ogden Ave. at Washington and Ashland Blvds., is a bit of green landscape at the north end of "Labor Row," a section of Ashland Boulevard with old mansions and new buildings housing various labor unions. The park is the starting point of the annual May Day parade and contains a Statue of Carter H. Harrison, the "martyred mayor," by Frederick C. Hibbard, and a Haymarket Riot Monument by Johannes Gelert, commemorating the policemen who lost their lives in the Riot of 1886. In a flat opposite the park lived the prototype of the heroine of Theodore Dreiser's novel *Sister Carrie*.

10. The PRAIRIE FARMER BUILDING (*open 9-5 Mon.-Fri., 9-1 Sat.*), 1230 Washington Blvd., contains the editorial offices and radio station, WLS of the journal devoted to the interests of farmers. Founded in 1841 by John Stephen Wright as *The Union Agriculturist and Western Prairie Farmer,* it has a circulation of 400,000. One of the paper's noteworthy campaigns was its successful agitation for a free school system in Illinois. West of the building is the site of the house where Mrs. Abraham Lincoln and "Tad" lived in 1866.

The SOUTH WATER MARKET, 15th St. between Racine Ave. and Morgan St., supplanted in 1925 the noisy picturesque market that for decades had occupied the south bank of the Chicago River. The 225 commission firms in the six, long, efficiently-planned buildings of the market, functioning independently under the guidance of the Market Service Association, supply the city with fruits and vegetables.

11. HOLY FAMILY CHURCH, 1080 W. Roosevelt Road, a large brick Gothic structure designed by Dillenburg and Zurber, and John Van Osdel, was dedicated in 1860. The parish, founded three years earlier by a Jesuit, Father Arnold Damen, the "Father of the West Side," in what was then largely open country, eventually numbered a congregation of 20,000 people. With the exodus of the Irish and Germans from the neighborhood, the membership has declined.

12. The JANE ADDAMS HOUSES (*open; apply at office*), 1002 S.

Lytle St., are a group of fireproof buildings erected in 1937 by the Public Works Administration. Built of brick in austere, well-arranged groups, the 52 houses of 4 and 5 rooms, and 975 apartments of 2 to 5 rooms provide low-cost modern housing in the midst of one of the most poverty-stricken areas of the West Side. More than three-fifths of the total ground area is devoted to lawns, gardens, and playgrounds. There are 20 recreation and social rooms, and a shower yard ornamented with sculptured animals.

13. The COOK COUNTY JUVENILE COURT (*open by appointment*), Roosevelt Road and Ogden Ave., was established in 1899 as the first children's court in America.

14. DOUGLAS PARK, Roosevelt Road at Sacramento Ave., a 182-acre retreat for the large Jewish and Bohemian population of the adjacent neighborhoods, has lily ponds and flower gardens, a lake for boating, an open-air natatorium, athletic fields, and an outdoor gymnasium. Near West Douglas Park Drive and Ogden Avenue stands a heroic bronze STATUE OF KAREL HAVLICEK, nineteenth century liberal writer, sculptured by Josef Strachovsky. Annually, on Rosh ha-Shanah (New Year's Day), which occurs on a variable date in early autumn, orthodox Jews gather at the lagoon for a ritualistic casting away of their sins.

15. The SEARS, ROEBUCK AND COMPANY PLANT (*tours* 9:45, 10:45, 1:45 *and* 2:45 *Mon.-Fri.*), Homan Ave. and Arthington St., houses the main offices of the nation-wide chain of retail stores and the largest mail-order system in the world. One of the bulkiest structural groups in the city, the building shelters the largest of the company's 10 mail-order plants. The precisely timed assembling of orders in the 2-block long merchandise building is a marvel of efficiency, as packages stream constantly along conveyor belts to cascade down chutes. Seven million catalogs, each 1,000 pages long, distributed semi-annually by the company have done more, perhaps, than any other one factor toward building the company's sales volume to hundreds of millions of dollars annually.

The business was originated in 1886 by Richard W. Sears, station agent of North Redwood, Minnesota. When a shipment of watches was refused by a local firm, Sears requested permission to sell the watches by mail to station agents along the railroad. The venture was successful, and led to the founding of the present firm. The man most prominently identified with the company was the late Julius Rosenwald, philanthropist.

16. The HEBREW THEOLOGICAL COLLEGE (*open* 9-8 *Sun.-Thurs.*, 9-12 *Fri.*), 3448 Douglas Blvd., a large three-story building with a classic façade, is an institution of higher Jewish learning, combining Jewish tradition and advanced methods of instruction. It trains young men to become modern orthodox Rabbis, teachers, and leaders of American Jewry. Its 400 students are drawn from all parts of the country. The LIBRARY BUILDING, dedicated in 1938, contains approximately 30,000 volumes, being noteworthy in the fields of Hebraica, Judaica, and Rabbinica. Included are many rare and out-of-print books.

17. The JEWISH PEOPLE'S INSTITUTE (*open* 9 *a.m.*-10:30 *p.m. Sun.-Thurs.*, 9-5 *Fri.*, 6 *p.m.*-10:30 *Sat.*), 3500 Douglas Blvd., is a social, recreational, and educational center in the heart of the Lawndale district. Largest Jewish community in Chicago, the section is portrayed in novels and stories by Meyer Levin, Albert Halper, Louis Zara, and others. Educational activities from grade school to college, instruction in the various arts, and a wide range of physical activities make the Institute an extraordinarily active place throughout the year.

In addition to numerous class and club rooms, lounges, gymnasium, theater, and roof garden, the four-story brick and stone building contains the Herman Schur Reference Library, with 16,000 volumes on Judaica and the social sciences, and a Museum of anthropology and natural history specimens gathered by Samuel Bornstein in his worldwide wanderings. Architects of the building were Eugene Klaber and Ernest A. Grunsfeld, Jr. The Museum of Antiquities, in the Spinoza Study, decorated with murals by A. Raymond Katz, exhibits ceremonial objects, rare books, and scrolls. Unique in Chicago is the mural-walled Blintzes Inn, a kosher restaurant with separate kitchens and dining sections for meat and for dairy dishes. An impressive wooden statue of Moses, by Enrico Glicenstein, stands in the center of the main hall.

18. HULBERT HALL, 1530 S. Hamlin Ave., (*open* 6:30 *p.m.*-9 *daily*), is the clubhouse of the Boys' Brotherhood Republic. With its novel plan of preventing juvenile delinquency by developing social relations by a form of municipal self-government, the organization, formed in 1914 by Jack Robbins, has been successful in providing for the recreational needs of thousands of underprivileged boys. Along

with a council, courts, and welfare departments, the Republic maintains a co-operative store and a bank.

19. The MARQUETTE STATUE, Marshall Blvd. and 24th St., is a bronze group of three figures representing Father Marquette, Jolliet, and an Algonquin Indian, sculptured by Hermon A. MacNeil.

20. The COOK COUNTY CRIMINAL COURTHOUSE (*jail open by warden's permission*), California Ave. and 26th St., includes the Criminal Court Building, the Cook County Jail Building, and four cell blocks. Designed by Eric E. Hall in rectangular neo-classic pattern, the Indiana limestone group was completed in 1929 at a cost of $7,500,000. Inmates of the jail are persons awaiting trial, transfer, or execution, and prisoners whose sentences for any single charge do not exceed one year.

The HOUSE OF CORRECTION (*tours arranged for groups*), immediately south of the Court House, is the municipal prison established in 1871 to supplant the old Bridewell. Around the castellated Gothic buildings are formal flower beds and an artificial stream.

21. The McCORMICK WORKS OF THE INTERNATIONAL HARVESTER COMPANY (*tours by arrangement*), 26th St. and Western and Blue Island Aves., occupying about 100 acres, produces a large part of the country's farm implements. It was established in 1872 after the destruction of the first harvester plant in Chicago, built in 1847 by Cyrus Hall McCormick near the north end of the present Michigan Avenue bridge. The plant normally employs about 4,500 men.

22. The MARQUETTE MEMORIAL, Damen Ave. Bridge on the South Branch of the Chicago River, marks the site of Marquette's dreary sojourn during the winter of 1674-75. E. P. Seidel modeled the bronze relief from a sketch by Thomas A. O'Shaughnessy.

Jackson Park

Through the 543 heavily wooded and informally landscaped acres of Jackson Park, which extends along Lake Michigan between 56th and 67th Streets, wind placid lagoons dotted with tiny islands and lined with cattails and other aquatic plants. Originally a swamp, it was converted into a park under the direction of Frederick Law Olmsted to be used first as the site of the World's Columbian Exposition of 1893, which was built here and along the Midway Plaisance joining

Jackson with Washington Park. Among other facilities in this third largest park in Chicago, the chief recreational area of the South Side, is an 18-hole golf course, first public course in Chicago.

At its narrow northern end the park is flanked with large apartment hotels. Facing them is (1) the MUSEUM OF SCIENCE AND INDUSTRY (*open* 10-6 *daily; guides for groups by appointment; special evening tour for groups of* 500 *or more by arrangement*).

The museum building incorporates a part and throughout closely follows the design of the Fine Arts Building of the World's Columbian Exposition. Designed by Charles Atwood, who adapted its detail from the Erechtheum, the Fine Arts Building won acclaim for its purity of style and excellence of composition. Two pavilions flank the great domed central pavilion, which they resemble in miniature, and are separated from it by transverse halls with free-standing Ionic columns. On each side of the main portico are caryatids, and the sides of the minor pavilions bear similar figures. The building, more than one-fifth of a mile long, has 600,000 square feet of floor space.

From the close of the Columbian Exposition until 1920, the original building was occupied by the Field Museum of Natural History, but as it had been erected for temporary use, it began to deteriorate rapidly. Agitation for the preservation of this sole major survival of the Exposition began and a $5,000,000 bond issue was floated for the purpose. In the reconstruction only part of the original structure was retained; wood and plaster were stripped away and replaced with Indiana limestone.

The present museum was conceived by the late Julius Rosenwald as a result of his young son's interest in the Deutsches Museum at Munich. When the bond issue proved insufficient to restore the building completely, Rosenwald donated funds and also provided a sum of $3,000,000 if the building would be used as a scientific and industrial museum. The first section was opened during the Century of Progress Exposition in 1933-34, and after the Exposition closed, many of its industrial exhibits were transferred here.

The museum stresses education, and many of the exhibits are elaborate working models; spectators set machinery and apparatus in motion by pushing a button. Such exhibits include a model airplane that realistically banks, zooms, and dives, controlled by a remote joystick. Elsewhere, steel ball bearings drop from a runway and bounce neatly one after another, all day long, through a revolving hoop, to

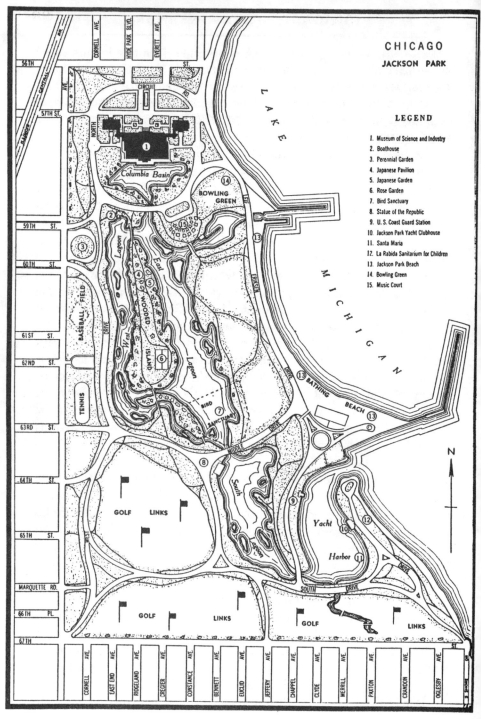

CHICAGO
JACKSON PARK

LAKE

MICHIGAN

LEGEND

1. Museum of Science and Industry
2. Boathouse
3. Perennial Garden
4. Japanese Pavilion
5. Japanese Garden
6. Rose Garden
7. Bird Sanctuary
8. Statue of the Republic
9. U. S. Coast Guard Station
10. Jackson Park Yacht Clubhouse
11. Santa Maria
12. La Rabida Sanitarium for Children
13. Jackson Park Beach
14. Bowling Green
15. Music Court

56TH
57TH ST.
59TH ST.
60TH ST.
61ST ST.
62ND ST.
63RD ST.
64TH ST.
65TH ST.
MARQUETTE RD.
66TH PL.
67TH

CORNELL AVE.
HYDE PARK BLVD.
EVERETT AVE.
ST.

CIRCUIT RD.
NORTH
Columbia Basin
BOWLING GREEN
Lagoon
East
WOODED ISLAND
West
Lagoon
BASEBALL FIELD
DRIVE
TENNIS
BIRD SANCTUARY
WEST
MIDDLE DRIVE
DRIVE
FRENCH
BATHING BEACH
GOLF LINKS
South Lagoon
Yacht
Harbor
GOLF LINKS
GOLF LINKS
GOLF LINKS

CORNELL AVE.
EAST END AVE.
RIDGELAND AVE.
CREGER AVE.
CONSTANCE AVE.
BENNETT AVE.
EUCLID AVE.
JEFFERY AVE.
CHAPPEL AVE.
CLYDE AVE.
MERRILL AVE.
PAXTON AVE.
CRANDON AVE.
OGLESBY AVE.

N

88

show the precision of machine-made bearings. In a large egg-shaped room principles of acoustics are demonstrated. Two people can carry on a whispered conversation from opposite ends of the room without being overheard by a third person standing between them. Other models graph the sound of a voice, transmit music on a beam of light, and X-ray the contents of a purse.

Lecturers operate more complicated apparatus at regular intervals, including demonstrations of the use of high-frequency electricity in lighting an electric bulb by wireless and of intermittent illumination, making readable the inscription on an airplane propellor revolving 1,400 times a minute. The full-sized coal mine, manned with miners and equipped with modern machinery, is the only exhibit for which there is a charge (*adults* 25c; *children* 10c).

In the theater, seating 1,000, motion pictures and popular lectures on scientific subjects are held (*hours vary; consult schedule posted weekly*). The library contains 25,000 volumes on science and industry.

Immediately behind the Museum is Columbia Basin, its waters lapping the rear steps of the great white building. Around it, to the right, a path leads to the West Lagoon and (2) a BOATHOUSE (*motor launches* 50c *a half-hour; row boats* 25c *an hour*). At the Midway Plaisance is (3) a PERENNIAL GARDEN. To the left of the boathouse a camel-hump bridge leads to WOODED ISLAND, planted with a large variety of trees and shrubs, many of them labeled. On the island are (4) the JAPANESE PAVILIONS, restored survivals of the Columbian Exposition. The three connecting pavilions, a gift of the Mikado, are patterned after the temple of Hoo-do, a shrine to the Phoenix bird. The central building symbolizes the body of the bird; the flanking pavilions, its wings. Tea is served in summer at the central pavilion. Adjoining the pavilions is (5) a JAPANESE GARDEN, with two small lily pools fed by a stream that splashes into it over boulders. Around the pools are junipers, dwarf pines, stone lanterns, and a tea house built of straw matting.

On the island, near the East Lagoon, is (6) the ROSE GARDEN, laid out during the Columbian Exposition and since expanded. Immediately south of the Wooded Island is (7) the BIRD SANCTUARY. An 8-foot fence keeps out predatory small animals; some domestic birds are kept here, but the majority are wild. In the shallow waters near the shore, many food plants have been set out for the birds.

The Middle Drive, which skirts the sanctuary, leads to (8) the

STATUE OF THE REPUBLIC, a gilded bronze of heroic proportions. The work of Daniel Chester French, it marks the site of the
Administration Building of the Columbian Exposition.

The statue faces the South Lagoon, which provides anchorage for
motor launches and small craft. Adjoining the South Lagoon is the
Yacht Harbor for larger boats. On its shores are (9) the U. S.
COAST GUARD STATION, a white building with an inclined run-
way leading to the water's edge, and (10) the JACKSON PARK
YACHT CLUBHOUSE (*private*).

Anchored at the clubhouse is (11) the SANTA MARIA (*open
when caretaker is available*), a copy of Columbus' flagship, built in
Spain, for the Columbian Exposition, together with reproductions of
its sister ships, the *Nina* and the *Pinta,* and sailed to America over
substantially the route followed by Columbus. In 1915, on its way to
the San Francisco Exposition, through the Great Lakes and St. Lawrence River, the *Santa Maria* was damaged in a storm near Halifax,
Nova Scotia. Held by the Canadian government for repair bills, the
boat was returned in 1918. Carrying 5,000 feet of canvas, it has an
over-all length of 100 feet. With its high bow and high poop over the
cabin aft, with clumsy masts and rigging, it contrasts sharply with
the trim modern sailboats in the harbor. The *Nina* sank in 1918; the
Pinta burned the following year.

On the rise of ground behind the clubhouse stands (12) LA
RABIDA SANITARIUM FOR CHILDREN (*open by arrange-
ment*). The original building, built for the Columbian Exposition,
was a copy of the monastery at Palos, Spain, where Columbus found
shelter before he secured aid for his expedition. Burned after more
than 20 years of service, it was replaced in 1932 with the present
building, designed by Graham, Anderson, Probst, and White; it accommodates 100 patients, offering free treatment to children suffering
from rheumatic heart.

North, across the harbor inlet, is (13) JACKSON PARK
BEACH (*bathhouse and pavilion, with picnicking facilities*), one of
the most popular in Chicago.

Farther north, beyond the beach, is (14) a BOWLING GREEN,
occupying the site of the Columbian Exposition's German Building.
Behind it stretches (15) the MUSIC COURT, an outdoor amphitheater, in which concerts are held during the summer.

University of Chicago

The University of Chicago, the youngest of the world's great institutions of higher learning, is less than a half century old. Unlike its rivals, it attained almost full stature at once, for it did not grow by slow degrees from a small college. Rather, it sprang fully fledged into the world as a large and splendidly equipped university, its entry smoothed by the oil millions of the Rockefellers. Today, it ranks among the best American universities in its scholastic standards, the scholarly attainments of its faculty, and its contributions to modern life and thought.

Founded in 1890 by John D. Rockefeller through the American Baptist Education Society, the university was placed in charge of the distinguished Hebraic scholar, William Rainey Harper. The latter gathered a most distinguished faculty of eminent scholars by offering them much higher salaries than any university was paying and by promising them freedom to carry on original research. The original faculty included nine college presidents and scores of younger scholars who had already made a name for themselves, or who were soon to do so. On the roster appeared the names of Thomas C. Chamberlin, noted geologist and collaborator with F. R. Moulton in developing the planetesimal hypothesis that revolutionized astronomical theory; Paul Shorey, perhaps the greatest of our classical scholars; Albion W. Small, a founder of modern sociology; John M. Coulter, a pioneer in the field of plant ecology; and Albert A. Michelson, the first American to win the Nobel prize in science, awarded for his measurement of the speed of light. By October 1, 1892, Cobb Lecture Hall was half completed, and the university opened its doors.

"President Harper's fondest wish was realized when the University started upon its practical life of instruction yesterday morning with the same confidence and absence of parade as if it had been running half a century," reported the Sunday *Inter Ocean,* October 2, 1892, adding that young men and young women, with books under their arms walked with lively steps and soon "everybody was working as industriously and earnestly as bees in a hive."

John D. Rockefeller, wonderful man is he,
Gives all his spare change to the U. of C.—

sang the students, as the faculty smiled, as well they might, for the "spare change" mounted to a $35,000,000 total and has since been

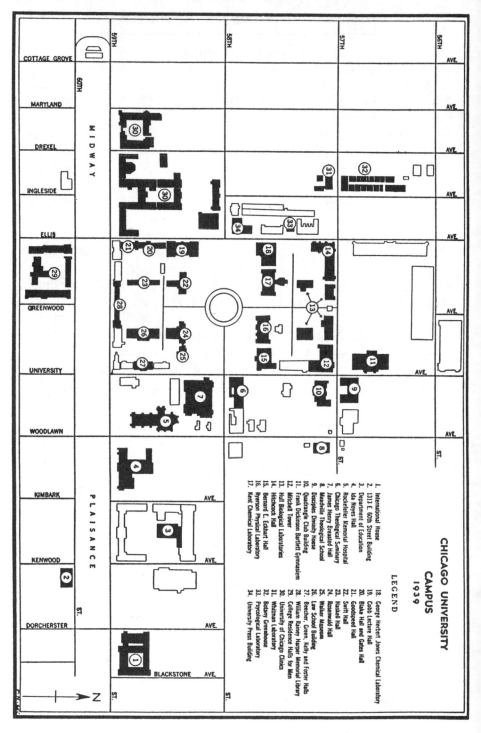

CHICAGO UNIVERSITY
CAMPUS
1939

LEGEND

1. International House
2. 1311 E. 60th Street Building
3. Department of Education
4. Ida Noyes Hall
5. Rockefeller Memorial Hospital
6. Chicago Theological Seminary
7. James Henry Breasted Hall
8. Meadville Theological School
9. Disciples Divinity House
10. Quadrangle Club Building
11. Frank Dickinson Bartlett Gymnasium
12. Mitchell Tower
13. Hull Biological Laboratories
14. Hitchcock Hall
15. Bernard E. Eckhart Hall
16. Ryerson Physical Laboratory
17. Kent Chemical Laboratory
18. George Herbert Jones Chemical Laboratory
19. Cobb Lecture Hall
20. Blake Hall and Gates Hall
21. Goodspeed Hall
22. Haskell Hall
23. Swift Hall
24. Rosenwald Hall
25. Walker Museum
26. Law School Building
27. Beecher, Green, Kelly and Foster Halls
28. William Rainey Harper Memorial Library
29. College Residence Halls for Men
30. University of Chicago Clinics
31. Whitman Laboratory
32. Botany Greenhouse
33. Physiological Laboratory
34. University Press Building

92

more than doubled by grants from the several Rockefeller foundations. John D. Rockefeller, Jr., personally contributed more than $5,000,000. Other gifts and bequests were received, many from Chicagoans, including a $4,500,000 donation by Julius Rosenwald, and the university's endowment today exceeds $125,000,000.

From the start the university has been noted for its reforms in the field of education. President William Rainey Harper created the university summer school by introducing the quarter system. He also pioneered in university extension work and in establishing a university press. The incumbent president, Robert Maynard Hutchins, instituted the "New Plan," with a curriculum designed to give students a comprehensive background in arts and sciences during their first two years, followed by more specialized work later. Under this plan compulsory class attendance has been abolished. Accomplishment is measured by comprehensive examinations taken whenever the student feels himself prepared. Approximately half of the 6,000 students are enrolled as undergraduates. There are six professional schools on the quadrangles. The downtown University College enrolls an additional 1,600.

The university grounds have expanded from 17 acres of sandy ridges and mucky swales, dotted with scrub oaks, to 110 trim landscaped acres. The 85 university buildings are in compact but uncrowded quadrangles and in single units on the Midway Plaisance, a mile-long parkway, lying between 59th and 60th Streets and connecting Washington and Jackson Parks. Built of Indiana limestone, almost all buildings are designed in late Gothic style, and possess an architectural unity rare among Midwestern universities; their mature dignity belies their age. Most of them are ornamented with symbols of their functions and bear the names of their donors.

CAMPUS TOUR

(Tours for groups by advance arrangement at the Information Office, 5758 Ellis Ave. Most buildings open 8-5 weekdays; permission to visit classes, except where otherwise noted, must be obtained from the appropriate dean. Information concerning lectures open to the public can be obtained from the weekly university calendar, posted on the bulletin boards of various buildings and in Chicago libraries. The university is closed in September. Official university guidebook 50c; chapel guidebook $1.00 at the University Bookstore, 5802 Ellis Ave.)

Easternmost of the university buildings on the Midway is (1) INTERNATIONAL HOUSE (*see announcements for activities open to public*), 1414 E. 59th St., an immense club with 507 dormitory rooms, lounges, assembly and dining halls, and national rooms, designed by Holabird and Root and completed in 1932. It is one of four such houses established by John D. Rockefeller, Jr., to promote mutual understanding among students of various races and nationalities as a means of fostering world peace. Thirty-six countries and 46 states are represented in the present membership (1939) of the House.

(2) The 1313 E. 60th STREET BUILDING, on the south side of the Midway, is owned and maintained by the university. It contains the national offices of such organizations and agencies interested in public administration as the American Society of Planning Officials and the International City Managers' Association.

(3) The DEPARTMENT OF EDUCATION occupies the second block to the west, on 59th St. between Kenwood and Kimbark Aves. A consolidation of several institutions formerly headed by such educators as Col. Francis W. Parker and John Dewey, the school conducts a complete pedagogical program from kindergarten through graduate work. EMMONS BLAINE HALL, on 59th St., houses the elementary school and some of the high school classes; HENRY HOLMES BELFIELD HALL, at the north end of Scammon Court, contains the University High School (*visitors welcome in laboratory school classrooms*). These buildings were designed by James Gamble Rogers, and completed in 1903 and 1904. The GRADUATE EDUCATION BUILDING, on Kimbark Ave., and the BERNARD E. SUNNY GYMNASIUM (high school) on the west side of Kenwood Ave., complete the group.

(4) IDA NOYES HALL, one of the most gracious of the campus buildings, designed by Shepley, Rutan, and Coolidge, and dedicated in 1916, rises like a great Tudor manor house from a flowered terrace, on 59th St., between Kimbark and Woodlawn Aves. Richly appointed and decorated, the hall is a clubhouse, refectory, and gymnasium for women. Murals by Jesse Arms Botke, the *Spirit of Youth*, adorn the walls of the theatre.

(5) The ROCKEFELLER MEMORIAL CHAPEL (*non-denominational services 11 a.m., Sun.*), 59th St., between Woodlawn and University Aves., designed by Bertram Grosvenor Goodhue and associates, is an original interpretation of Gothic architecture, extra-

ordinarily massive, simple and vigorous. The immense striding 40-foot bays, the glazed tile in the vaulted ceiling, and the placement of the tower over one of the transepts, are striking and unusual. Of solid masonry construction, the walls of the 207-foot tower are eight feet thick at the base.

A rich array of sculpture relieves the severity of the exterior. Designed by Lee Laurie and Ulric Ellerhausen, the 24 free standing and 53 demi-figures are, in general, archaic in style and symbolic in character, suggesting the religious continuity of the present with the past. The exquisite interior wood carvings were done by Alois Lang.

The LAURA SPELMAN ROCKEFELLER Carillon in the tower (*tours* 1-3:30 *Wed.*, 1-5 *Sat.*, 12-3:30 *Sun.*) ranks with the largest in the world; the tuning of the 72 bells (ranging from 10½ pounds to more than 18 tons in weight) is said to be the finest ever achieved.

North of the Midway, on 58th St., between Woodlawn and University Aves., is (6) the CHICAGO THEOLOGICAL SEMINARY, affiliated with the Divinity School of the University. It was founded in 1855 by the Congregational Church. The main buildings, designed by H. H. Riddle, and completed in 1928, are dominated by the graceful Lawson Tower. Hammond Library contains an important collection of source materials for the history of American Christianity. The Thorndike Hilton Chapel and Graham Taylor Hall have stained glass windows modelled on those of Chartres Cathedral. The WOMEN'S RESIDENCE HALL, on the east side of Woodlawn Ave., was originally designed as a private house by Frank Lloyd Wright in 1909.

(7) JAMES HENRY BREASTED HALL (*open* 10-5 *Mon.- Sat.; 11-5 Sun., June-Nov.; 9-5 Mon.-Fri.; 10-5 Sat.; 11-5 Sun., Dec.-May*), SE. corner of 58th St. and University Ave., contains the museum and the offices of the Oriental Institute, a great center of research on the rise of civilization. Named for the professor who directed the Institute until his death in 1935, the building was designed by Mayers, Murray, and Phillip, and completed in 1931. Most of the objects in the museum were unearthed by the 12 expeditions sent by the Institute to the Near East. The sites of present field operations are marked on a map in the lobby, where the publications of the Institute are displayed.

The exhibits in the Egyptian Hall, left of the lobby, illustrate the life story of the Egyptians—their dress and tools; the masterful craftsmanship of their artists revealed in delicate glass and pottery ware, carvings, paintings, and writings; their ways of life; and their manner of burial. The exhibits, arranged chronologically except for two topical alcoves, range from pre-historic implements taken from terraces along the Nile to Greco-Roman portraits of the second century A. D.

Dominating the Egyptian Hall near the entrance to Assyrian Hall stands a 40-ton stone figure of an Assyrian winged bull with human head, discovered in the ruins of the palace of King Sargon II (724-705 B. C.) near ancient Nineveh. A colossal red quartzite statue of Tut-ankhamen (Thebes 1350 B. C.) stands to the right of the bull. In the Assyrian Hall are relief sculptures from Sargon's palace, fine examples of the Assyrians' gift for portraying movement and force. The screen cases in this and the next hall illustrate the work of the Institute's various field expeditions by means of photographs, diagrams, maps, and color plates.

The gateway at the entrance of the Assyro-Babylonian Hall repro-duces the style of the palace of Nebuchadnezzar at Babylon (sixth century B. C.). The objects in this hall represent some of the most important archeological work of the Institute. The Sumerian cult statues, with large noses and big eyes, are the only ones yet discovered. The cylinder seals in the same collection are ornamented with animals unknown to the Babylonians—the elephant and rhinoceros—and sig-nificantly link the history of the Sumerians with that of India.

In the Iranian-Moslem Hall are ancient Persian pottery and bronzes; manuscripts in Arabic, Persian, Syriac, and Hebrew; and Egyptian Arabic tombstones and book-bindings. Soon to be installed (late 1939) are decorations from the palace of Xerxes—a massive bull's head, and reliefs still black with smoke from fires set by Alex-ander the Great in the fifth century B. C.

The Hittite-Palestinian Hall exhibits are from excavations at Alishar in Anatolia, and Megiddo in Palestine. In the collection are gold jewelry, carved ivory objects, and the oldest extant Biblical document—a stamp seal dating from early Christian centuries contain-ing a verse of scripture from the Book of Jeremiah.

(8) The MEADVILLE THEOLOGICAL SCHOOL, 57th St. at Woodlawn Ave., founded in Pennsylvania in 1844, is associated with the Divinity School of the University; there is no denominational control. The Wiggin Library contains more than 50,000 volumes, being rich in source material on the liberal movement in religion.

(9) The DISCIPLES DIVINITY HOUSE, NE. corner of 57th St. and University Ave., is a residence hall and social center for Disciples of Christ students registered in the Divinity School and affiliated institutions.

(10) The QUADRANGLE CLUB BUILDING, SE. corner of 57th St. and University Ave., was designed by Howard Van Doren Shaw and opened in 1922. Membership is drawn chiefly from the Faculties.

(11) The FRANK DICKINSON BARTLETT GYMNASIUM, NW. corner of 57th St. and University Ave., provides athletic facilities for the men of the university. The murals in the entrance hall, by Frederic Clay Bartlett, depict medieval athletic contests. The window above the main door, designed by Edward D. Sperry, portrays the crowning of Ivanhoe by Rowena. The remainder of the block is occupied by STAGG FIELD, a stadium seating 57,000. Professor Amos Alonzo Stagg, known affectionately as "The Old Man," was athletic director of the university for forty-one years, and was the first football coach to achieve faculty status. The immense new FIELD HOUSE stands north of the Stagg Field on University Ave.

The central Quadrangles occupy four blocks extending south from 57th St. to 59th St. and west from University to Ellis Ave. The entrance through Mitchell Tower, at the SW. corner of 57th St. and University Ave., is the busiest traffic artery on the campus. In the other corners of the Quadrangles are all of the university dormitories, except the College Residence Halls. All but one were completed before 1900; they were designed by Henry Ives Cobb, university architect of that period.

(12) MITCHELL TOWER closely reproduces the tower of Magdalen College, Oxford. From the studios on the second floor is broadcast the discussion around the Sunday Round Table, one of the first university programs with a national hook-up. The Alice Freeman Palmer Chimes peal the close of each college day, 10:05 p.m., with "Alma Mater." HUTCHINSON HALL, opening on the main floor of the Tower, is patterned on Christ Church Hall, Oxford. On the wood paneling of this great dining hall hang the portraits of benefactors and members of the university; above, are the shields of English and American colleges.

Also connected with the Tower are the REYNOLDS STUDENT CLUBHOUSE for men, and the LEON MANDEL ASSEMBLY HALL. The entire

Tower group was designed by Shepley, Rutan, and Coolidge in 1903, and decorated by Frederick Clay Bartlett; the buildings stand on two sides of Hutchinson Court, a sunken English garden, scene of the popular "University Sing" in June.

Westward, (13) the HULL BIOLOGICAL LABORATORIES (1897) stand on three sides of Hull Court; connected by cloistered walks are the BOTANY, ZOOLOGY, and ANATOMY BUILDINGS, and CULVER HALL, formerly the Physiology Laboratory, the first in America, now occupied by the Biology Library and various laboratories. Entrance from 57th St. on the north is through the massive stone Cobb Gate, richly ornamented with grotesques; from the south, through a delicately arched iron gate. Landscaped Botany Pond is one of the most charming spots on the Quadrangles, except during the annual muddy melée of the Freshman-Sophomore tug-of-war in Homecoming Week.

(14) HITCHCOCK HALL, designed by D. H. Perkins, (1902) and SNELL HALL, men's dormitories, stand in the NW. corner of the Quadrangles. Easternmost of an imposing row of Physical Science Laboratories, facing south on the Circle, at the center of the Quadrangle, is (15) BERNARD A. ECKHART HALL, designed by C. Z. Klauder and completed in 1930 for use of the Mathematics, Astronomy, and Physics Departments.

(16) The RYERSON PHYSICAL LABORATORY (1894) has rooms specially designed for control of sound, temperature, humidity, and vibration. Much of the work of the three Nobel prize winners of the university was performed here.

(17) The KENT CHEMICAL LABORATORY (1894) contains a large theater.

(18) The GEORGE HERBERT JONES CHEMICAL LABORATORY, at the west end of the row, was designed by Coolidge and Hodgdon and completed in 1929. Graduate and research work is carried on in the Laboratory, which contains student social halls.

(19) COBB LECTURE HALL, westernmost of the row of buildings on the south side of the Circle, houses various administrative offices and college classrooms. Named for its donor, Silas B. Cobb, the Hall and adjoining dormitories, extending south along Ellis Avenue in a solid row to the Midway, were the first of the university buildings.

(20) BLAKE HALL and GATES HALL, originally men's dormitories, are now women's residence halls.

(21) GOODSPEED HALL, at the corner, was a dormitory for divinity students until 1938, when it was taken over by the Department of Art. In the Gallery (*open 2-5 daily*), on the first floor, the Renaissance Society of the University of Chicago exhibits the collections and works of its members, and those drawn from other sources. In the Art Reference Library are some 200,000 reproductions of paintings and drawings, duplicating the collection of Sir Robert Witt of London, most notable in the world.

(22) SWIFT HALL, facing north on the Circle, east of Cobb Hall, is used by the Divinity School of the university. The school was originally organized in 1867 as the Baptist Union Theological Seminary but its present faculty and student body include representatives of all the leading Protestant churches. Connected with Swift Hall by a stone cloister is the charming JOSEPH BOND CHAPEL. Both structures were designed by Coolidge and Hodgdon and were completed and dedicated in 1926.

(23) HASKELL HALL (1896), south of Swift Hall, formerly the Oriental Museum, now houses the School of Business.

(24) ROSENWALD HALL, east of Swift Hall, designed by Holabird and Roche and completed in 1916, is occupied by the Departments of Geology and Geography. The first floor contains a museum with collections of minerals and rocks, and one of the largest map libraries in the country. The official Chicago station of the U. S. Weather Bureau (*open 9-4 Fri., 9-12 Sat.*) is in the tower. The seismograph in the basement rests on a concrete pier sunk 62.5 feet below floor level to bedrock.

(25) WALKER MUSEUM (1893) adjoining Rosenwald Hall (*open 9-5 Mon.-Fri., 9-1 Sat.*), is the foremost center for materials relating to Permian reptiles and Paleozoic invertebrates. Each of the alcoves on the first floor exhibits specimens of a particular geologic period. The fossil invertebrate collection on the second floor containing over a million specimens, is especially rich in Paleozoic material from the Mississippi Valley region. The paleobotanical collection on the third floor, gathered from all continents, includes extensive exhibits of specimens from the coal regions of southern Illinois.

(26) The LAW SCHOOL BUILDING, south of Rosenwald

Hall, was designed by Shepley, Rutan, and Coolidge. The cornerstone was laid by President Theodore Roosevelt in 1903.

(27) BEECHER, GREEN, KELLY and FOSTER HALLS, women's dormitories, extend south along University Ave. to the Midway.

(28) The WILLIAM RAINEY HARPER MEMORIAL LIBRARY (*open 8 a.m.-10 p.m., Mon.-Fri.; 8-6 Sat.*), facing the Midway, is the central unit at the south end of the Quadrangles. One of the great libraries of the world, it contains more than 1,250,000 volumes. The impressive main reading room is on the third floor. The American drama collection, among the best in the United States, includes a large group of Chicago playbills. Many collections of rare books and manuscripts, totaling 23,000 items, are housed in the west tower. The Lincoln Library (*open 9-11:45 and 1-5 Mon.-Fri.; 9-1 and 2-5 Sat.*), on the second floor, has 5,000 volumes, and 14,000 manuscripts and facsimiles of Lincolniana, one of the nation's largest collections. Notable among the Lincoln portraits are two original oils by George Frederick Wright. The principal motif of the elaborate interior and exterior decorations is based on the coats-of-arms of eminent universities and the devices of famous European printers. The building was completed in 1912.

The SOCIAL SCIENCE RESEARCH BUILDING (1929) opening into Harper Library from the east, is unusual among university structures in its provision of facilities for cooperative research on social problems by members of various departments. Many of the public lectures offered by the university are given in the Assembly Room; musical recordings are played here (12:30-1:15 *Tues.-Fri.*).

WIEBOLDT HALL (1927), forming a west unit of the library building, is the center of modern language study. The Modern Poetry Library, on the second floor, has as a nucleus the collection of books and manuscripts gathered by Harriet Monroe during her editorship of *Poetry* magazine.

The CLASSICS BUILDING: HIRAM KELLY MEMORIAL (1915), at the west end of the library group, is devoted largely to the study of classical languages and literatures. The small Classics Museum on the fourth floor contains architectural models and ancient pottery. The Classics and Harper Memorial Library Buildings were designed by Shepley, Rutan, and Coolidge; Wieboldt Hall and Social Science Research Buildings by Coolidge and Hodgdon.

(29) The COLLEGE RESIDENCE HALLS FOR MEN, on 60th St. between Ellis and Greenwood Aves., are stately dormitories, surrounding Judson Court and Burton Court. They were designed by Zantzinger, Borie and Medary, and completed in 1931.

(30) The UNIVERSITY OF CHICAGO CLINICS, on 59th St. between Ellis and Maryland Aves., are dominated by the ALBERT MERRITT BILLINGS HOSPITAL, for medical and surgical cases; included are the Max Epstein Clinic for out-patients, and the Walter G. Zoller Memorial Dental Clinic. The north wings house the laboratories of the Departments of Medicine, Pathology, and Surgery. Across the court on 58th Street stands the PHYSIOLOGY AND BIOCHEMISTRY BUILDING. East of Billings is the HOME FOR DESTITUTE CRIPPLED CHILDREN, conducted in affiliation with the university; to the west is the BOBS ROBERTS MEMORIAL HOSPITAL FOR CHILDREN. Across Drexel Avenue is the CHICAGO LYING-IN HOSPITAL; founded by Dr. Joseph B. De Lee, noted obstetrician, the hospital has been a part of the university since 1938. The building was designed by Schmidt, Garden, and Erickson. Coolidge and Hodgdon planned the other buildings of the group. All were built between 1927 and 1931. The hospitals have 630 beds in all. Maintenance and operation of clinics constitute the largest single item on the university budget.

(31) The WHITMAN LABORATORY, a block north of the Clinics, on the SW. corner of 57th St. and Ingleside Ave., is devoted to experimental zoology. Hundreds of chickens and guinea pigs are kept in the surrounding pens.

(32) The BOTANY GREENHOUSE occupies a quarter acre at the NW. corner of 57th St. and Ingleside Ave. The cycad collection is the largest in the world. At the north end of the greenhouse is the C. R. BARNES BOTANY LABORATORY.

(33) The PSYCHOLOGICAL LABORATORY, 5730 Ellis Ave., is flanked on either side of the two units of the HOWARD TAYLOR RICKETTS LABORATORIES, used in the study of bacteriology and parasitology.

In (34) the UNIVERSITY PRESS BUILDING, NW. corner of Ellis Ave. and 58th St., are printed various departmental journals, books and pamphlets, and all official documents of the university. More than 1,000 books and pamphlets have been published and 16 departmental journals are issued regularly. On the main floor are the Faculty Exchange and the Information Office.

The South Side

A varied and complex city in itself, comprising more than half of Chicago, the South Side lies between the South Branch of the Chicago River and 138th St. Up to 1889 it extended only as far as 39th Street, embracing less than 10 square miles, but in that year the municipalities of Lake and Hyde Park were annexed, adding 84 square miles and shifting the geographical center of the city close to the stock yards, previously outside the city limits. Later, an additional 23 square miles of towns were added so that today, in area, the South Side is larger than the District of Columbia by some 40 square miles, and in character, is a plexus of highly diverse communities, many of which have retained their original names.

Edged by the landscaped lake shore in the north half of the South Side, are some of the most elegant houses in Chicago, including the old and frequently dilapidated mansions of the 'former Gold Coast along Prairie, Calumet, Ellis, Lake Park, and Michigan Avenues, some occupied by institutions of various kinds, others converted into rooming houses. Southward are the communities of Kenwood, Hyde Park, and South Shore, laid out in fine avenues, and dotted with impressive schools and churches, and swank apartments.

In a narrow north-south belt known as the Black Belt, extending the length of the north half of the South Side immediately west of the lake shore communities, live most of Chicago's Negroes. Many of them find employment in the vast central manufacturing districts, packing plants, and switch-yards to the west. Monotonous acres of cottages of Polish, Lithuanian, and Czecho-Slovakian workingmen fill much of this industrial district, which is bordered on the south by the boisterous Irish section pictured in James T. Farrell's *Studs Lonigan* trilogy, and by Englewood, a middle-class community with a commercial center second only to the downtown district in magnitude.

From 79th Street to the southern limits of the city, the lake shore near the Calumet River, and the area along the Indiana border, are covered with the black clutter and confusion of industry. Great hulks of mills and furnaces and grain elevators rise along the banks and slips of the Calumet River. In spite of heavy industrialization, parts of the grimy but impressive Calumet region are still marshy and untamed, particularly in the neighborhood of Wolf Lake; its reedy waters are frequented by countless birds and contain many rare species of aquatic plants.

Pullman and the old Dutch community of Roseland occupy slightly higher ground west of Lake Calumet. Farther west lies the Blue Island Ridge, a thick glacial deposit about two and one-half miles long, the most conspicuous elevation in Chicago. It was an island left high and dry before the waters of glacial Lake Chicago receded from the rest of the Chicago area. Spreading among the huge oaks on the ridge are the leafy residential communities of Washington Heights, Morgan Park, and Beverly Hills.

POINTS OF INTEREST

1. The COLISEUM, 1463 S. Wabash Ave., retains the battlemented stone façade of the Civil War Libby Prison, removed from Richmond in pieces and rebuilt here in 1888. The structure served as a war museum; in 1900 it was replaced, and the façade incorporated in the present building, an indoor stadium seating 13,000. Here Taft, Theodore Roosevelt, and Harding were nominated for the presidency, and the notorious First Ward Balls were held in the early part of the century.

2. The HUMAN ENGINEERING LABORATORY (*open* 9-5 *weekdays; closed every fourth Sat.*), 1800 Prairie Ave., was established here in 1938 by the Armour Institute of Technology; people are here tested for vocational aptitudes. The laboratory, a branch of the organization created by Dr. Johnson O'Connor at Stevens Institute of Technology, occupies the John J. Glessner House, built in 1886 for the late director of the International Harvester Company. The Glessner House is the only remaining work in Chicago of H. H. Richardson. Its low lines, rugged construction, and crisply carved ornament are characteristic of the Romanesque Revival that he introduced.

3. The ARCHITECTS CLUB OF CHICAGO (*open daily*), 1801 Prairie Ave., occupies the W. W. Kimball house, the home of one of Chicago's pioneer piano manufacturers. Designed by Solon S. Beman after the 16th century Chateau de Josselin in Brittany, and built in 1887, it is a fine example of the Francis I style. Its many pinnacles and high gabled roof make a singularly romantic silhouette. The interior of the house has a sedate grandeur, with its rich oak and

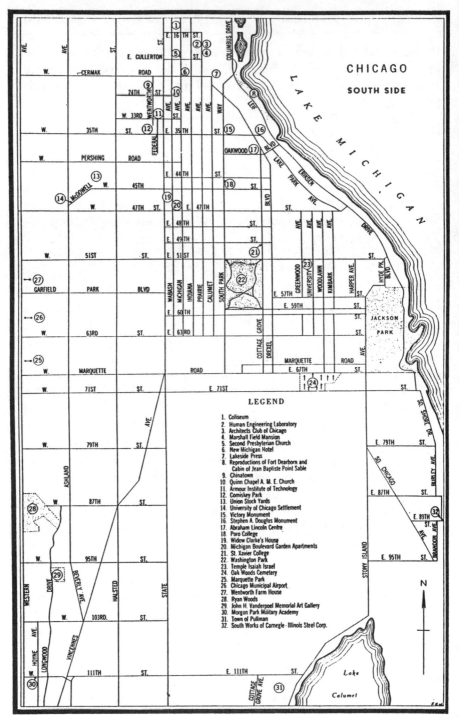

CHICAGO

SOUTH SIDE

LEGEND

1. Coliseum
2. Human Engineering Laboratory
3. Architects Club of Chicago
4. Marshall Field Mansion
5. Second Presbyterian Church
6. New Michigan Hotel
7. Lakeside Press
8. Reproductions of Fort Dearborn and
   Cabin of Jean Baptiste Point Sable
9. Chinatown
10. Quinn Chapel A. M. E. Church
11. Armour Institute of Technology
12. Comiskey Park
13. Union Stock Yards
14. University of Chicago Settlement
15. Victory Monument
16. Stephen A. Douglas Monument
17. Abraham Lincoln Centre
18. Poro College
19. Widow Clarke's House
20. Michigan Boulevard Garden Apartments
21. St. Xavier College
22. Washington Park
23. Temple Isaiah Israel
24. Oak Woods Cemetery
25. Marquette Park
26. Chicago Municipal Airport
27. Wentworth Farm House
28. Ryan Woods
29. John H. Vanderpoel Memorial Art Gallery
30. Morgan Park Military Academy
31. Town of Pullman
32. South Works of Carnegie - Illinois Steel Corp.

mahogany panelling, majestic staircase, and many fine fireplaces. The base of the monument *The Fort Dearborn Massacre* stands a few feet to the east, near the site of the massacre of 1812.

4. The MARSHALL FIELD MANSION (*closed*), 1905 Prairie Ave., was designed by Richard Morris Hunt and erected in 1879. The interior was extensively remodeled and a wing in the modern "International" style was added during its occupation by the New Bauhaus in 1937-38.

5. The SECOND PRESBYTERIAN CHURCH, Michigan Ave. at Cullerton St., was designed by James Renwick, and completed in 1874. Two small windows, executed by William Morris from designs by Sir Edward Burne-Jones, flank the front entrance.

6. The NEW MICHIGAN HOTEL, Michigan Ave. at Cermak Road, known during prohibition days as the Lexington Hotel, gained wide renown as the headquarters of Alphonse Capone, from whose suite the powerful Capone vice and alcohol ring operated.

7. The LAKESIDE PRESS, 350 E. Cermak Road, a handsome 8-story brick and stone building, is one of the largest in the United States devoted to the production of printing. The Press is noted for its typography and color work; the Exhibition Hall on the eighth floor (*open* 9-5 *Mon.-Fri.*) has displays of fine binding, printing, and illustration.

BURNHAM PARK, newest and second largest of Chicago's major parks, was envisaged by Daniel Burnham as a connecting link between Grant and Jackson Parks at least ten years before he drew up the comprehensive Chicago Plan, but construction was delayed until 1920 by negotiations for riparian rights held by the Illinois Central Railroad. Sand was pumped in and debris dumped to raise above the lake waters this strip of land one-eighth of a mile wide and five miles long, 598 acres in extent. Northerly Island, also "made" land, consists of 91 acres facing the north end of the park. In 1933-34 the park and island were the scene of the Century of Progress Exposition. Extensive grading and landscaping have since been carried out by Works Progress Administration.

There are striking views of the Chicago skyline from Leif Eriksen Drive, which traverses the length of the park, unimpeded by cross traffic. Southward, in Hyde Park, rises the sharp, bright cluster of towering apartments; along the shoreline curving to the east spread the gaunt black stacks of the Calumet district, overhung with a pall of smoke. The view northward is rivalled in magnificence in few other cities of the world. Angling in towards the open front of the downtown district, the drive affords a line of vantage for the greatly varied but somehow harmoniously grouped towers of central Chicago. Particularly splendid is the night scene approached along the light-streaked drive.

8. REPRODUCTIONS OF FORT DEARBORN AND THE CABIN OF JEAN BAPTISTE POINT SABLE (*not open*) stand in Burnham Park at Leif Eriksen Drive and 26th St., nearly three miles southeast of the original sites. Built for the Century of Progress Exposition, the reproduction of Fort Dearborn, complete with stockade, blockhouses, powder house, and barracks, is based on sketches of the first fort drawn in 1803 by its builder, Capt. John Whistler, later discovered in the War Office files.

9. CHINATOWN extends about three blocks from the corner of Cermak Road and Wentworth Ave., mainly along these two streets. Commercial and social center of Chicago's 6,000 Chinese, and the home of half of them, it ranks next in size to the settlements in San Francisco and New York. At first glance little distinguishes Chinatown from many other small outlying business sections. Cermak Road has been widened into one of the broadest streets in Chicago, and Wentworth Avenue resounds with the rumble of one of the most heavily used car-lines in the city. Architecturally, most of the district is old, consisting of a miscellany of two- and three-story shop and flat buildings, but some of the brick structures have been interestingly remodeled with recessed balconies, and the new Chinese "City Hall" is one of the finest examples of Chinese architecture in America. The numerous Cantonese, some slipper-shod, gliding along the sidewalks, and the store fronts with Chinese names and inscriptions in Chinese characters advertising Oriental foods and merchandise, attract thousands of visitors to Chinatown.

Jade and soapstone ornaments, incense, back scratchers, and all manner of charms and baubles are found in dim little shops, in the brightly lighted CHINESE EMPORIUM, Cermak Road at La Salle St., and in the LING LONG MUSEUM, 2238 Wentworth Ave., which contains a score of dioramas depicting the history and customs of China. Many food markets display a curious assortment of preserved foods from China and strange Chinese vegetables. Barbecued pork loins hang near boxes of succulent lotus roots; bright bitter-greens with yellow blossoms and fat bitter-melons nestle in window trays beside baskets of butter fish; flaky birds' nests, mud-caked "thousand year" eggs, shark fins, and beetles rest in jars and tins on store shelves.

The center of the district is the CHINESE CITY HALL (*open except during Tong meetings*), 2216 Wentworth Ave., headquarters of the On Leong Tong, an association of prosperous Chinese merchants. Adjoining the reception hall is the shrine room, with portraits of George Washington and Sun Yat Sen, father of the Chinese Republic. Teakwood chairs along the walls have backs of striped marble, selected to suggest seascapes, landscapes, and fantastic creatures of Chinese folklore. An elaborate memorial shrine to Quan-Kung, a teacher of the third century who emphasized honest dealings in business, has a painting of Quan-Kung half hidden in its gilded recesses. Here joss sticks are burned, and a perpetual oil light glimmers on ceremonial objects and ornaments symbolizing various qualities and virtues of the good life. In the building are meeting halls, a courtroom for settling business disputes between tong members, and a schoolroom for the instruction of Chinese youth in the language and customs of China.

On a variable date, between the end of January and the beginning of March, the Chinese celebrate their New Year. Fireworks pop, a 30-foot paper dragon and a grotesque lion dance in the streets, and the tables of the many good restaurants in Chinatown groan under the weight of 27-course dinners.

10. QUINN CHAPEL A. M. E. CHURCH, Wabash Ave. at 24th St., a massive Gothic structure of rough cut stone, houses a congregation that was organized in 1847, and in 1853 built Chicago's first Negro house of worship, the race's civic and social center, near Jackson Boulevard and Dearborn Street. Many of the members are descendants of the founders.

11. The ARMOUR INSTITUTE OF TECHNOLOGY, 3300 Federal St., founded in 1892 by Philip D. Armour, offers college courses in various branches of engineering in the red brick and sandstone laboratory buildings of modified Romanesque design. The Department of Architecture is housed downtown in the Art Institute. The school enrolls some 1,300 full-time students and about twice as many in its evening courses.

12. COMISKEY PARK, 35th St. and Shields Ave., is the home of the White Sox, Chicago's American League baseball club. Here Joe

Louis knocked out James J. Braddock for the world's heavy-weight boxing championship, in June 1937.

13. The UNION STOCK YARDS, Halsted St. and Exchange Ave., and PACKINGTOWN, Racine Ave. and Exchange Ave., the world's largest unit for the marketing of livestock and the processing of meat, consist of a square mile of pens and packing plants, in which some 12,000,000 animals, valued at $250,000,000, are received annually. Livestock is the chief source of cash income for the American farmer, and the Union Stock Yards handle approximately one-fifth of the total sales. About 75 per cent of the animals received are slaughtered and processed here. The remainder are shipped largely to feeders in the corn belt and to packers in the East. Most shipments of cattle and lambs go to Jewish packing houses in New York City, for by Mosaic law kosher meat must be eaten within a few days of slaughter.

Hundreds of latticed freight cars rattle into the yards each night with their noisy cargo. Transferred to the pens that fill the east half of the square mile, the animals are watered, fed, and prepared for sale in the morning. Cattle buyers, frequently mounted, representing large and small packers, traders, butchers, and feeders, inspect the day's offerings and bargain with the commission men to whom the livestock is consigned.

In busy seasons the streets within and around the yards swarm with men who have accompanied their stock to market—drawling Texans with wide-brimmed Stetsons, bearded men of rural religious sects, and Midwest farmers in ordinary business clothes.

The LIVE STOCK NATIONAL BANK BUILDING, 4150 S. Halsted St., is a reproduction of Independence Hall in Philadelphia. The STOCK YARDS INN, 4178 S. Halsted St., Tudor in design, with dormered roof and overhanging gables, contains paintings of animals and hunting scenes. The INTERNATIONAL AMPHITHEATRE, adjoining the Inn, is the scene of the International Live Stock Exposition, held annually during the last week in November.

From the roof of the EXCHANGE BUILDING, Exchange Ave. and Laurel St., is a fine view of the pens and barns, the connecting alleys, the chutes and platforms along the network of rails, and the overhead driveways leading into the solid wall of Packingtown buildings to the west. The CHICAGO DAILY DROVERS JOURNAL BUILDING, 836 Exchange Ave., houses a newspaper for the livestock farmer, and radio station WAAF.

Slaughter houses were established early in Chicago's history, but there were no centralized stock yards until John B. Sherman opened the Bull's Head Stock Yards at Madison Street and Ashland Avenue in 1848, from which the several packing plants along the Chicago River and its branches drew their supplies. In 1856 Sherman replaced the Bull's Head with yards along the Illinois Central Railroad at 29th Street, and in 1865 organized the Union Stock Yard and Transit Company and opened the present yards. Within a few years, Philip D. Armour, Gustavus F. Swift, Nelson Morris, and others built their plants adjacent to the stock yards. The rapid growth of the packing industry was stimulated by the development of the refrigerator car in the 1870's and by the utilization of by-products after 1885. But the poor working conditions in the plants and the unsanitary methods of waste disposal took their toll in human misery. Upton Sinclair's novel of protest, *The Jungle,* caused a public reaction; the report of an investigating committee, appointed by President Theodore Roosevelt in 1906, led to effective reform legislation.

Meat packing is Chicago's chief industry in value of its products. The Armour, Swift, and Wilson plants, largest in Packingtown, do most of the business.

The SWIFT PLANT (*tours* 9-2:30 *Mon.-Fri.;* 9-12 *Sat.*), Exchange and Racine Aves., normally employs 7,000 workers in its cluster of more than 100 buildings. The ARMOUR PLANT (*tours* 8:30-11, *and* 12:30-3:00 *Mon.-Fri.;* 8:30-11 *Sat.*), Racine Ave. and 43rd St., is comparable in size. Both of these companies provide 90-minute tours of their plants, which include the slaughter rooms if desired. The rapid "disassembling" operations—the conversion of cattle, calves, hogs, and sheep into wholesale cuts of meat, canned and smoked products, and by-products—are as smooth as on the production line of an automobile factory. But "Judas goats," trained rams, are still used to lead lambs from their pens to the slaughter.

14. The UNIVERSITY OF CHICAGO SETTLEMENT (*open* 9 *a.m.*-10 *p.m. daily*), 4630 McDowell Ave., was founded in 1894 by William Rainey Harper and a group of Christian Union workers. The "back of the yards" district was chosen as the best field near the University of Chicago for actual social service work and for study. Mary McDowell, selected by Jane Addams to head the settlement, won wide renown for her militant welfare work. Opened in a 4-room tenement apartment, the institution now covers most of a city block.

The BLACK BELT, known also as Bronzeville, forms a narrow rectangle from about 16th St. to 67th St. Although members of the Negro race have been identified with Chicago's earliest history, it is only since the World War that they have come in sufficient numbers to make the city the world's second largest metropolitan settlement of Negroes. In these few years they have developed a large and successful professional and semi-professional class, welfare organizations, modern hospitals, hotels, manufacturing concerns, department stores, and from time to time a score or more newspapers, one of which is known as the "World's Greatest Weekly." Extensive settlement began at the north end of the belt and spread rapidly southward. White residents in the path of expansion abandoned substantial dwellings in many cases, particularly along South Park Way. As a result, much of Bronzeville compares favorably in outer aspect with the rest of Chicago. But the low income of most of the Negroes, the terrific pressure of some 250,000 people living in an area of six square miles designed for a much smaller population, and the resistance to the expansion of the district by the owners of adjacent property, have created serious housing and racial problems.

The desolation in the older part of Bronzeville contrasts sharply with the gay, cornucopia air of the business section. The largest shops, theaters and ballrooms center on South Park Way at 47th Street, a corner alive with people most of the time. On adjoining side streets are small shops selling mystic charms and potions; curbstone stands with smoke rising from wood fires over which chicken and spareribs are being barbecued; lunchrooms serving hot fish, sweet potato pie, gumbo, and other Southern dishes, markets bulging with turnip tops, mustard greens, and chitterlings; taverns and night clubs that resound with blues-singing and hot-foot music. The SAVOY BALLROOM, 4733 South Park Way, is a counterpart of its more famous namesake in New York City. Once a week the ballroom is converted into an arena in which ambitious pugilists, their mind's eye on Joe Louis, jab warily at each other. Louis' victory over Max Schmeling on the night of June 22, 1938, catapulted thousands of Bronzeville's residents onto the streets to participate in one of the wildest celebrations ever witnessed in Chicago.

15. The VICTORY MONUMENT, 35th St. and South Park Way, the work of Leonard Crunelle, was dedicated in 1927 to the memory of soldiers of the old Eighth Infantry of the Illinois National Guard who died in France. Around the central shaft stand three heroic

figures in bronze symbolizing the tragedy and the glory of war. The bronze statue of a Negro doughboy surmounts the monument.

16. The STEPHEN A. DOUGLAS MONUMENT, foot of 35th St., memorial to the "Little Giant," overlooks the tracks of the Illinois Central Railroad, which he helped to organize. In the small square a tall granite pillar supports a heroic bronze statue of Douglas. The base of the monument, adorned with four seated figures representing *Illinois, Justice, History,* and *Eloquence,* contains the Douglas sarcophagus. The oldest sculptured monument in Chicago, it was executed by Leonard W. Volk in 1879. Nearby are the sites of Camp Douglas, famous Civil War training camp and prison, and the first university in Chicago (1857-1886), built on land given by Douglas.

17. The ABRAHAM LINCOLN CENTER (*open 7 a.m.-12 p.m. daily*), 700 Oakwood Blvd., occupies a massive, foursquare brick building designed by Frank Lloyd Wright. Founded in 1905 by the Reverend Jenkin Lloyd Jones to foster international, inter-religious, and inter-racial fellowship, the institution is an outstanding educational and recreational center. Among the noteworthy activities are the Friday Morning Forum (*Oct.-March*), and the Sunday Evening Discussion Club.

18. PORO COLLEGE, 4415 South Park Way, headquarters of a nation-wide chain, is a Negro school of beauty culture, occupying approximately half a city block. The plant includes four three-story buildings, housing dormitories, cafeteria, beauty shop, and school. The college faces on a beautiful lawn, available to the public for entertainment, as are the parlors. The college, accredited by the Illinois State Board of Education, was founded by Mrs. Anne Pope Malone, known for her philanthropy and work for the social betterment of her race.

19. The WIDOW CLARKE'S HOUSE (*private*), 4526 S. Wabash Ave., the oldest in Chicago, is a spacious two-story house of oak and Georgia pine. Built in 1836, it is in good repair and is still used as a residence. The original porch, with its columns and balcony, has been removed, but the cupola remains. The house was erected near Michigan Avenue and 16th Street for Henry B. Clarke, who died in 1849. His widow sold the house in 1872 to John Chrimes, merchant tailor, who moved it almost four miles south to its present site, then beyond the city limits.

20. The MICHIGAN BOULEVARD GARDEN APARTMENTS, Michigan Ave. and 47th St., is a group of modern brick buildings erected in 1928 by the late Julius Rosenwald, widely known for his philanthropic work among American Negroes. The development covers six acres, three of which are given over to gardens and courts. Other features include a playground and day nursery for children of the families occupying the 421 apartments. Klaber and Grunsfeld were the architects.

21. ST. XAVIER COLLEGE, Cottage Grove Ave. at 49th St., founded in 1912, is an outgrowth of Chicago's first Catholic private school, opened by the Sisters of Mercy in 1846 as the Saint Francis Xavier Female Academy. About 350 women are enrolled for courses which lead to the standard degrees of a liberal arts college. The college building of tan brick and limestone, approached by a semicircular drive through a landscaped block, rises four stories to a steep sloping slate roof with dormer windows.

22. WASHINGTON PARK, S. from 51st St. to 60th St., and E. from South Park Way to Cottage Grove Ave., is the largest inland park in Chicago, embracing 371 acres. In the eighties and nineties gay parties of Chicago's elite rode through in polished carriages and tallyhos to attend the races at the former Washington Park Racing Course, a block south of the park. With the extension of the Negro district in the last decade, the park is now used largely by this group. Large crowds of spectators and participants are attracted to the archery ranges; 'football, baseball, and cricket fields; tennis and roque courts; bridle paths, casting pools, and bowling greens. Pathways wind around the beautifully landscaped lagoons in the south half of the park.

The STATUE OF GEORGE WASHINGTON, South Park Way at 51st St., sculptured by Daniel Chester French and Edward C. Potter, pictures Washington taking command of the American Army at Cambridge. The statue is a replica of one presented to the government of France by the Daughters of the American Revolution.

Behind the Refectory at 56th St. and South Park Way are the SWIMMING POOLS, built by the Works Progress Administration.

The FOUNTAIN OF TIME, Midway Plaisance at Cottage Grove Avenue, masterpiece of Lorado Taft, illustrates in sculpture the line of Austin Dobson's poem:

"Time goes, you say? Ah, no!
Alas, Time stays, *we go*."

The figures of people in various stages and stations of life appear to move from the surging waters at the right to the engulfing waves at the left—a procession of mankind from birth to death crossing a bridge along the border of a quiet pool, under the brooding gaze of Father Time.

The Washington Park Open Forum, an outgrowth of the historic "Bug Club," meets near 56th St. and Cottage Grove Ave. Crowds gather on Sunday afternoons to hear noted speakers and to discuss the problems of the day. In the SUNKEN GARDENS, a block northward, stands a monument, sculptured by Albin Polasek, of the philosopher Gotthold E. Lessing, holding a book and a pen. The new ARMORY, Cottage Grove Ave. at 52nd St., one of the largest buildings of its kind in the United States, houses the 124th Field Artillery, 33rd Division, Illinois National Guard.

23. TEMPLE ISAIAH ISRAEL, Hyde Park Blvd. and Greenwood Ave., one of the most impressive houses of worship in Chicago, was designed by Alfred Alschuler for a reform Jewish congregation. Built of tawny brick of interesting texture and pattern and trimmed with limestone, the octagonal auditorium is roofed with a gold-tiled dome, behind which rises a slender minaret. The whole effect is early Byzantine. Interior and exterior ornamentations were based on photographs of fragments of a second century synagogue unearthed at Tiberias, Palestine.

The JACKSON PARK ART COLONY, 57th St. between Stony Island Ave. and Harper Ave., is a forlorn row of sagging barn-like shacks, erected during the Columbian Exposition to serve as souvenir stores and popcorn stands. After the turn of the century they were taken over by artists and writers. In *Midwest Portraits,* Harry Hansen tells of the carefree but productive life of the colony, and of the inspiration he derived from association there with Floyd Dell, Margaret Anderson, Theodore Dreiser, Edgar Lee Masters, Carl Sandburg, Sherwood Anderson, and many more. Later, there arrived lesser but no less industrious figures. Many of them live and work in GOUDICH CASTLE, an old apartment house at 5642 Harper Avenue, another relic of the fair.

24. The OAK WOODS CEMETERY (*open* 8:30-5 *daily*), 1035 E. 67th St., is one of the oldest of Chicago's cemeteries. Within this 187-acre garden spot rest 123,000 dead. In the southwest corner of the cemetery, in a small mound, are buried some 6,000 Confederate

soldiers who died while imprisoned in Camp Douglas. A large shaft of Georgia granite, surmounted with the bronze statue of a sorrowing Confederate infantryman, commemorates them. The names, companies, and regiments of 4,275 are inscribed on bronze plates around the base of the monument.

25. MARQUETTE PARK, Marquette Road and California Ave., second largest inland park in Chicago, contains 322 acres, extensively improved by the Works Progress Administration. Recreation facilities include a nine-hole golf course. At the entrance on California Avenue stands a red granite monument of striking modern design by the sculptor Raoul Josset, commemorating Captain Steponas Darius and Lieutenant Stasys Girenas, and their attempted flight from New York to Kaunas, Lithuania, July 17, 1933. In the form of a faceted irregular pyramid suggesting the broken wing of an airplane, the front face bears a bronze globe with the figures of ten airplanes tracing the route of the flyers, who crashed to their deaths just short of their goal.

26. The CHICAGO MUNICIPAL AIRPORT, a square-mile tract near the edge of the city at Cicero Ave. and 62nd St., is one of the busiest airfields in the world. Eight lines operate more than 100 schedules daily; the total of scheduled passengers carried to and from the field exceeds 250,000 annually.

27. The WENTWORTH FARM HOUSE (*private*), NE. corner of 55th St. and Harlem Ave., is a rambling white 19-room frame structure, once the seat of the vast country estate of "Long John" Wentworth (1815-88). Wentworth who arrived in Chicago in 1836, barefoot, as legend has it, was closely identified with the rapid transition of Chicago from a mudhole to a metropolis. Editor of the *Democrat,* mayor, congressman, he was also the largest landholder in the city.

28. RYAN WOODS, 87th St. and Western Ave. is one of the few tracts of the magnificent 33,000-acre Cook County forest preserve system that lies within Chicago. A bit of native woodland, it covers the north end of the Blue Island Ridge.

29. The JOHN H. VANDERPOEL MEMORIAL ART GALLERY (*open 9-5 weekdays; 2-5 Sun.*), occupies a wing of the Ridge Park Fieldhouse, Longwood Drive and 96th st. Vanderpoel was an instructor, artist, and author; three years after his death in 1911, his friends organized an association to perpetuate his memory, and

bought one of his paintings, *The Butter Makers,* as the beginning of a permanent collection.

Largely through the efforts of John A. Campbell, volunteer curator, who invited artists to contribute some of their work, the collection includes 600 paintings, water-colors, etchings, and sculptures. The collection, only part of which is shown at a time, includes works by Maxfield Parrish, Ralph Clarkson, Lorado Taft, Louis Betts, and Albin Polasek.

30. The MORGAN PARK MILITARY ACADEMY, 111th St. and Hoyne Ave., attracts thousands of visitors to its full dress parades and military maneuvers on Sunday afternoons during the school year.

31. The TOWN OF PULLMAN, centering around 111th St. and Cottage Grove Ave., at the northwest edge of Lake Calumet, is the result of a grandiose experiment in town planning, and its still beautiful old houses and public buildings give evidence of the proprietary Utopia that briefly flourished here. In 1881 George M. Pullman, inventor and manufacturer of the Pullman sleeping car, hired a group of experts, including the architect Solon S. Beman, to build a model settlement within the municipality of Hyde Park for the employees of his immense new manufacturing plant. This gigantic enterprise attracted world-wide attention as an "extension of the broadest philanthropy to the working man, based on business principles." Some of the employees, however, resented what they considered undemocratic town management. Shortly after the great strike of 1894, the Illinois Supreme Court ruled that the Pullman Company was exceeding the rights of its charter in leasing houses to its workers, and thereafter the cottages and apartments passed into the hands of private owners.

North of 111th Street are the CAR SHOPS, low rambling buildings, strangely ornate in contrast with the austerely practical factory buildings to be seen across Lake Calumet. Above the gabled roofs rises the old campanile-like Water Tower that once supplied water for Pullman. Rows of staunchly built brick cottages, simple in design, gracious and homelike, extend south to 115th Street. Some are well kept, with garden plots bright with zinnias and balsam. Interesting among the dwellings are the "blockhouse tenements," large apartment buildings designed for Pullman's lower-wage workers.

At Cottage Grove Avenue and 111th Street stands the FLORENCE

HOTEL, completely Victorian in the furnishings of its public rooms. Several fine houses, once occupied by executives of the Pullman Company, are grouped near the hotel square. The MARKET HOUSE, in the center of a tiny square at 112th Street and Champlain Avenue, is surrounded by curved arcades with apartments above. The old GREENSTONE CHURCH at 112th St. and St. Lawrence Ave., with its gabled roof and towering spire, is perhaps the handsomest building in Pullman. Its serpentine stone walls, of a faded green, delicately complement the subdued red tones of the surrounding houses.

32. The SOUTH WORKS OF THE CARNEGIE-ILLINOIS STEEL CORPORATION (*tours by arrangement*), 3426 E. 89th St., occupy 591 acres along the lake front at the mouth of the Calumet River. Established in 1880 by the Chicago Rolling Mill Company, it is the second largest steel plant in America, chiefly manufacturing stainless steel for all U. S. Steel Corporation subsidiaries.

By daylight the external aspect of the plant is grimly dark and cold, a rather confusing, heavy conglomeration of materials and equipment: huge cranes that scoop Mesabi ore out of block-long boats, 11 bulky furnaces capable of reducing mountainous cocoa-colored ore piles and coke and limestone heaps to 10,000 tons of pig iron each day, 43 open-hearth furnaces and 3 Bessemer converters that purify and convert the iron into thousands of tons of steel daily, long black sheds that mill slabs, rails, blooms, plates, and bars; and thick nets of rail-lines, that remove the finished products.

At night, like a huge fireworks sparkler almost instantaneously consumed, fountains of sparks leap from the Bessemer converters into the sky, projecting a weird quavering glow on the clouds, visible for miles along the lake shore.

POINTS OF INTEREST IN ENVIRONS

Baha'i House of Worship, 16 *m.*, Ravinia Park, 26.9 *m.*, Dunes Park, 48 *m.* (*see Tour* 2) ; Chicago Zoological Park, 13.4 *m.*, Morton Arboretum, 26.1 *m.* (*see Tour* 13) ; Illinois and Michigan Canal Parkway, 44 *m.* (*see Tour* 14).

ELGIN

Railroad Stations: 156 Douglas Ave. for Chicago & North Western Ry.; W. side of river at foot of Chicago St. bridge for Chicago, Milwaukee, St. Paul and Pacific R. R.; 3 E. Chicago St. for Chicago, Aurora, and Elgin R. R. (electric).

Bus Stations: Union Motor Coach Station, 9 N. Grove Ave., for Northland Greyhound Lines and Fox Valley Coach Line.

City Buses: 5c fare, transfer 1c.

Accommodations: Three hotels.

Information Service: Elgin Motor Club, 109 S. Grove Ave. and Elgin Association of Commerce, 164 Division St.

Golf: Municipal links, Wing Park, on Wing Blvd., 9 holes, daily fee.

Swimming: Wing Park, South Elgin Quarry Pool on State 31, and Y.M.C.A., 2 E. Chicago St.

Tennis: Municipal courts at Wing Park and at Lord's Park, E. end of Park Ave.

Annual Events: Elgin Industries Week, second week in May; Elgin Agricultural Fair and Old Settlers' Picnic, latter part of August; motor boat races on Fox River, Labor Day.

ELGIN (717 alt., 35,929 pop.), an industrial town in the midst of wide farmlands, lies on the gentle bluffs of the Fox River. Although only an hour's ride from Chicago, Elgin is sufficiently self-contained so that only 2 per cent of her wage earners commute to Chicago, and yet her industrial plants are not of the sort that cluster in an industrial wasteland. A few blocks from Fountain Square—described by Elgin wits as a triangle without a fountain—rises the city's major factory, while some of the finest houses are no greater distance down other radial streets. Concerned with more than industry, Elgin possesses an excellent art museum, a small zoo, and an extensive park system. "A midwest factory town," remarked an anonymous Boston reporter, "is not the place where one would ordinarily look for such things."

To Protestant ministers throughout the country, Elgin is the source of many of their Sunday School pamphlets; to Emerson Hough it is the city in which he wrote *The Covered Wagon;* to midwestern creameries it is the place their butter-tubs come from; but Elgin is known to the world at large as the manufacturer of the watches that bear the city's name. The seven-story clock tower of the watch factory, visible for miles, rises high above the central section, and the factory with its related industries employs the major portion of the city's workers.

The Black Hawk War was over when the first settlers, James and

117

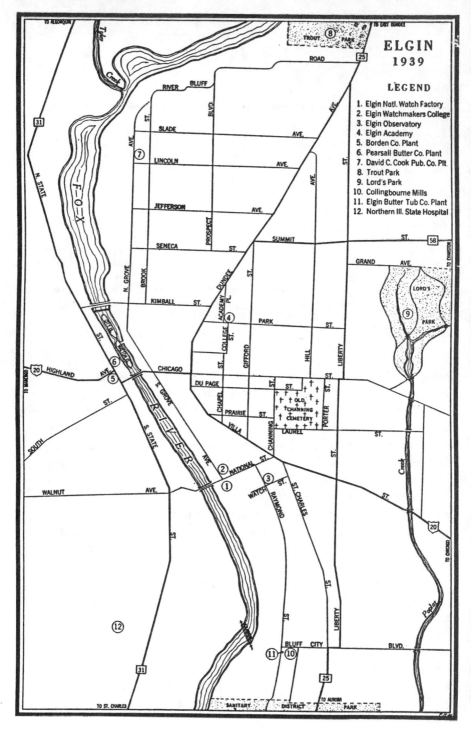

ELGIN
1939

LEGEND

1. Elgin Natl. Watch Factory
2. Elgin Watchmakers College
3. Elgin Observatory
4. Elgin Academy
5. Borden Co. Plant
6. Pearsall Butter Co. Plant
7. David C. Cook Pub. Co. Plt.
8. Trout Park
9. Lord's Park
10. Collingbourne Mills
11. Elgin Butter Tub Co. Plant
12. Northern Ill. State Hospital

118

Hezekiah Gifford, came here from New York in 1835. An Indian ferried them over the Fox River on their way here, but by the following year northern Illinois was cleared of the red men, and the Giffords built up their little settlement without interference. Intent upon having the Chicago-Galena stage routed past his cabin, James Gifford laid out a road, with the assistance of Samuel Kimball, to Belvidere. "Anyone would think," scoffed his wife, "that you expected this farm to become a city, with stagecoaches going through." Within a year they were, twice weekly, with a great blare of horns.

Elgin's industry from the first was bound to the river. Kimball and James Gifford co-operated again in 1837 in damming the river, and a sawmill was built on one side and a gristmill on the other. Hezekiah occupied himself running a tavern for the stagecoach passengers, who noted with "astonishment" that he ran it according to the new-fangled temperance plan then gaining strength in the East.

In 1838 B. W. Raymond purchased a portion of Gifford's tract, and although he lived in Chicago and served as its third mayor, soon interested himself in the development of Elgin. Throughout the forties he invested in several local enterprises, and by 1847 Elgin was able to incorporate as a village. The following year Raymond, by pledging much of his property, had the Chicago and Galena Railroad routed into Elgin. For two years the village was the terminus of that road, and the great stream of west-bound pioneers here transferred to covered wagons. In 1854 Elgin was incorporated as a city.

Elgin began to ship milk to Chicago in 1852, and soon processed a growing surplus into cheese and butter. The city's importance as a dairying center was greatly enhanced by Gail Borden. During his youth he had observed the difficulty encountered by Western travelers in transporting food and began experimenting with condensed foods. Following a stormy trans-Atlantic voyage, during which the ship's cows refused to give milk, he concentrated on condensed milk, and soon had a successful plant running in Elgin. By 1875 it was using the milk from a thousand cows, and the product was being hawked from push-carts in New York and other metropolitan centers.

The watch industry came here in 1866, and by the application of new principles of manufacture soon rivaled dairying. Adopting much the same methods that Ford later used in the automobile industry, the Elgin plant standardized parts and introduced a modified assembly-line whereby craftsmen ceased to be watch-makers and became watch-workers. Low prices had widened the market, and the plant began to turn out thousands of watches monthly.

The booming dairy trade resulted in the formation of a local Board of Trade, in 1872, and for forty years Elgin served as the Midwest marketing center. The Board was an important factor in setting the national prices of butter and cheese; the Elgin *Dairy Report* bore the slogan "Elgin makes the price—We tell you what it is." The peak year for cheese was 1883, when board members marketed 12,500,000 pounds; in 1911 they reached a high in butter sales with 57,000,000 pounds. During the World War the Food Administration requested the Board to suspend operations, and after the Armistice it was not reorganized.

Because of changes in transportation, Elgin no longer manufactures butter, but some 5,000,000 pounds of milk are handled annually, half of it as fluid milk for Chicago, the rest processed as dried and malted milk or used in the manufacture of margarine, mayonnaise, and spreads.

In 1935 the city celebrated the beginning of its second century. A reproduction of James Gifford's log cabin was built, and descendants of the founders told stories of pioneer life. One of the floats in the parade carried an old Frink and Walker stagecoach of the type that James Gifford, laying out his road to Belvidere a century before, had hoped could be lured past his little log cabin.

POINTS OF INTEREST

1. The ELGIN NATIONAL WATCH FACTORY (*reception room only open, 8-4*), National St. and Grove Ave., is set in spacious landscaped grounds along the Fox River. In the reception room is displayed every model produced, from the first in 1867, a railroad movement named the B. W. Raymond for the company's first president, through the key-winders of the late sixties, down to the current models. The factory interior, which has a special dust-removal system, resembles a huge watch itself, what with the whir of belting, miles of shafting, and the myriad wheels running in precise synchrony to the master ticks transmitted from the observatory. Much of the work is done under high-powered lenses, because some of the screws used are so small that 20,000 would barely fill a thimble. Weighing a pencil mark on a piece of paper would be a comparatively rough operation

for some of the balances employed. The plant has produced more than 40,000,000 watches since its establishment.

2. The ELGIN WATCHMAKERS COLLEGE (*open to members of the trade only*), 267 S. Grove Ave., was established in the 1920's in response to a demand for skilled watch-makers, particularly in repair departments of jewelry stores. A non-profit institution controlled by the Elgin National Watch Company, it provides training in clockmaking, watchmaking, engraving, and jewelry work. The courses of 12 to 15 months' duration teach the drawing of patterns, tool-making, and the manufacture of parts. Every type of clock and watch a watch-maker would be called upon to service is available.

3. The ELGIN OBSERVATORY (*apply Elgin National Watch Company for permit*), Watch and Raymond Sts., is housed in a small white stone building that caps a green hill. The observatory was built in 1909 by the Elgin Company to obtain sidereal time for the regulation of Elgin watches. From a list of 800 fixed stars, 10 or 12 are chosen nightly, and are followed across the heavens. An automatic electric recording device graphs time on a revolving drum. Variations of one-thousandth of a second in the master clocks can be checked. These clocks, of the Riefler type, are mounted on a concrete pier, separate from the building, in vacuum glass cases maintained at a temperature varying not more than one-tenth of a degree from 85° F. Secondary clocks relay the impulses by which workers time watches in the factory. A direct line conveys the impulses to the Chicago office of the company in the Pure Oil Building, where they are relayed to radio stations, utility companies, and other agencies requiring exact time.

4. The ELGIN ACADEMY, Park and College Sts., one of the oldest preparatory schools in Illinois, was chartered in 1839 but did not open until 1856. The spacious campus is on the highest ground in the city, and the academy is popularly referred to as "The School on the Hill." The curriculum includes a two-year junior college course. Only boys are boarded, but girls may enroll as day students. The main building, a three-story Greek Revival structure, was built in 1855.

The LAURA DAVIDSON SEARS ACADEMY OF FINE ARTS (*open 2-5 daily except Mon.*), a Georgia marble building with Doric columns, is an adjunct to the academy. The bulk of its exhibits were drawn from the private collection of the late Judge Nathaniel Sears, donor of the building. Some 250 canvases hang in five rooms, four of them devoted to American artists, arranged chronologically. There is a Gilbert Stuart equestrian portrait of Washington, and one by Charles Wilson Peale (c. 1770) picturing Washington in the uniform of a British colonel. Others include a portrait by Samuel Morse, who gave up painting when forty years old to tinker with telegraphy, Whistler's *On the Beach at Ostend,* and work by John Singleton Copley and Winslow Homer. The small but distinguished foreign gallery has a representative collection of the Barbizon School, and several paintings by early Italian masters, including Parmigiano and Bellini. Rosa Bonheur's *An Old Buffalo* was painted when "Buffalo Bill" Cody took his Wild West show to France.

5. The BORDEN COMPANY PLANT, 16 N. State St., erected in 1911, is one of the largest malted milk and dried milk plants in the country.

6. The PEARSALL BUTTER COMPANY PLANT (*tours by advance arrangement*), 31 N. State St., is one of the few plants still using the water power of the Fox River. Formerly a major factor in the production of Elgin butter, and purchaser of the entire output of 300 dairy farms, the firm now manufactures butter at branch plants elsewhere, and at Elgin produces mayonnaise, margarines and similar products.

7. The DAVID C. COOK PUBLISHING COMPANY PLANT (*tours by advance arrangement*), Grove and Lincoln Aves., has 13 acres of one-story buff brick units. Publishers of 37 religious periodicals and many pamphlets, with an annual production of over 100,000,-000 copies, and distributors of 7,000 mail order items, ranging from handkerchiefs to clocks and razor blades, the company accounts for half the income of the Elgin postoffice.

8. TROUT PARK, on State 25 at the NE. city limits, was a trout preserve on a private estate before it was acquired by the city in 1922. A large portion of its 57 acres is purposely untended, save for the paths that make it accessible. Trees blown down by the great storm of 1920 lie where they fell, clothed now in mosses and ferns. Throughout, the section is substantially as it was found by the pioneers. Many of the trees are tagged, and botanical classes from the University of Chicago and elsewhere frequently use the park as an outdoor laboratory.

9. LORD'S PARK, E. end of Park Ave., 110 acres in extent, was given to the city by Mr. and Mrs. G. P. Lord in 1892. Poplar Creek,

which winds through the park, has been dammed to produce lagoons on three levels, willow-shaded and connected by splashing little falls. The small Zoo, containing monkeys, black bears, coyotes, deer, raccoons, and snakes, was built into the side of a bluff, so that the animals may be viewed from above as well as from cage level. The AUDUBON MUSEUM *(open 1-5 daily during summer months)* contains a varied collection of mounted animals, including both American and foreign specimens, and historical relics associated with the pioneer history of the Fox Valley region.

10. The COLLINGBOURNE MILLS *(apply at office)*, Grace St. just off Bluff City Blvd., employ about 500 mill-workers in the spinning of silk, wool, and rayon threads and yarns.

11. The ELGIN BUTTER TUB COMPANY PLANT *(apply at office)*, Bluff City Blvd. and Raymond St., ships five carloads of tubs daily during the peak months. One of the by-products, a fine wood dust known as "flour," is sold to manufacturers of bakelite and linoleum.

12. The NORTHERN ILLINOIS STATE HOSPITAL *(9-11:30 and 1-4:30 for friends of patients only)* occupies 820 acres bordering S. State St. at the southern city limits. The three-story main building, opened in 1872 for 300 patients, now serves as the nucleus of a group of buildings housing 4,600 mental cases. The institution applies occupational therapy in its attempt to cure rather than merely incarcerate its patients.

POINTS OF INTEREST IN ENVIRONS

Yeoman City of Childhood, 4 *m.;* Illinois Pet Cemetery, 8.7 *m.* *(see Tour* 11).

EVANSTON

Railroad Stations: Main St. and Custer Ave., Dempster St. and Sherman Ave., Davis St. and Maple Ave., Central St. and Green Bay Road for Chicago and North Western Ry.

Interurban Stations: North Shore Line, running between Chicago and Milwaukee, five stations; Rapid Transit Line (elevated) to Chicago, nine stations.

Bus Stations: 305 Howard St. for Greyhound.

Local Buses: 7c fare.

Taxis: 5c to 15c per half mile.

Accommodations: 12 hotels.

Information Services: Chamber of Commerce, 518 Davis St.; Chicago Motor Club, 1011 Davis St.; Illinois Automobile Club, 1233 Chicago Ave.

Street Directions: Avenues and Courts run N. and S., Streets and Places E. and W.

Motion Picture Houses: Three.

Golf: Community course, 9 holes, Central St. and the canal, 50c fee.

Tennis: Bent Park, Central St. and Hastings Ave.; Ackerman Park, Central St. and McDaniels Ave.; Mason Park, Hamilton St. at Lake Michigan; Foster Park, Foster St. and Dewey Ave.; Leahy Park, Central St. and Simpson St.

Swimming: Free beaches at foot of Greenwood St. and of Davis St. Five fee beaches.

Annual Events: North Shore Music Festival, Dyche Stadium, variable date in May.

EVANSTON (601 alt., 63,338 pop.), fronting largely on Lake Michigan, and with an extension stretching westward at the northern edge of the city, is roughly L-shaped. It is the first of the North Shore suburbs, divided from Chicago only by Calvary Cemetery. Although its development hinged somewhat on the tremendous expansion of Chicago, Evanston retains a distinct individuality and runs a temperature at being referred to as an off-shoot of that city. Aristocratic and self-sufficient, it considers its proximity to Chicago little more than a geographic accident. In appearance it is almost an Illinois anomaly, the dignity and spaciousness of its residential districts contrasting sharply with the noisy, virile metropolis on the south. Untouched by the peculiar tumult that Sandburg calls the "harr and boom" of the early 1900's, Evanston felt no need to conform its city plan to the intense concentration of the new industrial age. The through traffic boulevard system that traverses Chicago's lakeside parks stops short at the threshold of Evanston. Here the lake front is given over to

124

quiet streets that wind through small parks and past brick walls enclosing spacious city estates.

Despite its rather sentimental regard for the narrower streets of the pre-automobile era, Evanston has been able to maintain an amazing traffic-safety record; in 1936 it had been named America's safest city in three of the four preceding years. Its system offers no formula, and functions by scrutinizing each general type of traffic problem closely and applying the best research methods to its solution. From 42 traffic deaths per 100,000 in 1928, the rate was reduced to 2.9 in 1935, in spite of the heavy burden of through traffic to the suburbs farther north. The Traffic Safety Institute, established at Northwestern University in 1932, works with and helps train the city police.

Pere Marquette and his Indian companions landed in 1674 in the natural harbor formed by the 25-foot bluff now named Grosse Point. Marquette's diary has an account of the incident and a sketch of his fleet of ten canoes drawn up on the sands. In pioneer days, as lake traffic increased, Grosse Point assumed some importance as a port, and a village grew up around it, settled by those who followed the inland seas. For some time a faint maritime atmosphere clung to the community; a number of families at the present time trace their descent from the early Great Lakes captains.

The first dwelling on the "Point" was built in 1826, but it was not until 1854, the year before Northwestern University opened, that the town was platted. At that time it was renamed Evanston, honoring John Evans, one of the university founders and a prominent early citizen. The subsequent blend of the maritime (enhanced by the Grosse Point lighthouse) and the academic, won Evanston the sobriquet of "the finest New England village in the Middlewest."

In the year 1855 Northwestern University opened, after its founding fathers had considered Chicago sites and rejected them. Although it was under the control of the Methodist Episcopal Church, the school proclaimed that it was "not intended to be sectarian, but the minds committed to its care will be induced to the practice of virtue and religion." In its second year the school charter was revised to prohibit the sale of liquor within four miles of the campus (Evanston is still dry). Shortly afterward, in nice coincidence, Frances E. Willard came here with her family from Janesville, Wisconsin. In the following forty years she became Evanston's most famous citizen, serving as Dean of Women and Professor of Æsthetics at Northwestern, and

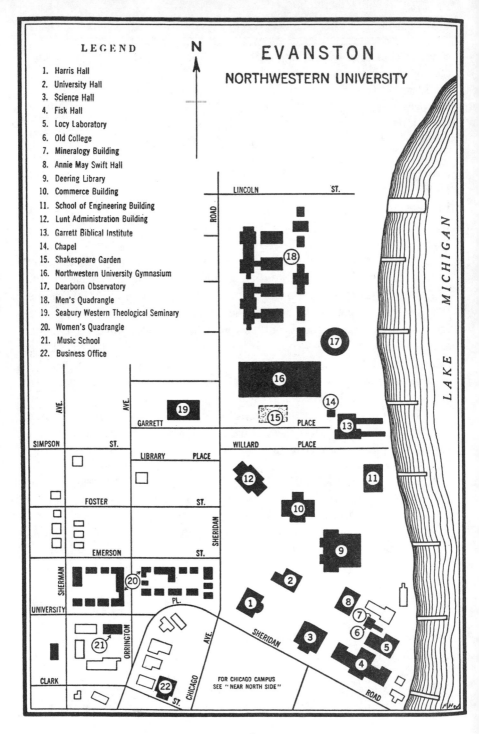

LEGEND

1. Harris Hall
2. University Hall
3. Science Hall
4. Fisk Hall
5. Locy Laboratory
6. Old College
7. Mineralogy Building
8. Annie May Swift Hall
9. Deering Library
10. Commerce Building
11. School of Engineering Building
12. Lunt Administration Building
13. Garrett Biblical Institute
14. Chapel
15. Shakespeare Garden
16. Northwestern University Gymnasium
17. Dearborn Observatory
18. Men's Quadrangle
19. Seabury Western Theological Seminary
20. Women's Quadrangle
21. Music School
22. Business Office

N

EVANSTON
NORTHWESTERN UNIVERSITY

LAKE MICHIGAN

LINCOLN ST.

ROAD

SIMPSON ST.

AVE.

AVE.

GARRETT PLACE

WILLARD PLACE

LIBRARY PLACE

FOSTER ST.

SHERIDAN ST.

EMERSON ST.

SHERMAN

UNIVERSITY

PL.

ORRINGTON

CLARK

SHERIDAN

AVE.

CHICAGO

ST.

FOR CHICAGO CAMPUS
SEE "NEAR NORTH SIDE"

ROAD

126

later organizing the World Women's Christian Temperance Union. Among her many writings was a glowing tribute to Evanston, entitled *The Classic Town.*

Early Evanston was a tiny town concerned largely with its university. Twenty-five years after the school was founded Evanston's population was only a scant four thousand, and not until 1892, when it annexed South Evanston, was it incorporated as a city. But after the turn of the century the city began to emerge as a suburb. Already cheap and efficient transportation had welded it economically to Chicago, and the booming of the metropolis could not help but be felt here. From twenty thousand in 1900, the population doubled in twenty years, and then almost doubled again in the decade ending in 1930.

In that last decade the city's economy underwent a sharp change. Today Evanston ranks twelfth among United States cities in per capita retail sales. Although a measure of this is consumed in good living by Evanstonians, the true significance of the statistics is the revealing of Evanston's lately acquired commercial importance. In the twenties large Chicago department stores began establishing branches in Evanston, local stores grew, and new ones were started. Increasingly Evanston has become the shopping center for much of the North Shore. But somehow this development has not greatly changed Evanston's suburban aspects; now and then, among the sleek modern cars of the North Shore shoppers, an archaic electric brougham still sedately whirs its way along.

Northwestern University

Northwestern University extends from Clark Street on the south to Lincoln on the north, and from Sherman Avenue on the west to Lake Michigan. Chartered in 1851 and opened in 1855, Northwestern was among the first institutions of higher learning in the Chicago area. The small group of founders, including Orrington Lunt, Grant Goodrich, and John Evans, were of the Methodist Episcopal faith, but the university is non-denominational. The first class, five in number, was graduated in 1857. The present enrollment of the university is about 12,000, which includes those enrolled on the Chicago campus, the majority of whom attend night classes.

The buildings of the Evanston campus are scattered informally about a wooded sward. Likewise informal is the architecture, from the stodgy red brick Romanesque of the Commerce Building, the eclecticism of Harris Hall, to the exquisite Gothic detail of the Deering Library. Back of the campus spreads Lake Michigan, its shore divided into beaches restricted to the University personnel. The pathways between the beach and the university buildings have an extra-curricular tradition as Lovers' Lanes.

CAMPUS TOUR

(The following walking tour [2 *hours*] begins at the main entrance, Sheridan Road and Chicago Avenue. A guide will be furnished for special groups upon application at the Administration Building. Buildings may be inspected between 8 *a.m.* and 5 *p.m.*)

One of the newer buildings, (1) HARRIS HALL, houses the social studies classes. Nearby rise the grey gables and spires of (2) UNIVERSITY HALL, effectively creating the intellectual atmosphere absent in some of the newer buildings, which are box-like and many windowed. It is given over to the departments of English and geology.

(3) SCIENCE HALL houses the departments of chemistry and physics. Here Winford Lee Lewis, professor of organic research, conducted the research leading to the discovery of lewisite, most deadly of poison gases. Immediately east is (4) FISK HALL, with the departments of classic and romance languages, and of botany.

In (5) LOCY LABORATORY is the department of zoology. Between it and the Mineralogy Building stands (6) OLD COLLEGE, a frame building, oldest on the campus. Its small rooms, still used by the School of Education, are connected by steep, narrow stairways, and lighted by many-paned high windows. In its tower is a huge candle, symbolic of the light of education, which is lighted once a year by the president of the university in a ceremony shared by alumni all over the world, who light similar candles at the same hour.

In (7) the MINERALOGY BUILDING there is a collection of specimens (*open daily during class hours*). The School of Speech, whose founder, John L. Cumnock, was widely known as a pioneer in his field, is in (8) ANNIE MAY SWIFT HALL.

(9) The beautiful new DEERING LIBRARY, from its central location above a sloping lawn known as the Meadows, presides aloofly over the campus. Its plan is an adaptation by James Gamble Rogers of the cathedral style of King's College at Cambridge, and is executed

in white limestone and marble. An interesting and unusual detail of its Gothic design is the omission of gables over the three exquisitely molded and carved arches of the porch, its dominating architectural feature. The entrance doors open into a broad, low-roofed hall, with groined arches decorated in mosaic of delicate colors. Two stairways mount to the second floor, where stained glass, the lofty ceiling and the fine Gothic carvings of the reading room give a grave and ecclesiastical air.

A million dollars of the initial cost of $1,250,000 came from the harvester fortune of the Deering family, who have contributed heavily to the university's endowment funds.

In (10) the red brick COMMERCE BUILDING, once the home of the Garrett Biblical Institute, are the School of Commerce and the Medill School of Journalism. East of this is (11) the SCHOOL OF ENGINEERING BUILDING. In (12) LUNT ADMINISTRATION BUILDING are the president's office and other administrative offices.

Across Willard Place and east toward the lake is (13) GARRETT BIBLICAL INSTITUTE, a school of divinity maintained by the Methodist Episcopal denomination, co-operating without affiliation with the university. The building is an exceptionally fine example of the perpendicular Gothic style of the Tudor period, finished in beautiful detail. On the first floor (L) is the BENNETT MUSEUM OF CHRISTIAN ARCHEOLOGY, with many reproductions of objects of use and beauty of early Christian and pre-Christian eras, vases, amphorae, chalices, and a large group of reliquary panels. To the west of the building is (14) a small CHAPEL, seating only 30, and open day and night for meditation and prayer. Its design is very early English Gothic. The entrance to (15) the famous SHAKESPEARE GARDEN is at the northwest corner of the Institute. Landscaped by Jens Jensen, it was the first in the country planned, like the one at Stratford-on-Avon, to display the flowers and herbs mentioned by Shakespeare in his plays. A double row of hawthorn encloses an oval in which there is an unbroken succession of bloom from earliest spring to fall. At one end is a tiny fountain inscribed with the quatrain from Midsummer Night's Dream beginning:

"I know a bank where the wild thyme blows."

North of the garden rises the great bulk of (16) NORTHWEST-

ERN UNIVERSITY GYMNASIUM. In it is a playing field large enough for football and baseball games, but the University's expansion now taxes even these ample 'facilities. Here are held the University's basketball games, between stands seating 5,000 spectators.

Behind the gymnasium is (17) DEARBORN OBSERVATORY (*open Thurs. evenings in clear weather*) used by the department of astronomy. Beyond the gymnasium on Sheridan Road is (18) the MEN'S QUADRANGLE, a group of houses for fraternity and non-fraternity men.

Across from the Shakespeare Garden stands (19) SEABURY WESTERN THEOLOGICAL SEMINARY, a handsome group of buildings of rough limestone in modernized Gothic. Offering training for the Episcopal priesthood, it is friendly but not affiliated with Northwestern.

(20) The WOMEN'S QUADRANGLE is bounded by Emerson Street, Sherman Avenue, University Place, and Sheridan Road. Here live the majority of Northwestern's women students, whose traditional beauty has given rise to the description of the university as a seminary that admits male students solely to provide escorts for her beautiful women.

Across University Place is (21) the MUSIC SCHOOL, whose long-time dean, Peter Christian Lutkin, built it into national prominence. At the end of the tour is (22) the BUSINESS OFFICE, which houses the offices of the university's business manager and the trustees' room. Here also is the ticket office for all major athletic events.

OTHER POINTS OF INTEREST

The EVANSTON PUBLIC LIBRARY, 1703 Orrington Ave., built in 1904 after a conventional Roman design, houses the exhibits of the Evanston Art Center, and those of the EVANSTON HISTORICAL SOCIETY MUSEUM (*basement:* 1:30-5 *weekdays except Sat.* 9-12; *closed from June 30 to Labor Day*). The society owns a notable body of historical material from Chicago and the North Shore, and scattered items from all over the country.

REST COTTAGE (*open weekdays 9-5 except Sat.* 9-12), 1728-30 Chicago Ave., is also known as the Frances E. Willard Home. A national shrine of the Women's Christian Temperance Union, Rest Cottage was the girlhood home of Frances Willard, second president of the organization and organizer of the World W.C.T.U. On the lawn behind the house, in a three-story brick building, are the national W.C.T.U. headquarters and the school of temperance instruction.

Rest Cottage consists of the Willard family residence, 1728, built in 1865, and No. 1730, which was added somewhat later to accommodate Miss Willard's brother and his family. Inside and outside, the cottage is a survival of another era. Gabled and with vertical weatherboarding instead of the usual horizontal, the house is surrounded by the same vines and shrubs which were planted by Miss Willard's father.

The sitting room of the Willard family has been dedicated to Miss Anna Gordon, Miss Willard's lifelong companion and later world W.C.T.U. president. The room contains, in addition to several pieces of the Willard furniture, a cup and saucer of John Wesley and a pair of earrings worn by Susannah Wesley.

The Willard parlor is at the left of the entrance. Archaic and prim, it appears much as it did in the days of the family's occupancy. Here are portraits of Miss Willard, her parents, her brother, and her sister Mary, whose biography Miss Willard wrote in *Nineteen Beautiful Years*. In the dining room, to the rear, stands the bicycle which Miss Willard learned to ride when she had passed fifty. A banjo clock, dated and signed by Simon Willard, eighteenth century clock-maker of Boston and an ancestor of Miss Willard's, hangs on the wall.

Miss Willard's study, upstairs, is the inner sanctum of the shrine. In an alcove is her ink spotted desk, and her bookshelves, filled with annotated books and faded family photographs. Nearby is the rocker where she held a tablet on her lap while writing her books and speeches. The grandfather's clock, still ticking, was also made by Simon Willard. On the wall is framed a piece of cloth used by Queen Victoria, as a child, for a doll's wrap. An inscription above the fireplace reads, "Let something good be said."

LEVERE MEMORIAL TEMPLE (9-5 *weekdays except Sat.* 9-12; 3-5 *Sun.*), 1856 Sheridan Road, houses the national headquarters of Sigma Alpha Epsilon and serves as a memorial to the fraternity's war dead. To the right of the entrance is a reference library chiefly devoted to fraternity books and publications. The chapel, Gothic and austere, has windows by Tiffany, and an everburning memorial light. The museum, on the second floor, contains S.A.E. relics, among which is the first saxophone owned by Rudy Vallee.

The EVANSTON CRADLE (10-4 *weekdays*), 2039-49 Ridge
Ave., occupies three buildings, the newest of which was completed in
1939. Organized in 1923 by Mrs. Florence Walrath and others, the
Cradle has become an internationally known child placement agency.
The efficiency of its management and its innovations in the care of
infants has won it the patronage of many headline names here and
abroad; its waiting list usually tops 2,000. Despite its small capacity
(28 cribs) by the beginning of 1936 it had admitted 2,904 infants. It is
supported by contributions, and among its sponsors, most of whom are
social leaders, the annual Cradle Ball is an event of first importance.

The EVANSTON WATER FILTRATION PLANT (*open;*
8-5 *daily*) is at Sheridan Road and Lincoln Street. Ultra modern and
distinctive in appearance, the Evanston plant is widely recognized by
engineers as a model of efficiency. Using a system adapted from the
tank type domestic filter, it daily treats 75,000,000 gallons of water
supplied by submarine pipes from a crib a mile and a quarter off-shore.
Visitors are shown the entire process of treatment.

The GROSSE POINT LIGHT HOUSE (*not open*) does much
to heighten the New England atmosphere of Evanston. Built in 1860,
it was the indirect result of the wreck of the *Lady Elgin,* in which
nearly 300 persons lost their lives in the lake off Evanston. In recent
years the old Fresnel light, installed in 1874, has been replaced by an
electric beacon visible for 20 miles and needing no tender.

The NATIONAL COLLEGE OF EDUCATION, 2770 Sheridan
Road was established in 1886 as the Chicago Kindergarten College,
and moved to Evanston in 1926 under its present name. It trains teachers for kindergartens, nursery and elementary schools, and also for
children's social and religious work. The demonstration school, maintained as a laboratory in child training methods, may be visited by
educators.

DYCHE STADIUM, Central St. and Asbury Ave., was named
for William A. Dyche, long time business manager of Northwestern.
Dedicated in 1926, it was designed by James Gamble Rogers and Gavin
Hadden, and has a capacity of 48,000.

POINTS OF INTEREST IN ENVIRONS

Baha'i House of Worship, 3 *m.;* Ravinia Park, 13.9 *m.;* Fort Sheridan,
18.9 *m.;* Great Lakes Naval Training Station, 26.7 *m.* (*See Tour* 2).

JOLIET

Railroad Stations: Union Depot, Jefferson and Scott Sts., for Chicago, Rock Island, and Pacific, the Alton, and the Atchison, Topeka, and Santa Fe.
Bus Stations: 301 N. Ottawa St. for Bluebird Coach, Gold Star, and Greyhound Lines; Union Bus Depot, 32 E. Jefferson St., for Joliet, Plainfield, and Aurora Lines, Kankakee Bus, National Trailways System, and Santa Fe Trailways.
City Buses: 5c fare.
Taxis: Rates from 15c per person to 15c for first half-mile.
Accommodations: Seven hotels.
Information Services: Association of Commerce, 436 Clinton St.; Illinois Motor Club, 224 Van Buren St.; Chicago Motor Club, 615 Van Buren St.
Radio Station: WCLS (1310 kc.).
Motion Picture Houses: Five.
Golf: One municipal, five commercial courses.
Tennis: Joliet High School courts, Jefferson and Eastern; Highland Park, Cass St., West Park, West Park Ave., Nowell Park, US 66 at Mills Road.
Swimming: Y.M.C.A. pool, 409 Ottawa St.; Michigan Beach, Rowell Ave. ½ *m.* S. of intersection with Second Ave.; Nowell Park and Pilcher Park.

JOLIET (607 alt., 42,993 pop.), the seat of Will County, lies 35 miles southwest of Chicago, on the Des Plaines River and the Illinois and Michigan Canal, a part of the Great Lakes to Gulf Waterway. Here the outer belt freight lines shunt much of the through freight around Chicago. Concerned with its freight handling and possessed of early transportation advantages, Joliet has developed as a self-dependent unit; here one senses little or no dependence upon the metropolis looming a scant hour's drive to the northeast. Joliet reveals its economic independence from almost every approach, in railway yards, warehouses, shipping platforms, quarries, factory stacks, and mountains of coal.

This is the Joliet of which Sandburg wrote, years ago:

> On the one hand the steel works
> On the other hand the penitentiary.
> Santa Fe trains and Alton trains
> Between smokestacks on the west
> And gray walls on the east . . .

But this is not all of Joliet; the man-of-the-street scarcely gives a thought to the penitentiary, so little does it intrude upon the life of the town. Across the north side of town stretches the Joliet park system, which, although planned too late to include areas in the city proper, is one of the finest among the small cities of the State. If the average resident were asked what is the most outstanding thing about his town, he would probably say the high school band, followed by the park system, and mention the penitentiary as an afterthought.

The city is one of the largest wall paper producers in the country, manufacturing enough daily to reach to New York and back. One hundred and fifty other factories produce more than 1,700 different articles. This diversification of products is the third stage of an industrial development that began some ninety years ago.

The first settler here was Charles Reed, who came in 1831. The following year he, along with numerous settlers in the vicinity, fled the region when the Black Hawk War broke out, but before the war was over they returned, and by 1834 a town was laid out and the first public sale of lots was held. By some unexplained quirk, the town was known as Juliet for years, and a nearby village romantically took the name of Romeo. When Will County was laid out in 1836, the designated county seat was referred to under the name of Shakespeare's heroine, and a year later it was incorporated with that name.

For ten years the fortunes of Joliet rose and fell as work went forward or languished on the canal. The first boat arrived here April 11, 1848, and was met by the entire population, with bands, booming cannon, and much oratory. With its new transportation means, Joliet entered into its first industrial era, based on the large-scale shipping of local limestone. In the fifties and sixties Joliet shipped blocks as far as New York, and its quarries provided the Middle West with material for such public structures as the Rock Island Arsenal, the Indiana penitentiary, and the State House and Lincoln monument at Springfield.

The first railroad, the Rock Island, came here in 1852, followed by five other lines. Although the railroad was eventually to cause the decline of the canal it brought, in the seventies, the new industry of steel manufacture, which was further attracted by the soft coal in the vicinity. The earliest mill manufactured spikes, track bolts, and other railroad items. Bessemer plants, rail and rod mills, blast furnaces followed, and then plants that made galvanized wire, barbed wire, nails, and other products for the growing agricultural west.

In 1894 Joliet pioneered notably in the elimination of grade crossings, seeking to require the railroads to elevate their tracks in the major portion of the city. In and out of courts the battle was fought, with the lines objecting strenuously to the ordinance that had been passed. Finally, in 1904, a compromise plan was effected, and within the next decade the work was completed. The program, which eliminated a score of dangerous crossings and consolidated all passenger service in one station, brought numerous queries from other cities that were spurred to emulate the plan.

The rise of the Chicago area as a steel-producing center wooed away from Joliet some of the mills engaged in heavier manufacture. But the lighter processing mills remain, surrounded by a plexus of plants that manufacture power corn shellers, soap, jewelry, packaging machines, flyspray, ink, sulphuric acid, steel washers, and shoes with which horses all over the world are shod. The outer belt railroad is still Will County's largest employer, but the glinting waterway, which Sandburg saw as "stripes of silver or copper or gold" still moves its freight through town, its quaint donkeys long discarded for power-boats as efficient as the factories they slip past.

POINTS OF INTEREST

The JOLIET WALL PAPER MILLS (*guides by arrangement*), 223 Logan Ave., is one of the six Joliet mills, which produce one-third of the country's wall paper. The visitor is first taken to the damp, warm boiler room, where dynamos generate electricity for the entire factory; from there to the raw material warehouses, which are piled high with chalky Georgia clay and huge bales of white paper already cut to wall paper width. Next visited is the color room, stacked with barrels of pigment and equipped with large grinding and mixing machines in which the colors are prepared in dry form.

In the actual printing room the air is pungent with the ammonia used to treat the soy bean color oils. Here are the printing machines, extending in vertical rows, a city block in length. The paper, fed from rolls in slow-moving festoons, is given a ground coating of the desired tint, picked up in loops by wooden fingers resembling broom handles, and slowly carried along drying units in a current of warm, dry air. Fed back into the machines, it is imprinted with as many as 12 different designs and colors. Carried back in dense scallops over the heaters, through a washing fluid, and into a long drying room, it is caught up by reels and wound into regulation rolls.

The AMERICAN INSTITUTE OF LAUNDERING VOCA-
TIONAL TRAINING SCHOOL (*guides at main office*), Chicago
St. and Doris Ave., was established in 1930. It conducts research for
members of a national laundry association, and maintains a separate
training school that gives a 40-week course in modern laundrying
methods.

In OAKWOOD CEMETERY, 1919½ Cass St., is the OAKWOOD
MOUND, situated on a steep rise of 30 ft., a conical structure 8 ft.
high, extending over an area 64 by 67 feet. Excavations conducted by
the University of Chicago in 1928, yielded 100 skeletons, in addition
to weapons, ornaments and implements, all now exhibited at the
University. There is revealed a preponderance of women and child
burials, and five instances where the mother and child were clasped in
an embrace. The mound, dating back some 1,000 years, contained the
scattered skeletal remains of over 300 persons. The confusion in placement and the lack of uniformity of the burials, which were characterized by both flexed and full length positions, indicate a great number
of sudden deaths, and a hurried disposal of the bodies, which were
probably gathered in a heap and covered with earth.

BIRD HAVEN is a 75-acre strip of land, reached by driving out
Cass St., through Hobbs Parkway and the south drive of Pilcher
Park. The dense natural growth of hawthorn, to which 300 ever-
green species have been added, serves as natural protection of small
birds from hawks and owls. Over two hundred kinds of birds, by
count, have nested here. The area includes a greenhouse with a desert
room containing about 170 kinds of cactus, and a chrysanthemum
show is given each fall.

PILCHER PARK ARBORETUM, US 30, from Maple to
Gauger Road, was presented to the people of Joliet by Robert Pilcher
in 1922 with the stipulation that it should remain in its natural state.
About 75 species of trees, including 9 kinds of oak, are native, as well
as many shrubs, bushes, and almost innumerable wild flowers. A
collection of imports started by John Higginbotham, original owner,
includes southern magnolia, sweet gum, cypress, tulip-tree, white
fringe, pecan, black birch, and hickories and black cherry trees. Plans
for development envisage introduction of trees from all over the world.
A five-acre picnic camp, across Hickory Creek, is connected with the
main park by foot bridge. One-way motor lanes are supplemented by
five miles of narrow footpaths and several miles of bridle paths.

The OLD PRISON, 1900 Collins St., functions as a unit under the same warden, with the new Stateville prison (*see Tour* 17). Its construction was begun in 1857 after long and bitter criticism of the first State prison at Alton by Dorothea Dix. Built on an impregnable limestone stratum from the stone quarried for the foundation, the prison was the model of its day. Corbelled walls five feet thick at the base surround the cell-block, which had a capacity for almost 3,000. Until 1928, much prison work, ranging from quarrying to match-making, was done by inmates, but income producing work has been discontinued. At one time one-hundred cells were reserved for women, but the entire prison is now given over to men.

The JOLIET HIGH SCHOOL, Jefferson St. and Eastern Ave., is a Tudor-Gothic building, constructed in 1899. The school band is nationally famous; so frequently did it win the national band competition that it was eventually barred and now attends the contests on an honorary basis only. On the main floor is a series of six murals by William Panhallow Henderson, painter, architect, and muralist. The murals depict the activities of Marquette and Jolliet among the Indians. Presented by the graduating class of 1906, they are considered among the finest of Henderson's mural work.

The COLLEGE OF ST. FRANCIS, 303 Taylor, is a Catholic senior women's college, and the only such one in Illinois outside of Chicago. Opened in 1925 as Assisi Junior College, it was rechartered in 1930 as an accredited college, awarding a bachelor's degree. It is conducted by the Sisters of St. Francis of Mary Immaculate, and is an outgrowth of the St. Francis Academy, a resident and day preparatory school for girls, established in 1869 and still functioning. The present enrollment of the academy is approximately 400, and that of the college, 500.

POINTS OF INTEREST IN ENVIRONS

Brandon Road Lock and Dam, 2.7 *m.* (*see Tour* 14). Illinois and Michigan Canal at Channahon, 11 *m.* (*see Tour* 14). Stateville State Prison, 4 *m.* (*see Tour* 17).

Part II

Chicago's Culture

ARCHITECTURE

THE FACTORS in Illinois that produced a clear and distinct new stream of architectural innovations have never been fully explained. It was in Chicago, generally speaking, that the conflict was fought between dead classicism and direct, vigorous functionalism, but what placed the battlefield in the prairie metropolis is perhaps too complex a tangle of circumstances for unraveling. Both geography and the economics of the city played their part. Separated by a thousand miles from the seaboard cities and their traditions, and given a city that was building at an unprecedented rate, Illinois architects experienced a subtle freeing of spirit that within a generation was to permeate the whole of American building. That the innovations they brought forth are now widely accepted has tended to obscure the daring they required, but from the first problems of the skyscraper, through the " Chicago School" of Wright, and down to the ultimate solution of skyscraper design, the significance of Illinois architecture has been that it was creative rather than adaptive.

While the Romanesque was at its height the revolutionary story of the skyscraper began to unfold one of the most exciting chapters in the history of building. The skyscraper has come to be accepted as America's outstanding contribution to architecture, and contrary to popular belief, it was in Chicago, not New York, that the technique of the tall building was developed in the two decades after the great fire of 1871.

The Montauk Block built in 1882 by Burnham and Root was the first all-fireproof building and embodied new developments in foundation design as well. This was a serious problem because of the yielding bed of clay underlying Chicago. In a striking innovation Root hit upon the idea of embedding a crisscross of steel rails in concrete to make a rigid support distributing the load, and this system was used until the development of caissons in 1893 by Adler and Sullivan in the Stock Exchange building.

But the basis of skyscraper construction is the underlying steel frame—the "bones" which carry walls and floors, and which have

141

given this method of building the name of "skeleton construction."
At the beginning of this period cast-iron columns inside the building
carried part of the floor loads, but the walls carried the rest. For low
buildings this was practical, until the soaring prices of Chicago real-
estate made tall buildings an economic necessity and the development
of elevators made them a possibility. But in order to carry the weight
of the additional upper stories the walls had to be so massive that
they took too much space from the ground floor. This can be seen in
the 16-story Monadnock building by Burnham and Root, the last
example of this type of construction, where the ground floor walls
are 6 feet thick. Its design, paradoxically, was admirably simple;
ornamentation was renounced and a sharp flare at the roof replaced
the traditional cornice.

The first step toward solving problems of height was the building
of cast-iron columns into the walls to carry the ends of the floor
beams. But in 1885 a more daring and satisfactory solution was
achieved by William LeBaron Jenney in the 10-story Home Insurance
building. There the outside columns of the two street-front walls
and court carried not only the floor loads, but also the wall panels
from floor to floor.

In 1887 Chicagoans were startled to see a building being built
"from the top down." This structure, the Tacoma building by Holabird and Roche, developed the skeleton construction further, and the
builders found it convenient to fill in the upper wall panels first. With
the development of the Bessemer and open-hearth processes, rolled
steel gradually displaced wrought and cast-iron, though the latter
persisted until 1904. Elevators were rapidly improved and engineers
soon solved the various other mechanical, electrical, and structural
problems involved in a high building.

Culminating this period was the 22-story Masonic Temple (later
renamed the Capitol Building) designed by Burnham and Root in
1892. Highest building in the world at that time, the throngs of
visitors to the World's Fair the following year gasped at its awe-
inspiring height.

The exposition's architectural success was largely due to the genius
of Daniel H. Burnham, Chief of Construction, who insisted that
the work be distributed among several architects, and by the fire of
his personality pushed the herculean task to completion. Though
dominated by Burnham, a galaxy of genius in all the arts was assembled to contribute to the work. Architectural firms were chosen

from the east and west about equally. Among the former group were McKim, Mead, and White, Richard M. Hunt, Peabody and Stearns, and Charles B. Atwood, whose lovely Palace of the Fine Arts has been preserved in Jackson Park. Chicago firms beside Burnham's (Root's death at the beginning of the work left him to carry on alone) included Solon H. Beman, Henry Ives Cobb, and Adler and Sullivan.

And yet there were other implications in the fair. An English architect, Banister Fletcher, expressed his disappointment in what he termed the fair's "collection of well-studied Parisian designs," and advised American architects to produce their own idiom. He wrote:

It is to be hoped that the imitative element will not cause these great Classic designs to be reproduced elsewhere for town halls, museums, and other buildings, but that American architects, already advancing so rapidly along certain new lines of departure will value the lessons they teach without copying their exact forms . . . it is certain that there is a great future for American architecture if only the architects will, as much as possible, express themselves in the language of their own times.

Unique among the exposition's buildings was Louis Sullivan's expression of exactly that credo. Sullivan bitterly condemned the architecture of the exposition as an unimaginative borrowing of dead forms to make a grandiose but fictitious stage set. However, he succeeded in obtaining a free hand in the design of his Transportation building, which stood out in warm colors amid the surrounding whiteness. In design it was fresh and original, though showing traces of Saracenic and Romanesque influence, and it was the one exposition building unanimously acclaimed by European critics, to whom the classic buildings were an old story.

At the time of the fair Adler and Sullivan were, next to Burnham and Root, the best-known architects in Chicago. Largest and most illustrious of their early commissions in Chicago was the Auditorium, built in 1887 and still used. This mammoth structure, combining a hotel, an office building, and a great opera house, was the boldest architectural conception of its time. Dankmar Adler successfully solved the difficult problems of structure and acoustics, while Sullivan was responsible for the design. On the exterior this showed a decided Romanesque influence, but in the interior Sullivan lavished his rich plastic ornament based on natural forms and imbued with a mystic symbolism.

Sullivan's chief contribution to architecture, however, lay in his all-embracing philosophy of design. To reduce it to the formula "form follows function" is to overlook the emotional and spiritual qualities which he held to be functions of a building as important as its utilitarian requirements. He pleaded for a living, democratic, American way of building, based on the laws of nature, and disregarding the forms of the past. His tall buildings before and after the fair embody these principles. First came the Wainwright building in St. Louis, then the Schiller Theater and the Stock Exchange in Chicago, all strongly vertical in feeling. The Carson Pirie Scott store, being lower, he treated in a horizontal pattern, with rich ornament around the show windows to enhance the displays.

Working in Sullivan's office up to the time of the fair was Frank Lloyd Wright, destined to become his disciple and chief exponent of the functionalist gospel. Wright first made his reputation in the residential field. Departing radically from previous styles, his houses first strike the eye by their strong horizontality achieved by low-pitched or flat roofs with widely projecting eaves and windows arranged in bands. By these devices Wright sought to make his houses appear to grow out of the prairie. Immediately the public spoke of his "prairie style," and evidently liked it, judging from the number of examples (and imitations) in Chicago's suburbs, especially Oak Park. But there was a principle underlying Wright's designs which proved to be more important than the more obvious external appearance. He objected to the current practice of regarding rooms as separate cubicles to be assembled into a house. His plans became more open; rooms had less definite limits; the outdoor and the indoor spaces "flowed" into each other in a more intimate way.

Wright experimented widely with new ideas in construction. Some he adapted from engineering practice for residential use, and some he himself developed. Many have since come into general use. Two examples are hollow walls of precast patterned concrete blocks, reinforced horizontally and vertically; and his method of supporting floors by the cantilever rather than the wall-to-wall principle.

For many years Sullivan and Wright were, in their own country, but voices in the wilderness. Sullivan's work dwindled to the vanishing point and Wright had to go to Germany to find a publisher for his books. Perhaps this was fortunate, for the drawings and text were hailed there with enthusiasm. His influence in Europe soon succeeded that of "L'Art Nouveau" (which many suspect was based on Sullivan's flowing ornament). Especially in Holland Wright's blocky forms were widely imitated.

Sullivan once exclaimed, "The damage wrought by the World's Fair will last for half a century if not longer." Certain it is that from then on architects turned to eclecticism, that is, a borrowing from the past, and the coincidence of eclecticism and the rise of the skyscraper could not have been more unfortunate. Of this paradox, Thomas Tallmadge has written:

There was one problem, however, that the lessons of the past could not help to solve, one Gordian knot that could not be untangled with Classic fingers, and that was the purely modern and American skyscraper. So we see a generation of distracted architects, vainly endeavoring to stretch the mantle of Phidias and the cape of Palladio to fit the gaunt form of the steel skeleton.

More than half of the tall buildings on Michigan Avenue facing Grant Park, built during the eclectic period, attempt to hide the fact that they are skyscrapers. Their skeletons are disguised, the vertical lines are broken at intervals, traditional cornices are used. And yet, in the early days of the skyscraper, Sullivan had indicated the ultimate solution. "What is the chief characteristic of the tall office building?" he asked. "And at once we answer, it is lofty . . . [which] must be in turn the dominant chord in the architect's expression of it, the true excitant of his imagination. It must be tall. The force and power of altitude must be in it . . . "

But in buildings where height did not intrude its troublesome head, the eclectic period fared well. A full account is impossible, and a few names, examples, and tendencies must suffice. The Boston firm of Shepley, Rutan, and Coolidge was responsible for two neoclassic buildings, the Art Institute and the Public Library, showing the influence of the fair. D. H. Burnham and Co. continued in importance, and after Burnham's death one of his designers, Pierce Anderson entered the partnership of Graham, Anderson, Probst, and White, whose best-known earlier work is the Wrigley Building, erected in 1921. Holabird and Roche were another important team, handling the Gothic vernacular in the University Club as skillfully as the Classic orders in the City and County building. Alfred S. Alschuler's outstanding building, the London Guarantee and Accident building, is decidedly classic, while Marshall and Fox's sumptuous hotels are French and Italian Renaissance.

The Gothic style's most accomplished exponents were Cram, Goodhue, and Ferguson in the East, who built the Fourth Presbyterian Church in Chicago. Gradually Goodhue developed a more personal and highly distinctive version of that style which reached a high point in the University of Chicago chapel. This was echoed to some extent by James Gamble Rogers in the Chicago campus of Northwestern University.

In 1922 a Gothic design by Raymond Hood and John Mead Howells of New York won the $50,000 first prize in the world-wide competition by the Chicago *Tribune* for its new building. Here, were it not for a strange quirk, the satisfactory solution of height was indicated; the shaft of the building was frankly vertical, and the Gothic detail and crown struck no incongruity and yet retained the note of traditionalism. The quirk was the second-prize design, the "building that was never built." The work of Eliel Saarinen of Finland, it followed no style but took Sullivan's creed and stated it more boldly than he had ever dreamed. It discarded the cornice, stripped the ornament away, and frankly exposed its structural plan, relying solely on set-back masses and strong vertical lines. The basic elements in the design were soon widely imitated, and the Gothic and Classic styles were completely discarded thereafter for skyscrapers.

Before long office-building architects began to work with even simpler surfaces and bold sculptural masses dictated by the set-back provisions of the zoning laws and the necessity of supplying light to as many offices as possible. Two firms led in designing a series of soaring, clean-limbed towers in this new style. One was Holabird and Root, beginning with 333 Michigan Avenue and ending with the Board of Trade and Palmolive buildings. The other was Graham, Anderson, Probst, and White with the Field building, Merchandise Mart, and Civic Opera.

While the new spirit revolutionized the design of skyscrapers, it was less felt in other fields. Residential architecture continued to be predominantly Colonial or Tudor in treatment, with occasional efforts in French or Mediterranean styles. However, there has been a strong tendency toward simplification, and now a few examples in the so-called International or functional style may be seen, harking back in principle to the teachings of Sullivan and Wright though in very different forms and not always with true understanding. Illinois architects have been experimenting also with methods of prefabricating houses for mass production.

Churches, schools, apartments, and public buildings have been for the most part eclectic, though many of their designers seem to have been obsessed with a desire to be startling and original. The net result is usually that ornament of the historic styles is replaced by "modernistic" ornament, but there is seldom a fresh approach to the problem as a whole. Fortunately signs of such an approach are here and there becoming evident.

The depression of 1929 put a stop to skyscraper building, but it saw another great Chicago fair, the Century of Progress Exposition of 1933-34. The need for economy dictated a light temporary form of construction and prevented lavishness in design. Intense colors were used instead, which produced an impressive effect until they weathered to pastel shades.

The architecture of this exposition was an attempt to crystallize the tendencies in modern design, but it was evident, as Frank Lloyd Wright was quick to point out, that to the designers "the modern" was just another style, and that the basic principles of functionalism were but half understood. He admitted, however, that the visitors might be impressed by the refreshing value of simplicity. This possibility and the experiments with new materials and methods of construction may prove to have been the main achievements of the fair architecturally.

But the architecture of a city applies to more than single buildings. The broader aspects of planning, namely the relation of buildings to each other and to the community, deserve mention. Until the World's Fair of 1893 few people were concerned with such questions. Cities "just grew" in chaotic haphazard patterns and the resulting evils of congestion and blight, as yet uncomplicated by the automobile, were taken for granted. But the openness and grandeur of the fair aroused some of Chicago's leaders to a desire for a greater civic orderliness, which Burnham stimulated by telling them how property values would begin to climb if the city were dressed up a bit. So from 1905 to 1908 the Commercial Club backed him while he worked on his famous city plan.

The plan was conceived along European lines with plazas, vistas, and radiating avenues. Some have called it "window dressing," but

Burnham studied the fundamental problems of Chicago: the need for better transportation both by highway and railway to relieve congestion, for better recreation facilities and parkways, and for the development of the lake shore waterfront into the show place of the country. All these things were incorporated in the plan. Though his proposals seemed at the time too visionary to admit of achievement, a host of them have been realized under the guidance of the Chicago Plan Commission, a perpetual advisory body appointed by the mayor. It seems probable that all of Chicago's future development will be around the basic scheme laid down by Burnham.

In recent years city dwellers have become more acutely conscious of another problem which the mushroom growth of the metropolis has produced. This concerns those once fashionable sections that have been left behind by the advancing waves of outward development. Early efforts by philanthropic agencies and limited-dividend groups to meet this problem proved inadequate. Recently, however, in answer to a growing demand for slum clearance and to demonstrate what can be done in group housing, the Public Works Administration has built several large open housing developments in run-down neighborhoods. It is possible that from a sociological point of view these projects may be more significant in the history of architecture than the towers of the Loop.

Now that America's population curve is flattening out, growth and development are likely to proceed more slowly. The problems of the future largely concern re-ordering the present situation, consolidating gains and rectifying mistakes. Builders of the future will perhaps find significance in the philosophy of Sullivan and in the oft-repeated exhortation of Daniel Burnham:

Make no little plans; they have no magic to stir men's blood and probably themselves will not be realized. Make big plans; aim high in hope and work, remembering that a noble and logical diagram once recorded will never die, but long after we are gone will be a living thing, asserting itself with growing intensity. Remember that our sons and grandsons are going to do things that would stagger us. Let your watchword be "order" and your beacon "beauty."

ART

Oscar Wilde came to Chicago in 1882 as a lecturer on art. Many of his eastern audiences had jeered and hooted, but in Chicago only the newspapers were outwardly rude. While the people were vexed at his disrespectful allusions to the medieval architecture of the water tower and his scoffing at the American worship of European culture, some noted that he spoke well of the possibilities of American art, and were impressed by his advice that "You can make as good a design out of an American turkey as a Japanese out of his native stork."

Wilde visited Chicago in an era when all manner of knick-knacks covered the walls, mantels, and tables of luxurious houses, and the popular conception of decoration had become a matter of filling the available space in rooms with useless and frequently absurd trifles. Most well-bred young ladies painted flowers, birds, cats, and landscapes, not only on canvas, but on almost any substance that would take oil pigments. The fine homes in Illinois were museums of the curious, and the more they overflowed with "artistic" pictures, screens, medallions, plaques, marble statuary, stuffed birds, figurines, and vases, the more "tasteful" they were considered. A decade passed before a reaction occurred—a reaction that was influenced more than was generally realized by the critical comments of the long-haired velvet-clad Oscar Wilde.

The promoters of the World's Columbian Exposition of 1893, ignoring Wilde's advice to develop American art along indigenous patterns and to break with the traditions of Europe, procured what were considered the best of the classical masterpieces and housed them in the imposing Palace of Fine Arts of classic design. Innovation and

149

experiment were felt to be unsafe and too iconoclastic for a fair that
was to show the world how Chicago had overcome provincialism and
how its citizens bowed to none in the appreciation of art. The neo-
classical influence exerted by the exposition was felt for more than a
generation. However unfortunate this may have been for the progress
of indigenous art, it did establish an art-consciousness that was tempered by a high standard of appreciation.

Between 1893 and 1895 the Central Art Association sent exhibits
of works by native painters throughout Illinois and the neighboring
States. In 1896 the first annual exhibition of the Society of Western
Artists was held, followed shortly by the organization of the present
Chicago Society of Artists, composed of a union of several art groups.
The year 1899 saw the formation of a Municipal Art League, and
within a few years Chicago had a city art commission.

Lorado Taft (1860-1937) injected a fresh stream into the art current of Chicago, with his native and transitional sculptures. His great
life-burdened figures, sorrowful and yet serene, cry out for comparison with Rodin. The similarity is not one of texture only, but of
spirit and philosophy, a new-world outlook realizing both the tragedy
and the dignity of life. Taft's classes in the Art Institute attracted many
young men and women of Illinois, some of whom have since become
well-known sculptors.

The School of the Art Institute of Chicago has contributed to art
and artists of Illinois the stimulating influence of other celebrated ar-
tist-teachers. Just before the turn of the century its faculty included
such men as Frank Duvenek and William Chase. Charles Francis
Browne, Hermon Mac Neil and Albert Herter conducted classes at
that time. The Spanish painter, Joaquin Sorolla came to the school
early in the second decade of the present century. Indeed, through the
years the faculty has included exponents of a wide variety of "schools."
The student has had his choice of such outstanding masters as George
Bellows, Randall Davys, Nicholas Roerich, Boris Anisfeld, and Francis
Chapin. Albin Polasek in sculpture, and Louis Ritman and Edmund
Giesbert in painting have been popular teachers for a number of years.

Until 1922 the director of the Institute was also director of the
school but in that year Raymond T. Ensign became dean of the school.
He was succeeded by Charles Fabens Kelley in 1927, and in 1938 Norman Rice succeeded to the deanship.

The permanent collections of the museum have consistently grown. At first limited only to plaster casts and a few nondescript originals, the Institute today owns one of the most notable collections of historic and modern paintings and exhibits a sequence of nineteenth century French painting unequalled elsewhere. Strong departments of Prints and Drawings, Oriental Arts, Decorative Arts, etc., have been created including many periods and civilizations. William M. R. French, Newton H. Carpenter, George W. Eggers contributed to the early development of both museum and school. In 1921, Robert B. Harshe was made director and under his brilliant leadership the Art Institute became one of the world's great institutions. Mr. Harshe's taste, knowledge and showmanship culminated in two great exhibitions of art for the Century of Progress Expositions in 1933 and 1934. After his death in 1938, the functions of directorship were divided. Mr. Daniel Catton Rich, who had assisted Mr. Harshe, became Director of Fine Arts and Mr. Charles H. Burkholder became Director of Finance and Operation.

Since the first American show in 1889 the exhibition of regional and contemporary art has become an increasingly important function of the Art Institute. The first exhibition of Artists of Chicago and Vicinity was held in 1897 and the first International Water Color Show, which is predominantly American, in 1922. More and more the Institute has been bringing the contemporary art of America and the world to Chicago. As a consequence the tendency among students to regard a period of study in Paris and New York as an indispensable part of a complete art education has been steadily diminishing.

Nevertheless, during the early 1900's, the attitude of most Chicagoans towards art was somewhat smug and complacent. Satisfaction with traditional forms lapsed into a kind of stagnation—a lethargy derived from too long familiarity with the great masters. So it was with the force of a bombshell explosion that the famous New York "Armory Show" descended upon Chicago in 1913. Here were the works of Picasso, Braque, Matisse, Kandinsky, and many others of the Expressionist and Cubist schools in all of their strange grotesqueness of color and form. This was the advent of modernism in Chicago, and its coming was heralded by jests and hoots, not only from the citizenry, but from established art critics. Only a few persons had the temerity to praise the vigor in these works, and to predict that they would have a salutary influence upon popular painting.

In 1915 Carl N. Werntz and Carl M. Newman staged in Chicago the "First Annual Exhibition of Independent Artists," a display which clearly demonstrated the effects of the Armory Show. In the same year the Cordon Club was organized by a group of artistic and professional women, and now holds continuous exhibitions of Chicago artists, and presents an annual show. The Arts Club of Chicago was founded in 1916; it had aided materially in bringing the best in modern art to Chicago, and has greatly encouraged artistic enterprise in the city.

During the great artistic and literary renaissance of the present century, numerous groups which fostered the creation and appreciation of art assembled in Chicago. Among these were the Renaissance Society, the Society of Artists and Sculptors, the Chicago No-Jury Society, the Chicago Professional School of Art, the National Academy of Design; and lesser but vigorous groups including the Neo-Arlimusc Art Club, the Dill Pickle Club, and the Seven Arts Club. Many new galleries and art stores that contributed to the creative ferment of the city sprang into life during this period, perhaps the most important of which is the Vanderpoel Art Gallery in Beverly Hills.

Instead of giving impetus to artistic production, the unprecedented prosperity between 1926 and 1929 caused many Chicago artists to turn to commercial work or enter the business world. The sale of a picture or two during those years was insufficient to combat the cost of living, and even lowly quarters in a run-down neighborhood were beyond the reach of many painters and sculptors. The ensuing depression brought even greater hardship. Artistic enterprise was almost at a standstill from 1929 to 1933.

Departing radically in architecture from the Columbian Exposition, the Century of Progress Exposition of 1933-34 accepted modernism in art. Sharing the spotlight with the old masters in the Art Institute were exhibits liberally sprinkled with works from the current "schools," and the fine photographic displays at the fair-grounds showed a strong preoccupation with experimental lay-out and design. American art was stressed in the exhibit of 1934, featuring Stuart, Trumbull, Copley, Melchers, Henri, Homer, Blakelock, Mary Cassatt, Inness, Whistler, Sargent, Weir, Eakins, Ryder, Bellows, and Luks.

The final influence of the fair on Illinois art is as yet undetermined. It brought to the Middle West the "International Style" in architecture and industrial arts. Some critics believe that it has had a deleterious effect upon interior decoration. Certain it is that the geometrical

forms outlined in black and chromium have pervaded the shops, restaurants, saloons, night-clubs, beauty parlors, and dress shops in
Chicago. But perhaps it is a mistake to attribute too much of this
modernistic trend to the fair, for the already flourishing movement
towards a revolution in painting and interior decoration was only
boldly and uncompromisingly realized in the exhibition halls of the
Midway.

Illinois' artists of the present period, unlike so many of her writers,
have not migrated to the East or to Europe in search of more congenial
atmosphere or better markets for their work. Although Chicago serves
as an art center for the vast hinterland of surrounding States, the rest
of Illinois has furnished its share of creative activity. As early as the
eighties, a union of art clubs for the study and appreciation of art was
organized in the central section of the State. Only a few of the smaller
towns held exhibitions at this time, but artists and critics journeyed
to Springfield, Decatur, Champaign, Lincoln, and other cities to read
essays on art and literature before large and enthusiastic audiences.
The All-Illinois Society of the Fine Arts, organized in 1926, has permanent galleries in the Stevens Hotel in Chicago, and holds annual
shows in the towns and cities of the Middle West.

The public library at Bloomington exhibits the works of Illinois
painters continuously from October to May. In 1919 the Decatur Art
Institute was organized for the promotion of the fine and applied arts.
Both the State House and the Centennial Building at Springfield house
large collections of paintings. The Laura Davidson Sears Academy
at Elgin and the Art Association of Peoria possess interesting canvases. Jacksonville, Aurora, and Rockford are supplied with exhibitions from the Grand Central Galleries of New York, the Federation
of Arts in Washington, the All-Illinois Society of the Fine Arts, and
other organizations.

Since its creation in 1933, the Federal Art Project has had the dual
effect of encouraging impoverished artists and creating popular interest in painting and sculpture. By paying all non-labor costs of production, tax-supported institutions of Illinois can obtain the work done
by the Project. This arrangement has enabled many public schools,
colleges, and charitable institutions to own works of art which would
otherwise have been beyond their means. The Federal art program
for Illinois fosters regional art in its best and broadest sense. Under
its influence, native artists have been led, as never before, to assert

the peculiar qualities of their surroundings and to interpret their lives
and experiences in thousands of easel paintings, murals, graphic
works, sculpture models, dioramas, posters, and plates for the index
of American Design. Among the most notable contributions of the
Federal Art Project in Illinois are the frescoes, murals, and sculptures of the University of Illinois Medical Unit and the paintings
selected by Mayor Edward J. Kelly for the Chicago city hall.

Present-day art in Illinois is absorbing the two main streams of
American art; realism and modernism. It is becoming more socially
conscious; it is becoming more experimental. In these two tendencies
lies its future.

LITERATURE

Chicago was an infant city of only 8,000 people when its first literary magazine was founded by a boy of 20. *The Gem of the Prairie* (1844) reflects the youthfulness of its editor, Kiler Kent Jones, and was much less substantial, judged by the literary standards of the times, than the *Illinois Monthly Magazine*. Its pages are enlivened, however, by a gossip column, signed "Man About Town," and by a series of entertaining sketches entitled *Slices of Chicago Life*.

In contrast to these self-conscious literary endeavors are the origin and growth of the talent through which Illinois gave world literature her first great gift, and still her greatest. It has been almost universally recognized that Abraham Lincoln was a great writer as well as a great man—that his letters and speeches, quite definitely unapproached in their kind in America, represent a literary achievement of the highest order. It has not been realized so generally that whatever nourished and sustained Lincoln, as a writer and as a man, he found in Illinois. He drew into himself and gave forth in supreme expression all that was best in a frontier society too often assumed to have been merely crude and ugly.

While Lincoln was being considered for the vice-presidency, in 1856, an old preacher sat at a table in his home at Pleasant Plains, Illinois, writing the story of his life. Peter Cartwright had been a Methodist circuit rider in Illinois for more than thirty years. He had traveled thousands of miles on horseback or on foot, baptized thousands of converts, organized scores of church societies. His autobiography, a frank and detailed account of day-by-day activities, with shrewd observation of the people he encountered and unstinting revelation of himself, is one of the minor classics of the American frontier. It belongs on the same shelf with David Crockett's autobiography and Timothy Flint's *Recollections of the Last Ten Years*.

After the Civil War Francis Fisher Browne, one of the most influential and least appreciated literary figures, appeared on the Illinois scene. In 1871 he founded the *Lakeside Monthly*, a periodical devoted to the cause of literary progress in the Middle West. Publishing stories and poetry as well as articles, this magazine replaced the less definitely literary *Western Monthly*, founded in 1869. After weathering the Chicago fire and other hazards through the efforts of its editor, the *Lakeside Monthly* suspended publication in 1874. In 1880 it was succeeded by a new magazine which Browne named the *Dial*. Throughout his editorship of more than thirty years the *Dial* maintained a high standard of thoughtful and informed critical comment on literature and literary affairs. The *Dial* left Browne relatively little time for the few books which bear his name. A characteristic achievement was his courageous and far-sighted defense of Governor Altgeld.

Perhaps as a result of the faithful endeavors of Browne as well as by the impact of other forces, Chicago and Illinois experienced in the last years of the nineteenth century an outburst of activity which justifies the description of this interval as the first major period of literary production in the State. During these and later years, many natives of Illinois won literary fame for work done elsewhere, dealing with other materials than those of Illinois life. Such writers will not be considered here.

Of all the writers in this Illinois movement of the 1890's, Hamlin Garland was the most conspicuous. Wisconsin born, product of Iowa farms and country schools and rural academy, Garland had gone to Boston and then returned to his early habitat to write the realistic stories of Middle Western rural life in *Main Traveled Roads*. Early in the 1890's he came to Chicago and continued his reporting of the Middle Western scene in *Jason Edwards,* a political novel, as well as in occasional short stories, and in the convention-challenging *Rose of Dutchers Coolly*. Born in Illinois, but never essentially orientated in the Middle West, was Garland's contemporary and friend, Henry B. Fuller, whose first novel, *The Chevalier of Pensieri-Vani,* a memorial of lyrical journeyings among the gardens and relics of the Old World, awed his western readers and threatened to brand him a condescending purist. But that he could deal objectively and uncompromisingly with Middle Western Life, Fuller soon proved by publication of another novel, *The Cliff Dwellers,* bristling with ironic and penetrating comments on the artistic Chicago of the 1890's. In the same vein are his *Under the Skylights, With the Procession,* and *On the Stairs.* In *Gardens of this World,* written shortly before his death in 1929, he resumed much of his early, nostalgic manner.

In this Illinois literary movement in the 1890's, Chicago publishing houses and newspapers played an important part. From 1880 until

1892 the *Dial* was owned and published by A. C. McClurg and Co.; after the purchase of the journal by Browne in 1892 it continued to be published by them. The firm of Stone and Kimball published for a time the *Chap-Book,* a Midwestern *Savoy,* or *Yellow Book,* later merged with the *Dial.* A new standard for literary columnists was introduced by the appearance of Eugene Field's "Sharps and Flats" column in the Chicago *Daily News.* Field's successive volumes of poems and essays won for him a loyal audience of discerning readers. A columnist of a different sort was Finley Peter Dunne, whose creation of Mr. Dooley in the pages of the Chicago *Times-Herald* added a new name to the brief and honorable list of homely commentators on the American scene. Also truly of America and of Chicago are George Ade's *Fables in Slang,* which present among other characters, the notable creations of Doc Horne and Pink Marsh.

Following the high standard set by Field, Dunne, and Ade, the Chicago *Tribune,* oldest newspaper of the city, brought zest to its pages through the wit of Bert Leston Taylor, a poet of genuine distinction who, as editor of *"A Line o'Type or Two,"* became the most beloved columnist of his day. Another *Tribune* columnist, albeit on the sports page, was Ring Lardner, who later attained a position of first rank among present day short-story writers. Also a noteworthy feature of the *Tribune* was the dramatic criticism of James O'Donnell Bennett and Percy Hammond. Literary supplements of Chicago newspapers have justified their existence under the editorship of authors and critics who gave them a weight and influence felt throughout the State and the entire Middle West. Identified with the old Chicago *Evening Post* were Francis Hackett, Henry B. Fuller, Floyd Dell, George Cram Cook, Lucian Cary, and Llewellyn Jones. Harry Hansen and Burton Rascoe made their reputations as literary critics in the 1920's while editing the book pages of the *Daily News* and the *Tribune.*

In things materialistic Chicago had attained, during the 1880's, a metropolitan prominence to be reckoned with throughout the State and the Nation. For many, in the city of over 500,000 population, business success had been swift and flattering. Economic security more assured, it was a time when the explicitly superior attitude of the East, with its cultural advantages and traditions, became for the clamorous market-metropolis a spiritual challenge. But in its struggle for material achievement, Chicago had not only become the central market for grosser commodities, it had also become the center of a vast book purchasing and book reading section of the country. By the beginning of the following decade there were rumors of a Middle Western school of literature; within the next few years Chicago was both censured and praised for its alleged pretensions of fostering the emerging school.

In the East criticism was carping, even vindictive; in England, sympathetic, encouraging, prophetic. In the opinion of the New York *Daily Tribune* there was something "funny" in Chicago's "getting up a school of literature over night," and in its "trying to establish a 'literary school' out of crudity and the froth and fury of the last new things, no matter what they may be . . . . Chicago needs a stiffening of her intellectual backbone." In 1896, Stanley Waterloo who in 1870-71 had been a reporter on Chicago newspapers, published a London edition of his *An Odd Situation*. For this novel Sir Walter Besant, the prominent English author, prepared a preface in which he declared ". . . . there has sprung up in the city of Chicago a new literary center and a new center of publishing. There exists in this city of a million inhabitants, which sixty years ago was but a kind of barbican, or advanced post against the Red Indian, a company of novelists, poets, and essayists, who are united, if not by associations and clubs, at least by an earnest resolution to cultivate letters. It may be objected that this is nothing but a provincial coterie . . . and that . . . it will presently disappear. I do not think that this will be the fate of the Chicago movement, for several reasons. First, the city is so huge that there must be continually born in it, or brought into it from the country, persons with the literary gift; next, there exists in the Northwest States an unbounded admiration for the literary calling—a feeling which ought by itself to raise up aspirants . . . ." In alluding to the *Dial*, he characterized it as "a journal of literary criticism, sober, conscientious and scholarly, from every point of view unsurpassed by any other literary journal in America or England." Further, he took account of Chicago's "daily papers by the dozens, which afford the aspirant the means of a livelihood while he is working at his real profession."

That Sir Walter Besant's reflections were indeed prophetic is borne out by the literary development that followed in less than twenty-five years. Perhaps by more than a coincidence, it was also in

London that Chicago came finally to be hailed as "the literary capital of the United States." H. L. Mencken's famous article, *The Literary Capital of the United States,* appeared in the English periodical, *Nation,* in 1920. He wrote:

It is, indeed, amazing how steadily a Chicago influence shows itself when the literary ancestry and training of present-day American writers are investigated. The brand of the sugar-cured ham seems to be upon all of them. With two exceptions, there is not a single novelist of the younger generation—that is, a serious novelist deserving a civilized reader's notice—who has not sprung from the Middle Empire that has Chicago for its capital . . . . All the rest have come from the Chicago palatinate: Dreiser, Anderson, Miss Cather, Mrs. Watts, Tarkington, Wilson, Herrick, Patterson, even Churchill. It was Chicago that produced Henry B. Fuller, the packer of the modern American novel. It was Chicago that developed Frank Norris, its first practitioner of genius. And it was Chicago that produced Dreiser, undoubtedly the greatest artist of them all . . . The new poetry movement is thoroughly Chicagoan; the majority of its chief poets are from the Middle West; *Poetry,* the organ of the movement, is published in Chicago. So with the little theatre movement. Long before it was heard of in New York, it was firmly on its legs in Chicago. And to support these various reforms and revolts, some of them already of great influence, others abortive and quickly forgotten, there is in Chicago a body of critical opinion that is unsurpassed for discretion and intelligence in America.

At the turn of the century, Frank Norris had returned to Chicago from his adopted California for the scenes and the actual writing of his most successful novel, *The Pit.* Theodore Dreiser, who had driven a laundry wagon and done his first reporting in Chicago, used Chicago settings and characters for his first two novels, *Sister Carrie* and *Jennie Gerhardt,* and returned to the same city for the settings and characters of *The Titan* and for parts of *The Genius.* Moreover, Chicago remained a symbol and a point of reference to Dreiser; his work was profoundly affected by the coarse vitality of the city as he knew it in a brief but crucial period of his life.

More significantly identified with Chicago in his life, though not in his writings, was William Vaughn Moody, one of the greatest American poets of his time. Moody taught at the University of Chicago, and wrote during the period of his teaching most of his best work, including the great *Ode in a Time of Hesitation,* in which he denounced the American attitude in the Spanish-American War.

If, during the 1890's and even in the first decade of the new century, the literary impulse of the region was sporadic, with little to bring it to a focus, a definite force for direction was supplied by the establishment in 1912 of a magazine which was, and is still, unique in America—*Poetry: A Magazine of Verse,* founded by Harriet Monroe. With the inception of this magazine began a second important period in the literary history of Illinois. Miss Monroe was a fine poet in her own right. She had been chosen to write and recite a dedicatory ode for the Columbian Exposition in 1893. She published several volumes of verse. In 1917, co-editor with Alice Corbin Henderson, she published *The New Poetry, An Anthology of Twentieth Century Verse.* Revised and enlarged in 1923, and again in 1932, this anthology has done much to promote recognition of the younger poets of America.

Miss Monroe's greatest achievement, however, was *Poetry,* which she maintained by funds largely obtained through her personal efforts and which she edited with consistent courage and acumen. On the eve of *Poetry's* twenty-fourth anniversary, Miss Monroe wrote the editorial which was destined to be her last. "We shall remind people once more, as we did with quite a din twenty-four years ago, of the meager and lackadaisical support given to the finest of the fine arts, the art most powerful for making the story of our deeds immortal by telling it to the next age," the editorial declared. "We shall insist again, as many times in our history, that great poetry is not a creation *in vacuo,* but antiphonal between a poet and his audience, that it is not enough to sing—the song must be heard. . . . What a printing may mean to a struggling poet in the way of spiritual food and refreshment, hundreds of letters in our files would show. It is that realization which has impelled me to continue the effort to finance and run *Poetry* all these years." Miss Monroe died in South America in 1936. Her autobiography, published in 1938, is a rich record of literary activities in Chicago and elsewhere during a long and fruitful life.

Early in its career the magazine established several annual prizes for poets. The Helen Haire Levinson prize betokens *Poetry's* highest honor, and is not restricted to work published in its own pages. Among recipients of the Levinson prize, first awarded in 1914, are eight poets of Illinois : Carl Sandburg, Vachel Lindsay, Edgar Lee Masters, Cloyd Head, Lew Sarett, Margery Allen Seiffert, Mark Turbyfill, Maurice Lesemann. Lew Sarett has been a member of the faculty of Northwestern University for many years, following an earlier connection with the University of Illinois. Sympathetic insight and rich personal observation are evident in his poems, particularly in those dealing with nature and with Indian life. Glenn Ward Dresbach, a native of Lanark, Illinois, and long a resident of Chicago, is another poet of importance whose best work has consisted of the poetic recording of the experience of nature. Eunice Tietjens and Alice Corbin Henderson, both editorially associated with the magazine *Poetry,* have written about Chicago, but have 'found the material for their best work elsewhere—Mrs. Tietjens in China, Mrs. Henderson in New Mexico. Margery Allen Seiffert of Moline is a poet whose work is noteworthy for its variety and versatility, though she too has found relatively infrequent inspiration in the Illinois scene.

Of the Illinois poets who emerged into positions of recognized importance during the decade following the establishment of *Poetry,* one was not introduced by that magazine, though much of his later work appeared in its pages. This was Edgar Lee Masters, whose Illinois epitaphs in the *Spoon River Anthology* were first published in William Marion Reedy's *Mirror* in St. Louis. *Spoon River Anthology* was a landmark in regional literature. It revealed to writers the possibilities of a new approach to life in the Middle Western small town, and impressed publishers by becoming a best seller. The bitterness of some of the poems and the sensationalism of others have blinded some readers to the compensating beauty and soundness of such epitaphs as those of Lucinda Matlock, Emily Sparks, and Ann Rutledge. Masters, a Chicago lawyer, who had besieged the citadel of literary fame persistently and ineffectually before the success of *Spoon River Anthology,* has continued to write voluminously. His successive volumes of poetry since 1915, though containing some fine work, have never approached the stature of *Spoon River Anthology.* In recent years he has written chiefly in prose. In *Skeeters Kirby* he gave a memorable portrayal of an Illinois boyhood. One of his later contributions is a biography of his fellow poet of Illinois, Vachel Lindsay.

Masters rightly describes the life of Lindsay as tragic. After a childhood dominated by religious bigotry, Lindsay early achieved control of singularly fresh and vital rhythms. When those rhythms are applied to the expression of profound experience, as in "Abraham Lincoln Walks at Midnight" and "Sleep softly, eagle forgotten" (his tribute to Altgeld), the result is poetry of a very high order. Even when, as in such longer poems as "The Congo" and "The Chinese

Nightingale," the emotional content is slight and the intellectual element even slighter, the involved rhythms and colorful language are a perpetual delight. Lindsay was as erratic and impractica   's are traditionally expected to be. He sought to add to the i   e income from his writing by lecturing and teaching, but was   al in establishing himself in a workable relationship to hi   —though he steadfastly refused to remain long away fr   Illinois. He died penniless at Springfield in 1931, by hi

Of the many writers whose early or first work was pi   pages of *Poetry*, none was more truly a product of Illi   Sandburg, and none has made a greater contribution to   ture. Born at Galesburg in 1878, Sandburg attended Lo   served as an organizer for the Socialist Labor party,   paper work in various towns. His volume, *Chicago P   with its famous dedicatory "Chicago," was the first   tempt to capture in verse the quality of life in a modern industrial metropolis. This work was followed by *Cornhuskers* (1918) in which Sandburg recorded with the same decisiveness and power the rural life he knew in Illinois. To the study of Abraham Lincoln and the interpretation of his life to the modern world, Sandburg has devoted the energies of his later years. His biography of Lincoln, begun in 1916 with *Abraham Lincoln: The Prairie Years,* is a unique achievement. Scholarly and authentic, it is at the same time a work of art, a genuine recreation in moving and appropriate words of the intimate experience of its subject. But Sandburg's preoccupation with the Lincoln biography has not interrupted his output of poetry. *The People, Yes,* his most recent volume of verse, shows a maturing and sharpening of his powers as a poet, and particularly a clarification of his faith in democracy. Though he now lives on a farm in Michigan, Sandburg is near enough to Chicago to play a part in the cultural life of the State. He is clearly Illinois' most distinguished man of letters in our time.

Sandburg was one of a brilliant group of writers who were employed by the Chicago *Daily News* under the editorship of Henry Justin Smith, himself a novelist, short-story writer, and historian of importance. Among the other members of this group were Ben Hecht, Harry Hansen, Keith Preston, and Howard Vincent O'Brien.

Sherwood Anderson was a resident of Chicago during this important period, and *A Story Teller's Story* contains an interesting reflection of his experience in the city. Much of his important work was written in Chicago ; the city is expressed in *Marching Men*, and both city and country in *Mid-American Chants*. Another Anderson—Margaret —established the *Little Review* in Chicago in 1914, but after three years of weathering "no compromise with the public taste," took it to New York and later to Paris. While in Chicago the "no compromise" policy of the magazine was once expressed by an issue of blank pages, intended as a reproach to readers and writers alike; and later in New York by publication of the first chapters of the epoch-making *Ulysses* by James Joyce. Throughout its stormy career the pages of the *Little Review* were open to the most radical literary experiments that were being made in both America and Europe.

The colleges and universities of Illinois have shared in the creation of its literature both directly and indirectly. At the University of Chicago, Robert Morss Lovett was closely associated with the brilliant achievement of successive groups of students, among them Elizabeth Madox Roberts and Glenway Westcott. In its brief history Mundelein College has made an exceptional record in the encouragement and development of young writers. Among the careers of creative writers with academic connections, that of Robert Herrick is noteworthy. As the author of such novels as *Together* and *Homely Lilla* he became a nationally important figure in the field of fiction.

Since 1930 the creative literature of Illinois has entered a new phase, too little matured as yet to allow of definite evaluation, in which the novel seems to be the most favored medium. Magazines and publishing houses have played a relatively unimportant part in this most modern phase of Illinois' literary development. *Poetry,* edited by Morton Dauen Zabel after the death of Harriet Monroe, and more recently by George Dillon, whose volume of poems, *The Flowering Stone* won for him the Pulitzer Award, has continued to print poetry of real worth and has made a valuable contribution to criticism as well. *The Midland,* founded and edited in Iowa by John T. Frederick, and moved to Chicago in 1930, introduced Albert Halper and many other important writers, and printed James T. Farrell's first story in America, before its suspension in 1933. Short-lived magazines, chiefly radical in emphasis, such as *Left,* published at Moline, and *Direction,* published at Peoria, have contained some valuable work.

It is natural that this recent Illinois literature should reflect the thought and feeling of the times. Significantly a part of the main current of critical realism in American fiction at the present time are the novels and stories of such writers as James T. Farrell, Albert Halper, and Louis Zara. Farrell in *Studs Lonigan* and *A World I Never Made,* Halper in *The Foundry* and *The Chute,* and Zara in *Give Us This Day* have written about industrial Chicago from within in terms frequently denounced as too harshly critical, but marked by sincerity and power. There is indication that Illinois literature in its current phase will continue to express the preoccupation of writers with the social and economic problems reflected in the unhappiness and insecurity of many of the people of the State, in both urban and rural areas. Among examples of this preoccupation are Nelson Algren's *Somebody in Boots,* Stuart Engstrand's *The Invaders,* and Tom Tippett's *Horseshoe Bottoms.*

In fields other than the narrowly creative, members of the faculties of Illinois colleges and universities have made extremely important contributions to the literature of the State throughout the period since the nineties. The writings of such men as William Rainey Harper, James A. Breasted, Thorstein Veblen, and Richard G. Moulton did much to build the world-wide reputation of the University of Chicago. Stuart P. Sherman was a professor of English at the University of Illinois when his *On Contemporary Literature* and *The Genius of America* established him as one of the major critics of the country. Among the many contemporary Illinois teachers whose writings have possessed general literary importance are Charles E. Merriam, Harold W. Gosnell, T. V. Smith, Ferdinand Schevill, Bruce Weirick, and Baker Brownell. No record of Illinois literature would be complete without reference to Jane Addams' *Twenty Years at Hull House* and Clarence Darrow's *The Story of My Life.* Particularly valuable is the interpretation of their city by Lloyd Lewis and Henry Justin Smith in *Chicago: A History of Her Reputation.* At an opposite pole of interest are Donald Culross Peattie's studies of nature, particularly the fine *An Almanac for Moderns.* Excellent contributions in the field of biography and history are Paul Angle's *Here I Have Lived;* E. E. Calkins' *They Broke the Prairie;* and Harry Barnard's *Eagle Forgotten.*

Contemporary Illinois novelists are recognizing more and more the value of the State's historical background as subject matter for their work. Margaret Ayer Barnes introduced a noteworthy study of Chicago's development on one social level in her *Years of Grace;* in *Bright Land* and *The Smiths* Janet Ayer Fairbank used rich material from nineteenth-century Galena and Chicago. Harold Sinclair in *A Prairie Town,* Donald Culross Peattie in *A Prairie Grove,* and Gareta Busey in *The Windbreak* have given appreciative treatments of the early days in other cities and in a rural community.

But notwithstanding the creative exploration of Illinois' present and past in recent years, great areas of Illinois life still lie untouched by writers. The builders of canals and railways, the workers in mines and mills, the members of varied ethnic groups in cities and rural districts, all are waiting for novelists, poets, and dramatists whose vision and power are worthy of their material. It would be wrong to think of Illinois literature of today in any terms save those of opportunity, of praise, and of continued growth.

THEATER

THE THEATER was always an afterthought on the hard fighting frontier and the hardships of pioneer life in sparsely settled Illinois gave little encouragement either to the itinerant actor or the aspiring amateur. Perhaps the first amateur Illinois theatricals were presented in Springfield, on December 3, 1836, as announced in the *Sangamon Journal.*

One of the first professional actors to visit Illinois was Joseph Jefferson III, later beloved throughout the country in the rôle of Rip Van Winkle. "In the year 1838," wrote Jefferson in his *Autobiography,* "the new town of Chicago had just turned from an Indian village into a thriving little place, and my uncle had written to my father urging him to join in the management of the new theater which was then being built there." The Jefferson family traveled part of the journey through the Erie Canal on a packet-boat. Her name, as Jefferson noted, was the *Pioneer,* and it was most appropriate, for the Jeffersons were among the first players to migrate to the West.

Traveling in open wagons over the rough prairie roads, the venturesome players made their way to Galena, Illinois. Turning south again, they were forced to give their entertainment at Pekin in a porkhouse, accompanied by the squealing of pigs. In Springfield, where they arrived for a season during a session of the Legislature, they were disheartened by a prohibitive license fee demanded by the town.

In the midst of our trouble, [wrote Jefferson] a young lawyer called on the managers. He had heard of the injustice, and offered, if they would place the matter in his hands, to have the license taken off, declaring that he only wished to see fair play, and he would accept no fee whether he failed or succeeded. The case was brought up before the council. The young lawyer began his harangue. He handled the subject with tact, skill, and humor, tracing the history of the drama from the time when Thespis acted in a cart to the stage of today. He illustrated his speech with a number of anecdotes, and kept the council in a roar of laughter; his good-humor prevailed, and the exorbitant tax was taken off. This young lawyer was very popular in Springfield, and was honored and beloved by all who knew him. . . . He now lies buried near Springfield, under a monument commemorating his greatness and his virtues—and his name was Abraham Lincoln!

167

How other early Illinois actors, managers, and their creditors fared
during their barnstorming is vividly described by the celebrated actor-
manager, Sol Smith, in his delightfully rambling *Theatrical Management*. Smith, who began his long career in the Middle West in 1824,
has this to say of Manager Potter, a male counterpart of the present-
day sob-sister. Smith wrote:

It ought to be mentioned that P. has a weakness in a nerve of one
of his eyes, from which a *tear* is always involuntarily starting. It is
supposed that in this weakness consists Manager Potter's strength,
no person having yet been found who could resist it. There is not a
town on any of the Western waters from Fever River in Illinois, to
the Bay of Mobile in Alabama, but has experienced him.

One of Potter's devices for moving from place to place without
money was to "abolish the salary-list." Another was to borrow additional sums from his creditors when they came to collect what was
already overdue. Enroute to Chicago in 1844, Potter and his company
came to St. Louis on a steamboat from Memphis. The captain swore
that no baggage would be taken off until the company paid its passage.
But before nightfall Potter had the whole company and its properties
on board a Galena boat; the captain who had brought him to St. Louis
had a note for his debt, and had been persuaded to endorse other notes
to pay not only the passage of the company to Galena, but across the
country to Chicago!

During the frontier period productions in the larger cities differed
little from those presented in the villages. To a measurable extent this
was due to the "star" system then practiced, for an actor's appearances
were limited only by his opportunity to travel. Many of the famous
actors of the day were well known in the remote parts of the State.

Essentially, however, the theater of the pioneer period was an
imported product. The classics of the English stage, particularly the
plays of Shakespeare, together with contemporary English offerings,
held the boards. In his *Literature of the Middle Western Frontier*,
R. L. Rusk, who has examined over seven thousand newspaper adver-
tisements appearing between 1799 and 1840, states that of the Shakespearean plays, *Richard III., Othello,* and *Hamlet* were the most popular. American dramatists, according to Professor Rusk, were given
slight attention, with the single exception of John Howard Payne,
whose greatest successes were *Therese, Charles the Second, 'Twas I,*

or the Truth a Lie, and *Clari.* Plays on Western life were not popular;
The Lion of the West, and *The Kentuckian, or a Trip to New York,*
for instance, had together less than a dozen performances. At first,
melodrama, farce, opera, and pantomime proved slightly more popular than forms of greater literary pretension: later, they were much
preferred to comedies, tragedies, and historical plays. But productions
of any sort were events, and audiences usually represented a well-
defined cross-section of frontier society.

During the pioneer period Chicago became the center of the theater
in Illinois. In 1837, the year the city was incorporated, the first actors
who came to Chicago, unlike the Jeffersons in Springfield, found no
champion who "only wished to see fair play," and were restrained
from performing because they could not afford to buy a license. Before long, however, two managers purchased a license, improvised a
theater in the dining room of the Sauganash Hotel, and drew a crowd
with their production of Kotzebue's *The Stranger.* The success of the
venture encouraged the opening of a new theater in the upper story
of a wooden building, and it was probably in this more pretentious
house that the Jeffersons appeared in 1839.

A vivid description of one of Chicago's earliest playhouses appears
in Jefferson's *Autobiography.*

And now for the theater, newly painted canvas, tack-hammer at
work on stuffed seats in the dress circle, planing-boards in the pit, new
drop-curtain let down for inspection, "beautiful"—a medallion of
Shakespeare, suffering from a severe pain in his stomach, over the
center, with "One touch of nature makes the whole world kin" written under him, and a large, painted, brick-red drapery looped up by
Justice, with sword and scales, showing an arena with a large number
of gladiators hacking away at one another in the distance, to a delighted
Roman public. . . . There were two private boxes with little white-
and-gold balustrades and turkey-red curtains, over one box a portrait
of Beethoven and over the other a portrait of Handel. . . . The dome
was pale blue, with pink-and-white clouds, on which reposed four un-
graceful ballet girls representing the seasons, and apparently dropping
flowers, snow, and grapes into the pit. . . . With what delight the
actors looked forward to the opening of a new theater in a new town,
where dramatic entertainments were still unknown—repairing their
wardrobes, studying their new parts, and speculating on the laurels
that were to be won!

In 1847 John Rice, soon to become Mayor of Chicago, erected the
first theater building in the city on Randolph Street near Dearborn.

Theaters continued to multiply until ten or more were playing at a time. Players who appeared in Illinois found enthusiastic audiences. Such famous actors as Edwin Forrest, the Jeffersons, John Drew, Charlotte Cushman, the Booths, Charles Kean, and others were often seen.

Stock companies, composed of permanent groups, which often gained prestige by the presence of an actor of distinction, flourished during this period. Visiting stars from Europe and the East, traveling alone, found ensembles ready to support them in stock performances. Comedy, burlesque, light and grand opera, minstrel shows, and pantomimes were presented. Foreign groups, particularly the Germans, were active, and supported three companies in Chicago.

John H. McVicker, a popular actor of the day, built the third theater in Chicago in 1857, at a cost of $85,000, and named it after himself. Crosby's Opera House, famed throughout the Midwest, was built in 1865 at a cost of $600,000. Two years later, this huge structure was won by an individual on a lottery ticket. Other well-known theaters were Wood's Museum, North's Amphitheater, Aiken's, the Academy of Music, the Globe, and the Dearborn. In 1871 the Chicago fire destroyed some fourteen showhouses.

Between 1871 and 1894 literally dozens of theaters arose in the city. Entertainment adjusted itself to the social stratum of its audience. For the well-to-do, sentimental melodrama was offered. A type of burlesque for the entire family appealed to those of lesser means. It was at this time that the burlesque houses of Sam T. Jack appeared. Although eastern companies toured the Middle West, competent local stock companies continued to thrive, and as Chicago took on the proportions of a metropolis, stars gradually confined their performances to its well-attended theaters.

Chicago, however, was not the only scene of the theater in Illinois. Though the drama presented along the rivers was unimportant from the viewpoint of literature, it merits attention as a phenomenon in the history of the American stage. In his *Theatrical Management*, Sol Smith states that the Chapman family "established and carried into operation that singular affair, the 'Floating Theater,' concerning which so many anecdotes are told. . . . It is said of this Floating Theater that it was cast loose during a performance at one of the river towns in Indiana by some mischievous boys, and could not be landed for half a dozen miles, the large audience being compelled to walk back to their villages."

Because of its depth and placid waters, the Illinois River became an early favorite of show boat operators. These craft ascended the stream as far as it was navigable, stopping at such towns as Morris, Marseilles, Ottawa, La Salle, Peru, Peoria, Pekin, and Beardstown. Along the Mississippi they docked at Galena, Rock Island, Moline, Quincy, Alton, and Cairo. Along the Ohio their itinerary included Shawneetown and Metropolis. Among the show boat plays were comedies, with the shrewd Yankee as hero; sentimental melodramas, like *Uncle Tom's Cabin*, effective as "tear-jerkers"; and dramas of horror. These three types formed the core of the repertory.

Outstanding "floating theaters" were the *Cotton Blossom*, the *Golden Rod, French's New Sensation*, and the *Princess*. The nineties were the big years for them, and whenever one of these "singular affairs" tied up at a town, it was a sign that festive days were to begin. Among the popular companies known in Illinois were those headed by Mencke and Billy Bryan. When the show boats became outmoded and their audiences small, the stock companies of the twentieth century followed a route that had as its basis the old river itinerary.

Between 1810 and 1830 James H. Caldwell, an English actor with several years' experience in the South, controlled a theatrical monopoly in the Mississippi Valley. The Cincinnati *Daily Gazette* of November 16, 1836 commented,

Mr. Caldwell of New Orleans, not satisfied with owning all the theaters between the falls of St. Anthony and the Balize, and managing two or three of them, with being the proprietor of a bank, and the largest bathing establishment in the Union—and with holding contracts for lighting three or four cities with gas, has a new project on foot—the formation of an Ocean Steam Company for running a line of packets between New Orleans and Liverpool.

But the shrewd English actor's monopoly was only a hint of what was to come. Following the trend of the industrial revolution, the season of 1895-96 saw the formation in New York of "The Syndicate," controlled by Charles Frohmann, Marc Klaw, Abraham Erlanger, Sam Nixon, Al Rayman, and Fred Zimmerman, which began at once to dominate the American stage. Some managers and players, however, refused to capitulate to the dictatorship of this new monopoly, among them David Belasco, Mrs. Fisk, Richard Mansfield, and Sarah Bernhardt. Because of her defection, Mrs. Fisk was forced to appear in halls, and Madame Bernhardt was reduced to playing in a tent. In the opinion of many observers, the effect of the trust on the theater was devastating. Dating from its origin, the theater in Illinois began to decline, and has now become but a catch-all for the conventional drama produced in the East.

Eastern managers shielded good plays by sending them on tour with their own companies, and as a protection against high rentals, gained control of a number of theaters in various cities. By 1880 the old style stock company was dead in the major houses. New York became the producing center, and the rest of the country served as a "road" for its productions. A successful play was regarded as a formula, and worn thin through repetition. This stifled initiative and originality, and also produced a revolt, out of which came the first drama in America that had any pretensions at all toward greatness.

In Illinois the theater trust touched only the larger cities, particularly Chicago, and as a consequence local stock companies, suffering from the impact of the eastern invasion, took on new form. Just as New York became the producing center for the commercial theater on a large scale, so did Chicago function for Illinois and its environs on a small scale. Stock companies which had been permanently situated took to the road, and nearly every settlement and village in the State saw one or another of them in at least a "one-night stand." A more or less standardized theatrical bill-of-fare—including such old favorites as *East Lynn* and *Uncle Tom's Cabin*—was served alike to cities and villages; the smaller communities, however, received an extra measure of emotional seasoning. Stock companies toured Illinois until the World War period, and most were successful financially.

About the turn of the century Illinois produced a few dramatists who strove to create a vital native drama, and chose their themes from the chaos of the rising industrial order. William Vaughn Moody, Robert Herrick, Edward Sheldon, among others, dramatized the maladjustments of this new society. But theirs was a short-lived battle, and the theater became more and more the genteel art of convention. As the independent companies in Illinois gradually disbanded, the better actors, playwrights, and technicians migrated to the East, drying up still further the sources of an indigenous Midwest theater.

With the establishment of New York as the theatrical producing center of America, a movement of protest began almost immediately. Although directed primarily against the type of drama presented by the commercial theater, and stressing its interest in "art," the revolt was at the same time an attempt to reincarnate the local theater. In Illinois many groups sprang up with these objectives; the most important were organized in Chicago. A theater was formed at Hull House with the aim of presenting dramas that reflected the problems of contemporary society.

The second movement of revolt against commercialism came in 1912, when Maurice Browne established the Little Theater in Chicago. Among the plays produced by Browne on the tiny stage in the Fine Arts Building were: *Trojan Women* and *Medea* by Euripides; *Creditors* and *The Stronger* by August Strindberg; *Joint Owners in Spain* by Alice Brown; *The Fifth Commandment* by Stanley Houghton; and *Grotesque* by Cloyd Head. This Little Theater venture lasted about four years, stimulated the local theater throughout the Middle West, and fostered native talent.

In 1913, asked to write an article on the book *The Ideals and Accomplishments of Little Theaters* by the late Theodore B. Hinckley, editor of the *Drama*, Mr. Browne replied, in part:

It is nearly half a generation since Laura Dainty Pelham established the Hull House Players and laid the first foundation stone in America of what is known as the Little Theater, in England as the Repertory Theater, movement. Our future dramatic historian . . . will certainly record the fact that Chicago was the first city in America where the movement came into active being, not only with the work of Mrs. Pelham, but also, a few years later, with the plucky and thorough pioneering of Donald Robertson and the earliest experiments of The Chicago Theater Society, which were none the less interesting and profitable for their being temporarily abortive.

In 1916 a theater was formed to produce experimental dramas and to encourage local playwrights. Kenneth Sawyer Goodman and Alice Gerstenberg were members of this organization, which started with great promise but dissolved with the coming of the World War. The Goodman Theater was the next important advance in the crusade. It introduced a number of talents, but was forced by the depression to close its doors as a repertory company. It now exists as a school of dramatic art. A short-lived venture in Shakespearean productions came to an end in 1931 with the closing of the Repertory Company.

Today a number of "little" and semi-professional groups, among them the Jewish People's Theater, the Mummers, the Chicago Repertory, and the Group, are actively engaged in theater work. They have been producing plays that deal with the more basic issues of present-day society. Among the dramatic schools in the State are the School of Speech at Northwestern University, the Goodman Theater, the De Paul Little Theater, and the Barnum School of Drama.

When, as a result of the depression, the Federal Government turned its attention to the rehabilitation of actors, technicians, and the many assistants necessary in the operation of playhouses, it offered a new hope for a professional theater in the Middle West. From the beginning the Federal Theater has neither sought to compete with nor rival the type of virtuosity displayed in the commercial theater. Along with the educational phase of the vast undertaking, the aim has been to bring a living theater to those people who could not afford to attend the regular offerings.

Recent offerings of the Federal Theater have been the highly successful, *The Mikado,* a modern swing version with an all-Negro cast; the ballets, *Frankie and Johnnie, Ballet Fedre,* and *Guns and Castanets;* and the plays, *Power, The Copperhead,* and *Prologue to Glory.* At present the Federal Theater is using two playhouses, the Great Northern and the Blackstone.

Although no great drama has come from Illinois, the State has had its prominent critics, the most influential of whom were associated with Chicago. The names of Burns Mantle and Percy Hammond received Nation-wide recognition. Amy Leslie stood out as one of the most competent critics in the country, and her authority was undisputed in the Midwest from the early nineties until the late twenties.

MUSIC

DESPITE her meager inheritance in the realm of music, Illinois has made a praiseworthy artistic contribution to the rapidly focusing national musical picture. Unfortunately America has not afforded her music-lovers the stimulation to be found in native ballads and ancient folk tunes. Since the songs of the American Indians have never struck a responsive chord in our nature, they have exerted a minute influence upon our cultural development in comparison with the music imported from Europe. But from the assimilation of the melodies of other countries has sprung an intense desire for a music of our own, and Illinois has produced a number of compositions conceived in an idiom recognizably American.

Eastern settlers, trappers, and hunters, who pushed westward into the Illinois wilderness, brought with them the tunes, hymns, and ballads from which much of our music of today has logically progressed. In New England, whence came many of the Illinois pioneers, an organized effort had been made to confine music to church use. But the traditional ballad singing and fiddle playing had persisted, and plays with music similar to our comic operas had been given since Revolutionary time. This type of music was further encouraged by the freer life of the migrants. In his *American Songbag,* Carl Sandburg has included several songs which were brought to Illinois directly from New England. "Down, Down Derry Down" is one of these colorful many-versed ballads.

From about 1800 to 1830, the unadorned struggle for food, shelter, and clothing fully occupied the Illinois pioneers. But eventually they picked up the threads of their former modes of life. Among the new settlers were ministers and missionaries. Churches were established, and soon the hymns of Wesley, Mason, Billings, and others floated out upon the prairie air. Singing schools also appeared. Often the teacher did not live in the settlement, but went about from post to post, encouraging groups to cultivate a love and appreciation of music.

In 1834 the Beaubien brothers, John and Mark, possessed two of the earliest musical instruments in the State. Mark owned the first violin recorded in Illinois, and John had the first piano in Chicago, if

175

not in Illinois. One year later the Old Settlers' Harmonic Society was founded at Chicago; its opening concert was given within a year at the Presbyterian Church. In 1837 a theater was opened in Chicago. This brought to Illinois a ballad singer and a group of minstrels who were soon followed by others.

In the 1840's and 1850's families of strolling singers and musicians were extremely popular throughout the State, and monopolized the musical entertainment field. The Sable melodist, the Negro minstrels, the Algerines, the Antoni, the Newhall, and the Peak families were welcomed warmly wherever they performed. In 1853 the Swiss Bell Ringers appeared before an overflow crowd of eight hundred persons at the Springfield courthouse. The trend toward musical self-expression also thrived at Alton, where "Professor" Van Meter conducted a music course attended by five hundred pupils, one hundred and fifty of whom appeared in graduation recitals. By the end of the period, bands and choral societies had been organized in many Illinois towns. Grierson's Band at Jacksonville, founded at this time, gained wide attention for its unique method of playing by notation instead of "by ear." The number of music lovers increased so rapidly that in 1852 a two-day State-wide convention was held at Springfield. A *Sangerbund* was organized in Belleville in 1865, followed by a Philharmonic Society in 1867.

Between 1840 and 1850 American music was further stimulated by the arrival of immigrants from Europe. Early music in Illinois had a distinctly German flavor. Hans Balatka, once a choral conductor in Vienna, was appointed to lead the newly organized Philharmonic Orchestra at Chicago in 1860. His first program included the Second Symphony of Beethoven and a chorus from Tannhauser, the first Wagnerian music to be played in the region. The Germania Orchestra of New York was one of the first large orchestras to tour Illinois. Among visiting artists at this time were Richard Hoffman, Gottschalk, and Rubenstein.

It is not to be supposed, however, that the arrival of the works of Wagner, Beethoven, and other European composers effected an immediate leavening of the musical taste in the cities of the Prairie State, much less in the rural districts. Music of another sort—robust, not to say coarse—played its part in both pastime and manual labor. An idea of the place occupied in Illinois by popular and utilitarian music is given in Charles Edward Russell's *A-Rafting on the Mississip'*.

If in the face of . . . fairly eloquent testimony, I continue to maintain that my rascals of the raft had sometimes a redeeming substratum of sentiment and poetry under their rowdyism, I may be judged merely eccentric. . . . Of a sudden, there would float over the water the sounds of a fiddle, or maybe an accordion, playing "Buffalo Gals," and we could easily make out the crew sitting in a semi-circle rapt upon the solitary musician. . . . It was not always hymnody of a kind to edify the youthful mind, but I am bound to say that, when there were children about, the raftsmen, if they happened to be sufficiently sober, would put some restraint upon both their language and their lyric offerings. They had a singular and absorbing passion for music— crude music, but still something approaching melody. Most rafts carried fiddlers as conscientiously as they carried cooks.

Of the old songs and tunes, Mr. Russell has said,

Those that provided a chorus or an opportunity to dance a few steps between the stanzas were the favorites. "One-Eyed Riley" went like this:

> He was prime fav'rite out our way,
> The women folks all loved him dearly;
> He taught the parsons how to pray,
> An' he got their tin, or pretty nearly.
> He's the man they speak of highly!
>   W-a-h-hoop!
> Riddle, liddle, linktum!
> *Pause—then all together, fortissimo*
> One-Eyed Riley!

. . . When "tum" is reached, all the boot-soles must slap the floor together. Then the dancers remain rigid until the refrain, which they deliver with roaring enthusiasm, "One-Eyed Riley!"

The "Big Maquoketa" and "Raftsman Jim" were other favorites of the period. The former, according to Russell, was the "flowerage of an undiscovered river laureate," although the tune, like that of "Raftsman Jim," was not composed in Illinois. Of "Buffalo Gals" Russell stated that he printed the text "with a sense of humiliation," but had "found this song on old Broadway programs as having been sung to audiences that ought to have known better, and there is evidence that East and West, it was the darling of its times."

Although music was steadily gaining the collective fancy of early Illinoisans, choruses and instrumental groups in the towns and cities almost entirely suspended their activities during the Civil War. Only minstrels singing war songs were popular with audiences at that time. But with Lee's surrender and peace, Chicago, Jacksonville, Peoria, Rock Island, Alton, Cairo, and many other growing places were again visited by musicians. Louise Kellog sang, and Camilla Urso came with her violin. A traveling artist, Gunge, spoke of the smaller towns as being quite as appreciative of music as Chicago, although he found the American taste was far below the European. Said Gunge, "In music he [the American] likes best—waltzes, the galop, quadrilles, and best of all, polkas. There are only a few exceptions. Minstrels have the best business."

Perhaps these "exceptions" were responsible for the establishment of music schools in Alton, Moline, Rockford, Elgin, and Chicago. Some of the foreign and local teachers who conducted early schools earned but a pittance; others received a thousand dollars a year, which was considered a good salary in a profession that twenty years earlier had been able to reward its followers with only a meager existence.

Soon conservatories were created to meet a definite need: the Chicago Conservatory of Music in 1866; the Illinois Conservatory of Music at Jacksonville in 1871; the Department of Music at Northwestern University, with Peter Christian Lutkin at its head, in 1873; the Knox Conservatory of Music at Galesburg in 1883; and the Chicago Musical College, founded in 1887 by Dr. Florenz Ziegfeld, father of the late producer of the Follies. These forerunners were followed by many others.

The development of music in the public schools was at first slow and difficult. With no American folk songs handed down from generation to generation, the early settlers from the East had only the European tunes and words their parents had taught them. But this music held little meaning in a frontier atmosphere, where an exotic culture might be remembered but could not thrive. The only hope lay in transplanting music training from the singing school. This was done gradually, a town here and there fusing music with academic study. As early as 1872 the State school laws provided that music and drawing might be insisted upon in the various districts by their respective boards.

In 1885 questionnaires were sent to the public schools throughout Illinois. Twenty towns and cities in the State were found to be teaching music. Freeport and Sycamore were not among these because of the expense. The Carlyle school was too crudely organized to admit of anything but compulsory subjects. Mount Vernon was hampered by the inability of its teaching force and want of money to pay a special music teacher. In Dwight only music by rote and some instrumental accompaniment were taught.

Twenty years later the situation was vastly different. Statistics taken in 1905, covering the whole of the United States, indicated that approximately 97 per cent of the cities in Illinois that answered the questionnaires taught music in their schools. By 1908 twenty-six conservatories, colleges, and universities throughout the State, offered courses in music. The State university credited music toward a degree. The course of study prepared in 1915 by the committee of county superintendents' section of the Illinois State Teachers' Association included an outline for music in elementary grades. Today the study of music is widespread in Illinois public schools, although no law exists forcing them to include it in their curricula.

School glee clubs and orchestras are as numerous today in the small towns as in the cities. Music festivals have become legion, beginning with competition in each town, then narrowing to a number of towns vying for honors in a district meet, and finally centering in a State contest. Winners from the various States meet in the early summer for national competition. The entries include vocal and instrumental solos, choruses of all kinds, orchestras, bands, and ensemble groups.

By 1885 nine Illinois towns boasted of large singing societies. A few years later Jacksonville had an excellent chorus; the Peoria Oratorio Society, during its first season, performed with seventy-five voices. The Northwestern University musical groups were giving well-attended chamber music recitals.

Opera made a start in Chicago in 1850 at the Rice Theater, but when a fire destroyed the building, enthusiasm waned until the Crosby Opera House was built in 1865. Several good productions were presented there. At the same time chamber music concerts under the management of the Briggs House were being given. About 1887 the city enjoyed a season of German opera, and an opera festival held soon afterwards in the Exposition Building encouraged the construction of Chicago's famous Auditorium Theater.

Shortly before 1890 the Auditorium was formally opened by President Harrison. The evening was momentous. Harriet Monroe's dedicatory ode was read, and Adelina Patti sang with the Apollo Musical Club. On the next night *Romeo and Juliet* was presented, the first of twenty-two operatic performances to be given that year. From then until 1914 Chicago enjoyed a succession of well-known singers, including Lillian Nordica, Schumann-Heink, Caruso, John McCormick, Mary Garden, and Carolina White.

Soon after the outbreak of the World War the Chicago Grand Opera Company went into bankruptcy. But a year later a new organization, the Chicago Opera Association, headed by Harold F. McCormick, was organized; Galli-Curci sang with this company in 1916. The Opera Association was disbanded in 1922, and its functions taken over by the Chicago Civic Opera Company.

In 1929, under the direction of Samuel Insull, a $20,000,000 Civic Opera House was built on Wacker Drive in Chicago. But what had seemed a triumph, presaging a brilliant future, turned out to be a finale, for in a few years the inverted pyramid of Insull finance suddenly collapsed, and with it went the Civic Opera Company. Several smaller groups were formed to carry on. Of these the Chicago Grand Opera Company is the most prominent today. Until 1931 opera stars from the Metropolitan and Chicago Opera companies appeared annually during the summer season in the open air pavilion at beautiful Ravinia Park, twenty-five miles north of Chicago's Loop.

Orchestral music paralleled the growth and struggle of opera in Chicago. From 1859 until 1905 the name of Theodore Thomas was synonymous with orchestral development in the Middle West. Thomas, often referred to as "Chicago's Father of Music," toured the region in 1859 with the operatic company of Karl Formes, the famous German basso. On October 9, 1871, the young violinist led his own symphony orchestra in a concert at the Crosby Opera House in Chicago, playing one of Beethoven's overtures to Fidelio, a scherzo from a Schumann symphony, and music by Chopin, Gounod, Schubert, and Wagner. Later that night the Chicago Fire began its furious assault upon the city, forcing the musicians of the Thomas Orchestra to flee from a North Side hotel. Despite this harrowing experience the popular Thomas was induced to settle in Chicago, and in 1891 he organized the Chicago Orchestra. With nearly 8,500 Chicagoans contributing to a popular subscription fund, the present Orchestra Hall building was erected on Michigan Avenue in 1904, but Thomas lived only long enough to direct three concerts there. He was succeeded in 1905 by

Frederick Stock, the present conductor (1939). In 1906 the orchestra was named the Theodore Thomas Orchestra and kept this name until 1912, when it was changed to the Chicago Symphony Orchestra.

Orchestral music flourished in Chicago following the World War. The Chicago Civic Orchestra was established in 1919; and the Woman's Symphony Orchestra in 1925. Ravinia Park was again opened to the public in 1936, with the Chicago Symphony Orchestra a major attraction. That same year symphony and band orchestras co-operating with city officials inaugurated a series of free summer concerts, in Grant Park on Chicago's lake front, which attracted thousands of music-lovers.

An organization unique in the Middle West was the Chicago Allied Arts, Inc., founded in 1924. The Chicago Allied Arts comprised a ballet company of about twenty-five dancers, under the choreographic direction of Adolph Bolm, formerly of the Diaghileff *Ballets Russes,* and Eric DeLamarter's Solo Orchestra of about twenty-five pieces. An air of novelty distinguished the organization's performances. The orchestral concerts, preceding the ballets, presented the works of John Alden Carpenter, Leo Sowerby, Honegger, Milhaud, Stravinsky, Schonberg, and many others. The ballets, too, their settings and costumes designed by Nicholas Remisoff, were mostly modern in treatment. An interesting feature of the organization was its presentation of guest artists. Among a number of guest dancers who appeared with the company was the distinguished ballerina, Tamar Karsavina, upon her first visit to America. Ruth Page, later ballet mistress of the Ravinia Opera Company and the Chicago Opera Company, was *première danseuse* throughout the three seasons of the Allied Arts, and introduced some characteristically American choreography. John Alden Carpenter acted as president of the organization during its first season. The Allied Arts closed its brilliant Chicago career in December 1926. The following year the entire company was invited to give joint performances with the League of Composers in New York. Among the ballets presented were the Chicago creations, *The Tragedy of the Cello,* with music by Alexander Tansman, and *The Rivals,* composed by Henry Eichheim.

At the close of the World War a new musical phenomenon, jazz, captured the entire entertainment field. Jazz, as every one knows, was once regarded as "an underground waif," a low noise in the scale of music, but some forget that Chicago made jazz its protegé, and gave it a vibrant send-off that imparted prestige. Paul Whiteman wrote:

There is considerable discussion over exactly who did invent the term "jazz band," with many authorities giving the honor to Bert Kelly of Chicago who described a group of musicians that he hired out to the Boosters' Club at the Hotel Morrison in Chicago as a "jazz band." The Boosters' club promptly raised all its prices, alleging that the new-fangled jazz came high.

But long before this, Brown's orchestra (a group Mr. Gorman had recently discovered in a frenzy of syncopation on the streets of New Orleans) had been taken over by Mr. Gorman and placed at the Lamb's cafe, also in Chicago. The players burst upon the unsuspecting pork-packer world with a bang that nearly shattered the roof. . . . This, so far as I can discover from cabaret history, was the honest-to-goodness beginning of jazz.

"Hot" bands appeared also in Peoria, Springfield, and East St. Louis; saxophones whined, banjos strummed, and drums beat a new kind of rhythm. Crowds filled the night clubs and ballrooms, dancing to the jazz of Wayne King, Ben Bernie, Duke Ellington, and Cab Calloway. Paul Ash and his orchestra enlivened the Oriental Theater in Chicago's Loop with his jazz renditions, while on Chicago's South Side the Negro jazz band of Erskine Tate, experimenting with new forms of rhythmic music, elevated from its ranks one of the Nation's foremost jazz composers, Louis Armstrong. Negroes also found an eager audience with such famous spirituals as "Go Down, Moses," "Steal Away," and "Swing Low, Sweet Chariot."

With the organization of the Federal Music Project in 1935, music in Illinois has for the first time been brought within reach of the masses of the people. Symphony orchestras and bands, choral groups and music classes, have kindled a desire for cultural development in communities weighed down by economic depression. This has been particularly true in the mining area of southern Illinois, where in the Negro settlement of Colp, paralyzed by unemployment, a chorus of twenty-five was assembled to travel about the countryside, singing their spirituals before enthusiastic crowds. In Chicago the Illinois Symphony, a WPA unit, presents weekly concerts, and encourages the work of native composers.

Of recent development is the working-class song. To the tune of "Jacob's Ladder," a Negro spiritual, the miners of southern Illinois, after the formation of the Progressive Miners' Union in 1932, sang

"We are Building a New Union." During a strike in the steel mill area of South Chicago, the labor song "Beans" was composed. These songs, together with older ones like "John Brown's Body," sometimes with new words, have been adopted by groups of industrialized and urban Illinois workers.

A number of composers in the State have contributed to the dignity and musical importance of Illinois. John Alden Carpenter is the author of many beautiful songs. In his "Adventures in a Perambulator" and in his ballet *Krazy Kat,* he has struck a persuasively American and original note. Leo Sowerby was the first American winner of the *Prix de Rome* musical scholarship. Hamilton Forrest's opera, *Camille,* was produced by the Chicago Civic Opera Company, with Mary Garden singing the principal rôle. The ballet, *Play of Words,* composed by David Van Vactor in 1932, was produced at the Goodman theater for the Originalists, a group whose members represented all of the arts and professions. Among many distinguished compositions by Eric DeLamarter, formerly associate conductor of the Chicago Symphony Orchestra, is his ballet *The Dance of Life.* Other well-known Illinois composers include: Frederick Stock, Felix Borowski, Robert Sanders, Rosseter G. Cole, Arne Oldberg, Dr. Albert Noelte, Wesley La Violette, Robert Whitney, Irwin Fischer, Max Wald, Edward Collins, William Lester, Radio Britain, and Daniel Protheroe.

Music critics and journals of music have rendered a valuable service to the art in Illinois. Both the *Musical Leader* and the *Music News* are published in Chicago. The late Edward Moore was author of *Forty Years of Opera in Chicago.* Karleton S. Hackett was vice-president of the American Conservatory of Music at the time of his death. Among the music critics writing today for the Chicago press are Eugene Stinson, Glenn Dillard Gunn, Herman Devries, Claudia Cassidy, Edward Barry and Cecil Smith.

Part III

Tours

TOUR 1

CHICAGO—CHICAGO HEIGHTS

Hard-surfaced roadbed throughout.
Chicago and Eastern Illinois Ry. roughly parallels the route between Chicago and Danville, the Cleveland, Cincinnati, Chicago & St. Louis Ry. between Danville and Marshall.
Usual accommodations throughout.

BETWEEN CHICAGO and Chicago Heights the metropolis dwindles across a lake plain, its weakening impulse relayed from suburb to suburb by intervening industrial plants and the weedgrown plots of thwarted subdivisions. South of Crete, State 1 traverses farmlands that were settled early in the nineteenth century. The trade center villages rising from the cornfields owe their founding either to the Hubbard Trail, the Chicago-Vincennes State Road, or the Chicago and Eastern Illinois Railway, built between Chicago and Danville in 1871. The Hubbard Trail, which State 1 approximates, was marked off in the 1820's by the wagon wheels of the fur-trader Gurdon S. Hubbard (1802-1886). The Chicago-Vincennes State Road was routed along the Hubbard Trail in 1833 and 1834.

CHICAGO, 0 *m.* (598 alt., 3,376,438 pop.) (*see Chicago*).

Points of Interest: Chicago Board of Trade Building, Union Stock Yards, Field Museum of Natural History, Art Institute of Chicago, Museum of Science and Industry, Adler Planetarium, Shedd Aquarium, University of Chicago, and others.

Chicago is at the junctions with State 42 (*see Tour* 2), US 41 (*see Tour* 2A), US 12 (*see Tour* 9), US 14 (*see Tour* 10), US 20 (*see Tour* 11), US 330 (*see Tour* 12A), US 66 (*see Tour* 17), and the Illinois Waterway (*see Tour* 22).

CALUMET PARK (R), 15.7 *m.* (604 alt., 1,429 pop.), a suburb, extends along the highway for half a mile.

Right from Calumet Park on Vermont Avenue to BLUE ISLAND, 2.1 *m.* (605 alt., 16,534 pop.), a residential suburb centering about Vermont and Western Avenues. First settled in 1835 and organized as a village in 1872, Blue Island has a population largely of German and Italian extraction. Its name indicates the nature of its site on a glacial ridge, the only appreciable hill on the Chicago lake plain. Rising like an island from the marshland that surrounds it, the ridge was named by settlers for the blue haze that cloaked its dense woods. The LIBBY, MCNEIL & LIBBY PACKING PLANT (*open* 8:30-4 *daily; conducted tours*), 13635 S. Western Ave., is the main canning plant of a company with branches throughout the world.

187

Left from Blue Island on Western Avenue (Dixie Highway) to a junction with 139th Street, 1.5 *m.*

Right on 139th Street to ROBBINS (602 alt., 753 pop.), 1 *m.*, one of the two all-Negro communities in Illinois (*see Tour 7*). Incorporated as a village in 1917, Robbins was named for Eugene S. Robbins, the realtor who developed the site expressly for Negroes. Save for a lumber yard and a dozen shops on Claire Boulevard, Robbins is wholly residential, its houses ranging from neat cottages to jerry-built structures of scrap materials. Despite a low per capita income, 15 churches and a public school system are maintained.

On Western Avenue (Dixie Highway) is POSEN, 2 *m.* (605 alt., 1,329 pop.), a community of industrial workers whose homes are surrounded by garden plots and small farms. Its homogeneous population (98 per cent Polish) reflects the enterprise of a Chicago realtor, whose 75 Polish salesmen sold 12,000 lots to their countrymen during 1893. Incorporation was in 1901 when neighboring Harvey attempted to extend prohibition to Posen.

RIVERDALE, 16.7 *m.* (597 alt., 2,504 pop.), a railroad center with a steel plant, had its genesis in a ferry operated across the Little Calumet River between 1836 and 1842 by George Dolton and J. C. Matthews.

HARVEY (R), 19 *m.* (608 alt., 16,374 pop.), is a manufacturing city, its industrial east side begrimed with smoke, its residential west side bordered by Kickapoo Grove, a forest preserve. When Turlington W. Harvey, Chicago lumberman and capitalist, bought this site in 1889, it was swamp and prairie, with one factory, a hotel, and a few dwellings. Two years later the village of Harvey had several factories, new schools and churches, and 5,000 inhabitants. Diesel engines, highway machinery, ranges and stoves, and railroad equipment are manufactured.

PHOENIX (L), 19.8 *m.* (605 alt., 3,033 pop.), a residential outgrowth of Harvey, is economically dependent on the factories of the latter city.

At 20.5 *m.* is a junction with US 6 (*see Tour* 14).

The 250-acre WASHINGTON PARK RACE TRACK (*racing in Aug. and Sept.; adm.* $1 *and* $2), 23 *m.*, is the annual scene of the American Derby; the CLUBHOUSE (R) is a reproduction of Mount Vernon.

HOMEWOOD, 23.3 *m.* (659 alt., 3,227 pop.), a residential suburb that adjoins Washington Park on the south, was originally named Hartford for James Hart, who platted the site in 1852.

On a 430-acre farm (L) is the GLENWOOD MANUAL TRAINING SCHOOL (*open*), 23.8 *m.*, established for underprivileged boys between the ages of 8 and 16. The institution is maintained by tuition fees and private philanthropy. The 345 pupils, enrolled on the recommendation of juvenile courts and social service agencies, receive grade school instruction and military and vocational training. There are 12 dormitories, a chapel, a schoolhouse, a clubhouse, a dining hall, and an administration building.

The route climbs the Valparaiso Moraine, 25 *m.*, which it crosses here at its widest point (15 miles). Deposited by the Wisconsin glacier, it is one of the largest terminal moraines in the world. It extends crescent-wise to the south shore of Lake Michigan, rising to a height of 200 feet above the lake plain on which Chicago is built. In contrast with the table-like lake plain, the moraine consists of low hills and marshy depressions.

CHICAGO HEIGHTS, 27.5 *m.* (694 alt., 22,321 pop.), is built on the comparatively high ground of the Valparaiso Moraine. In the days of exploration and settlement, the site was a meeting point for travelers from the east and south. Here the Hubbard Trail from Vincennes to Fort Dearborn crossed the Sauk Trail, along which the Indians had for generations traveled between their hunting grounds and the fur post and garrison at Detroit. The Sauk Trail became the westward artery for trappers, soldiers, settlers, and the mail. Covered wagons traversed it to lands beyond the Mississippi; the forty-niners followed it to California; New Englanders hurried over it to settle Kansas with abolitionists; and Negro slaves used it to escape from Missouri to Indiana.

The settlement at the junction of the trails became known as Thorn Grove in the 1830's. German settlers renamed it Bloom in 1849, honoring Robert Bluehm, a German patriot executed at Vienna in 1848. The present name and industrial character of Chicago Heights date from 1890 when the Chicago Heights Land Association induced manufacturers to establish plants here, bringing with them hundreds of workmen and their families. Chicago Heights was the earliest and, for a time, the most important of the steel-making communities of the Chicago district. But the blast furnaces have since been transferred to newer centers on Lake Michigan, reducing local production to steel fabrication.

Industrial plants and millworkers' houses occupy the east side of the city; the west side consists of the more spacious residences of mill officials and Chicago commuters. Many plants, including OWENS-ILLINOIS GLASS FACTORY, welcome visitors; others—among them INLAND STEEL, AMERICAN MANGANESE, and COLUMBIA TOOL AND STEEL PLANTS—owing to inherent occupational dangers, may be visited by special permission only.

Chicago Heights is at the junction with US 30 (*see Tour* 12).

SOUTH CHICAGO HEIGHTS, 29.7 *m.* (708 alt., 1,691 pop.), is a residential suburb of comfortable houses whose occupants—largely of Polish, German, and Italian ancestry—are employed in Chicago Heights industries. West of the community is the SAUK TRAIL FOREST PRESERVE.

STEGER, 30 *m.* (712 alt., 2,985 pop.), was named for John V. Steger around whose piano factory the town was built. The factory (L), a series of three-story brick structures, sections of which are closed, is now used for the manufacture of radio cabinets.

CRETE, 31.2 *m.* (720 alt., 1,429 pop.), a farm center and residential community, was platted in 1849 by William Wood, who operated a tavern here for travelers on the Chicago-Vincennes Road. Wide-girthed trees line the streets. In spring, front yards are bright and fragrant with lilacs. Crete is in the public spotlight each September when the season opens at the LINCOLN FIELD RACE TRACK (L), 34.5 m.

In the late 1820's droves of hogs owned by Gurdon S. Hubbard roamed the prairie between Crete and Danville. At intervals Hubbard and a crew of what might be termed "pigboys" rounded up the half-wild animals and drove them to Chicago where they were slaughtered.

BEECHER, 38.2 m. (723 alt., 772 pop.), named for Henry Ward Beecher (1813-87), noted divine and leader of the anti-slavery forces, provides retail facilities for the surrounding farm country. The village was platted in 1870 as a shipping point on the Chicago and Eastern Illinois Railway, then in construction. On Beecher's east side is the SHADY LAWN GOLF CLUB (18 holes; 50c weekdays, $1 Sun. and holidays).

TOUR 2

(MILWAUKEE, WIS.)—ZION—WAUKEGAN—WILMETTE—
CHICAGO; STATE 42.

Wisconsin Line to Chicago, 53 m.

Hard-surfaced roadbed throughout.
The Chicago & North Western Ry. and the Chicago, North Shore and Milwaukee R. R. (electric) parallel the route throughout.
Ample accommodations.

BETWEEN THE Wisconsin Line and Chicago, State 42 (Sheridan Road) follows the shore of Lake Michigan, which stretches toward the eastern horizon. Traversing a brief agricultural area, the route crosses the heavy industrial region of Waukegan and North Chicago and, winding and dipping through thickly forested sections, proceeds south past Chicago's wealthy North Shore suburbs.

State 42, a continuation of Wisconsin 42, crosses the Wisconsin Line, 0 m., 8 miles S. of Kenosha, Wisconsin (see Wisconsin Guide).

WINTHROP HARBOR, 1 m. (598 alt., 661 pop.), grew out of the acquisition in 1892 of 2,700 acres of dairy farm land by the

Winthrop Harbor and Dock Company, which planned to develop a harbor and establish an industrial town. With the collapse of the plan, dairying continued as the chief occupation of the community, and today its sole industrial plant is an ultra-modern dairy near the North Western station.

ZION, 3 *m.* (633 alt., 5,991 pop.), was founded by a man who believed the world to be flat despite his having taken a trip around it. The town enforces one of the most stringent sets of blue laws in the country.

In 1899 Chicago real estate offices were buzzing with rumors of a big land deal on the North Shore. On the night that marked the end of the nineteenth century, the man behind the deal revealed himself as John Alexander Dowie (1847-1907), Scottish faith-healer who, four years before, had founded the Christian Catholic Apostolic Church. He announced his plan for the city of Zion, a community where the tenets of that church would govern every phase of life. "Our motto," affirmed Dowie, "the unalterable and unassailable truth that where God rules, man prospers . . . our object, the establishment of the rule of God in every department of the government."

To the hastily erected town flocked hundreds of Dowie's followers, and within a few years Zion's population reached 10,000. Although Dowie planned the physical features of the town before a spade of earth was turned, he ignored the economic structure, except to establish a lace factory, for the operation of which he imported skilled workers from Nottingham, England. The real industrialization of Zion was largely the work of Wilbur Glenn Voliva, who succeeded Dowie upon his death in 1907.

Under Voliva, Zion has had a roller-coaster existence. Bankrupt in 1906, redeemed from bankruptcy in 1910, booming with prosperity in the 1920's, into receivership again in 1933, Zion had not, until recently, modified the essential structure of theocratic government. The church, under the tight control of its overseer, owned all industries and commercial establishments but one. The use and sale of liquor, tobacco, playing cards, oysters, pork, and clams are prohibited. Through a special ruling obtained from the Illinois Commerce Commission, no trains stop in Zion on Sunday. In 1939 Voliva lost his control as overseer; titles to real estate were being transferred to individuals; and other modifications of the theocratic government and managed economy seemed imminent.

In ZION AUDITORIUM, 27th St. and Enoch Ave., a 3-story, gray stone building, an elaborate Passion Play is given annually (*Sundays, Palm Sunday through June,* 3 *P.M.*). Research for the settings was done by the play's conductor, who made a special trip to Palestine for that purpose. ZION HOME, on Elijah Avenue, a gray frame, block-long building erected in 1904, serves as a hotel and divine healing home. A ground-floor porch extends along the entire front exposure, and an upper porch in the center of the structure separates a belfry and a short, square, box-like tower. A green Moorish turret, supported by pillars, guards the southern end of the building. Zion Home, the only available eating place on Sunday, strictly observes the ban on oysters, clams, and "swine's flesh," offering for the latter a substitute called "Zion beef bacon." The square, gray frame ZION ADMINISTRATION BUILDING, across the street from the Home, has a gray-green roof with gables, and is faced by a porticoed entrance. The building houses the offices of Zion Industries, Inc., and serves as the general administrative quarters for the town.

The ZION LACE INDUSTRIES PLANT (*open only to those affiliated with the trade*), on 27th Street, is the sole Zion industry operated by outsiders. It was acquired by the Marshall Field Company of Chicago following the bankruptcy of 1906.

At 5.5 *m.* is a junction with a graveled road.

Left on this road is the entrance to DUNES PARK (*adm.* 10c), 0.5 *m.*, 1,500 acres of duneland along three and a half miles of beach. This typical dune region, with pine and oak woods, cactus, juniper, and bearberry clinging to windblown sandhills, has been kept in its natural state.

WAUKEGAN (Ind., fort or trading post), 10 *m.* (669 alt., 33,499 pop.), the seat of Lake County, is on the site of an Indian village that was known to seventeenth-century explorers. La Salle and Hennepin are reported to have recommended the establishment of a trading post in the village. The post, listed on eighteenth-century maps as Little Fort because of the small stockade that the French erected, remained a minor French outpost until about 1760. Potawatomi continued to occupy the Little Fort region long after the area became part of the United States (1783). Pioneers who would have attempted settlement were restrained by an Act of Congress and an Indian treaty that forbade the entry of white men until after August 1836, and, in turn, provided for the evacuation of Indians from the territory before that date.

Thomas Jenkins of Chicago, anticipating the departure of the Potawatomi, came to Little Fort in 1835 and set up a general store. The decayed timbers of the old French fort were still visible near what is now the intersection of Water Street and Sheridan Road; for that reason the flourishing settlement that arose around Jenkins' establishment retained the traditional name.

Little Fort superseded Libertyville as county seat in 1841. As totaled several years later the community had "three commodious public houses, seven stores, two blacksmith shops, one chair and cabinet factory, one pier, and a second being constructed, and two brickyards." Designated as a United States port of entry in 1846, Little Fort became the chief outlet for the region's abundant furs, hides, pork, oats, wheat, and wood. When it was incorporated as a village in 1849, the inhabitants voted to change the town's name to Waukegan. A decade later, caught up in the same expansion that boomed Chicago, Waukegan was organized as a city.

The shops and residences of Waukegan are on a bluff overlooking Lake Michigan. The lowlands between the base of the bluff and the waterline of the city harbor are jammed with factories that back the piers and railroads. Here are produced gas, tool steel, locks, chemicals, machinery, sausage, babbitt, envelopes, asbestos products, outboard motors, refrigerating units, ornamental and industrial steel fences, ignition contacts, and pharmaceuticals. Coal, coke, and raw materials comprise the bulk of the cargoes landed at Waukegan.

On April 2, 1860, Abraham Lincoln visited Waukegan and spoke at Dickinson Hall. His speech here was the only one he did not finish. While addressing the audience of 400 people, he was interrupted by a fire alarm from outside. One of his listeners arose and stated his belief that the alarm was a Democratic plot to break up the meeting. However, the uneasiness among the people continued and Lincoln finally stopped and said, "Well, gentlemen, let us all go, as there really seems to be a fire, and help to put it out."

NORTH CHICAGO, 12 *m.* (673 alt., 8,466 pop.), and Waukegan constitute a continuous industrial area with 65 diversified industries manufacturing more than 200 commodities. In North Chicago, State 42 is the main business street, along which are the more important shops and restaurants and the City Hall. Along the lake-shore east of the business district is Foss PARK (*May* 30-*Sept.* 15; *camp sites* 50c *a night or* $2 *a week, including stoves, tables, chairs, and running water*), a 34-acre recreational tract. The stretch of wooded bluffs and sandy beach has complete playground equipment, with facilities for boating, tennis, baseball, dancing, and swimming.

From the FANSTEEL METALLURGICAL CORPORATION PLANT, 2200 Sheridan Rd., a long, two-storied brick building of modern industrial design, 63 sit-down strikers were driven by tear gas in 1937. Two years later, in March 1939, the U. S. Supreme Court, by reversing an order of the National Labor Relations Board that the strikers be rehired, ruled, in effect, that sit-down strikes are illegal.

The GREAT LAKES NAVAL TRAINING STATION, 13.3 *m.* (9 *to sunset; guides at entrance gates*), only major naval unit in the Middle West, is one of four in the United States. In 1937, 2,943 recruits, ranging in years from 18 to 25, trained here. About 245 men leave the station each month, after 12 weeks of intensive training, for assignment to ships or naval trade schools. The station was first designed to accommodate 1,500, but during the World War (1918) the area and structures were increased to receive and train 50,000 men. Closed for some time after the war, it was reopened in July 1935.

The station is in a wooded area, an excellent setting for the Colonial style of its architecture. The grounds cover 507 acres, with

117 buildings, including barracks, marine hospital, field house, swimming pool, bowling alleys, auditorium, and library. Dress parade is held during the summer months on Wednesday, at 3 P.M., with music by the Great Lakes Band. The HOSTESS HOUSE (*open to public*) contains a restaurant and rest rooms. The Navy Day celebration, October 27, is the station's chief "show" day.

At 13.6 *m.* is a junction with a paved road, reached by a sub-pass.

Left into this sub-pass; R. on the road to the VETERANS ADMINISTRATION FACILITY HOSPITAL (*2-4 Tues., Thurs., Sat., Sun., and holidays*), 0.6 *m.* The hospital, maintained and operated by the Veterans' Administration of the Federal Government, is for the care of veterans afflicted with mental illness necessitating hospital care. In a wooded area of 590 landscaped acres, the hospital is an almost self-sufficient unit, with its own slaughter house, laundry and power house.

The entrance, 14.6 *m.,* to ARDEN SHORE, a year 'round recuperative center operated by the Gads Hill settlement of Chicago for underprivileged mothers and children of the settlement neighborhood, also leads to the THORNE DONNELLY EXPERIMENTAL RADIO STATION W9TZ (*private*), on Mr. Donnelly's estate.

In June of each year scientists, amateur radio operators, and owners of amateur stations gather as Mr. Donnelly's guests for what they call a "hamfest," to interchange ideas and discuss matters pertaining to the development of radio. The station was in direct contact with Commander Eugene F. McDonald, Arctic explorer, on his last polar expedition, and was one of the key stations in the pick-up for the McMillan and Byrd expeditions.

LAKE BLUFF, 15.6 *m.* (683 alt., 1,452 pop.), is the most northern of the North Shore suburbs, separated by the Great Lakes Naval Station from the nearby industrial districts of North Chicago and Waukegan.

Lake Bluff first became generally known in 1874, when it was chosen as a camp-meeting ground by a group of Methodist ministers and laymen. A tabernacle in the campground was the scene of an important State W.C.T.U. convention in 1881 and of a conference of the Prohibition Party in 1885. The campgrounds and buildings were disposed of in 1898, but residents exhibit as relics garden benches made of the tabernacle wood.

LAKE FOREST, 18 *m.* (713 alt., 6,554 pop.), is known as the wealthiest of the North Shore suburbs. Magnificent estates, many surrounded by high iron fences, border both sides of State 42. Large groves of timber outline beautifully landscaped lawns; statues, formal gardens, pavilions, and stone benches are placed with an eye to beauty and functional use; occasionally a tennis court or swimming pool is visible from the road. The architecture of the costly homes, many silhouetted against the blue waters of Lake Michigan, ranges from the elaborate pre-World War styles to the straight-line modernity of Frank Lloyd Wright.

Lake Forest was first settled in 1835. Deerpath Avenue, once an actual deer and buffalo path leading to the lake, made a convenient portage track to the Des Plaines River and was a thoroughfare for trappers, traders, and explorers in early days. Green Bay Road, west of the North Western tracks, was once an Indian trail to the Green Bay region. In 1856, two years after the railroad went through, a company of Chicago businessmen bought 1,300 acres of land and planned the town. David Hotchkiss, a St. Louis landscape architect, laid it out, making use of the beauty of the deep ravines and wooded bluffs. The winding streets through which Sheridan Road twists are part of his handiwork.

Fifty-two acres were reserved for school purposes and every alternate lot was assigned as an endowment for LAKE FOREST COLLEGE, Sheridan Rd. and Deerpath Ave. The college is divided into two campuses; the most outstanding building on the North Campus, at Deerpath Avenue, is of ivy-covered red stone, with a red roof; the South Campus, a few blocks away, comprises a group of gray stone and red and yellow brick buildings, set among handsome trees and well-kept lawns. The first unit of the college, a preparatory school for boys, LAKE FOREST ACADEMY, 677 E. Rosemary Rd., was opened in 1857. The second unit, a school for girls, FERRY HALL, 541 N. Mayflower Rd., was opened in 1869. The coeducational college, opened in 1876, provides higher education for graduates of the two lower schools. In 1925 the Academy and Ferry Hall withdrew from the college and became independently controlled.

Across Sheridan Road from the college stands the PRESBYTERIAN CHURCH, organized in 1859 in connection with the college. The bituminous limestone used in the construction of the present building, erected in 1871, was salvaged after the Chicago fire from the Second Presbyterian Church in that city. The PUBLIC LIBRARY, 360 Deerpath Ave., of pink Holland brick and white stone, won the 1931 Craftmanship award of the Chicago Architects Club. The building is surmounted with a large glass dome that serves as an effective skylight. North two blocks from Deerpath on Western Avenue is MARKET SQUARE, a group of stores housed in Elizabethan styled buildings surrounding a village green.

At the intersection of Sheridan and Westleigh Rds. is the entrance (R) to the grounds of SACRED HEART ACADEMY and BARAT COLLEGE. The preparatory school and liberal arts college operate in connection with a convent, vicariate headquarters for the order. The red stone main building, all but hidden from the road by trees, dates from 1904.

FORT SHERIDAN, 21.1 m. (*grounds open to public during day*), a United States Army post, consists of about 725 acres of wooded bluffs rising in places 100 feet above Lake Michigan. The fort was used as a camp during the Spanish-American War, and 3,000 officers were trained here during the World War. For two years after the war the post was given over to the rehabilitation of wounded soldiers; thousands passed through the hospital and received vocational training. In addition to serving as an Army post, Fort Sheridan is now used to train reserve officers, CMTC recruits, and ROTC members during the summer months.

HIGHLAND PARK, 24.1 *m.* (691 alt., 12,203 pop.), one of the largest residential suburbs of the North Shore, stands on the site of two Potawatomi villages. White settlement began with the construction of the Green Bay House (1834), a tavern on the Chicago-Milwaukee post road, now Waukegan Road. The name Port Clinton was used in 1850, during the city's brief career as a lake port. The railroad company named its station Highland Park in 1854, and the town was incorporated under that name in 1867. It was laid out to take full advantage of the natural beauty of its lake shore, bluffs, woods, and ravines. Cottages of modified Colonial and English designs are features of the residential districts.

On Sheridan Road, opposite the entrance to Lake Shore Country Club, is an INDIAN TRAIL MARKER, a bent tree that the Potawatomi twisted as a sapling to mark one of their trails.

The DEERFIELD-SHIELDS TOWNSHIP HIGH SCHOOL, Vine and St. John's Sts., is an L-shaped, red brick building, with white trim around its windows. The functional design of the original building has been duplicated in the large annex, which forms the north portion of the ell. Each year the students of the vocational training department build a five- or six-room house, which is sold to finance a similar undertaking the following year.

In Highland Park along the highway (R) is RAVINIA PARK (*adm. 75c, reserved seats in the roofed pavilion 75c add.; free parking*), long the summer music center for the Chicago area. Like a faded diva, Ravinia has seen great days. Begun as a privately operated amusement park, it was taken over in 1910 by North Shore residents who promoted a series of symphony concerts each summer. After 1916 the burden of sponsorship was largely assumed by Louis Eckstein, Chicago real estate dealer and mail order executive, who changed the programs from symphony to grand opera. Audiences of 10,000 were common, but the policy of maintaining popular prices while presenting top-rank opera stars resulted in a deficit each year. Year after year Eckstein met the deficits, which often exceeded $100,000, but in 1931 the burden became too great and the programs were discontinued. Five years later the park was reopened with a series of more modestly budgeted symphony concerts, which were repeated in 1937 and 1938.

GLENCOE, 27.9 *m.* (673 alt., 6,295 pop.), was first settled about 1836, and was incorporated as a village in 1869. The name is a compound of "glen," suggestive of the site, and "Coe," the maiden name of the wife of Walter S. Gurnee, one of the founders. The GURNEE HOUSE (*private*), a three-story yellow brick building with elaborate porches and gables, still stands on Green Bay Road, opposite the North Western station. It was built in the 1870's. Glencoe's public schools are rated among modern educators as models of progressive teaching. The method of study guidance draws a close parallel between the subjects studied and the daily life of the community.

WINNETKA, 31 m. (651 alt, 12,166 pop.), a suburban village incorporated in 1869, also is known for its public school system. The Winnetka schools were organized in 1919 under the direction of Carleton Washburne, superintendent. The program advocates self-reliance and allows children a great deal more freedom than is customary in the average school system. The child studies arithmetic and spelling by himself, sets his own pace, checks his own work, and receives aid from his teacher only when necessary. Social ideals are obtained through group activities, during which the pupil translates many of his studies into action. The child thus in large part educates himself, and his own goal card, which he keeps and on which he records his progress and social attitudes, becomes more important to him than the record kept by his teacher.

The NORTH SHORE COUNTRY DAY SCHOOL is a private organization for children from kindergarten through high school. It occupies the former Garland Mansion, 310 Center St., and Leicester Hall, 301 Forest Ave., the latter built in the 1880's to house a preparatory academy for the original Chicago University.

The HADLEY CORRESPONDENCE SCHOOL FOR THE BLIND has headquarters at 584 Lincoln St. Organized and incorporated in 1922, it offers extension courses to the blind free of charge. The school was founded by William A. and Jessie H. Hadley, and is conducted by the former, now blind, a prominent educator once connected with the Chicago public schools. Directors of education for the blind throughout the country make up the advisory board, and the school is supported by donations and a community chest.

On Tower Road, L. of the highway, is the WATER TOWER (1893) of the community-owned and operated water plant. The plant, at the base of the steep bluff on which the tower stands, is integrated with the municipal electric plant, resulting in numerous economies in the operation of both.

KENILWORTH, 33.2 m. (615 alt., 2,501 pop.), is named for Sir Walter Scott's novel, and many of the streets in its hilly residential section commemorate places or characters in the book. In the cloistered yard of the CHURCH OF THE HOLY COMFORTER (Episcopal), 333 Warwick Rd., is the GRAVE OF EUGENE FIELD. The remains of the "children's poet" were brought here from Graceland Cemetery, Chicago, in 1925. Those of Mrs. Field, his survivor by more than forty years, were buried beside him in 1936.

No MAN'S LAND, 33.7 *m.*, offers a brief and sharp contrast to the remainder of the North Shore. Brightly colored stucco buildings with Spanish names provide commercial recreation—dancing, drinking, dining, and movies. Access to the lake and beach, exclusive elsewhere in the North Shore, may be had here for a nominal price. This bright spot, which on a summer's day contrasts strikingly with the quiet of the residential suburbs, is so named because a strip of lake shore frontage was not included in the corporate limits of either Kenilworth or Wilmette.

WILMETTE, 34.7 *m.* (614 alt., 15,233 pop.), the largest of the residential North Shore suburbs, was named for its first white settler, Antoine Ouilmette, a French-Canadian whose Indian wife received the land under a Government treaty in 1829.

Visible along the North Shore from a distance of several miles is the graceful white dome of the BAHA'I HOUSE OF WORSHIP (*visiting,* 10-4 *daily; open meetings,* 3:30 *Sun.*), R. of the highway at Linden Avenue. Designed by the late Louis J. Bouregeois, the temple is the sole North American house of worship of the faith founded in the 1860's by Baha'u'llah (1817-92), a Persian religious leader. The Baha'i faith correlates the major religions with the tenet that God has periodically revealed, through such prophets as Buddha, Zoroaster, Moses, Christ, and Mohammed, such of the truth as man has been capable of assimilating. Members of the faith believe that Baha'u'llah was the latest of these prophets, or "Manifestations." The unity of all religions and peoples is taught, as well as universal education, world peace, the equality of the sexes, and a universal language; a simple life of service is advocated. There is no clergy; teachers of the faith work without remuneration; no formal services are held; contributions are accepted from members only, and only from those members who are free of debt. The faith spread to America in the early 1900's through the teachings of the son of Baha'u'llah, Abdu'l-Baha (1844-1921), who laid the cornerstone of the temple. Actual construction was not begun until 1930.

The building, in process of construction, employs the elements of many architectural styles, blended into a harmonious pattern that is distinguished for its lightness and grace. A nine-sided structure, it rests upon nine caissons of steel and concrete; the nine sides of the clerestory and of the dome are staggered upon the nine sides of the base. Glass, mounted in metal, is used extensively, both in the dome and clerestory and in the lower part of the building. When completed, the steel and concrete of the structure and the metallic forms that hold the glass will be concealed by delicate traceries in molded materials that will overlay the exterior walls and dome and cover the interior as finely traced grills. The design of the ornamentation is geometric; the symbols employed are largely astronomical. The color will shade from white on the dome to light buff at the base.

From the auditorium, beneath the great dome, open nine chambers separated by nine hallways. These smaller rooms, which will be used for study and meditation, are comparable to the chapels of a cathedral. The numbers nine and nineteen, recurrent throughout the structure, illustrate, according to a Baha'i publication, the "basic principle of Unity—nine being the number of perfection, containing in itself the completion of each perfect number cycle, and nineteen representing the Union of God and man, as manifested in life, civilization and all things."

In the financing of the temple, the East has contributed to the West, the coppers of impoverished Persians supplementing the generous gifts of affluent Americans. Eventually the grounds will be landscaped in the Eastern manner, and the temple will be the center of a group of Baha'i buildings which will include a hospital and a school.

EVANSTON, 40 *m.* (603 alt., 63,338 pop.) (*see Evanston*).

Points of Interest: Northwestern University, Gross Point Lighthouse, the Cradle, and others.

CHICAGO, 53 *m.* (598 alt., 3,376,438 pop.) (*see Chicago*).

Points of Interest: Chicago Board of Trade Building, Union Stock Yards, Field Museum of Natural History, Art Institute of Chicago, Museum of Science and Industry, Adler Planetarium, Shedd Aquarium, University of Chicago, and others.

Chicago is at the junctions with State 1 (*see Tour* 1), US 41 (*see Tour* 2A), US 12 (*see Tour* 9), US 14 (*see Tour* 10), US 20 (*see Tour* 11), US 330 (*see Tour* 12A), US 66 (*see Tour* 17), and the Illinois Waterway (*see Tour* 22).

TOUR 3

(MILWAUKEE, WIS.)—CHICAGO—HAMMOND, IND; US 41

Wisconsin Line to Indiana, 64 *m.*

Concrete road-bed throughout; four lanes divided by parkway.
The Chicago & North Western Ry.; the Chicago, Milwaukee, St. Paul and Pacific R. R.; and the Chicago, North Shore and Milwaukee R. R. (electric) parallel the highway at varying distances throughout.
Limited accommodations.

US 14 crosses the Wisconsin Line, 0 *m.*, 38 miles S. of Milwaukee, Wisconsin (*see Wisconsin Guide*).

Compared with State 42 (*see Tour* 2), the lake-shore route to the east, or US 45 (*see Tour* 3), the scenic road to the west, US 41 is an uninteresting express highway. Such charm as it may possess lies more in its clean-cut lines and freedom from dangerous intersections than in beauty of scene or history of settlement. It is the direct through traffic highway between Milwaukee and Chicago.

Points of scenic or historic interest in the region are largely along the highways that parallel US 41 to the right and left. Yet the route is not devoid of aesthetic appeal. South of the Wisconsin Line the valley of the Des Plaines is followed for 10 miles. Then the road rises to the upland to sweep over gentle grades from the crests of which broad pasture lands and vast estates stretch to the wooded horizon. Southward for 30 miles, the embanked road runs down the center of Skokie Valley, until recent decades a continuous marsh that resisted settlement. Today much of the valley remains in wild lands, but some sections have been drained, and small suburban communities or rich, black farm lands have replaced quaking bogs and peat beds. Near Chicago, country clubs and golf courses are numerous.

Entering Chicago from the north, the highway quickly reaches the lake shore, and follows outer drives through lake shore parks, past Chicago's skyline, to the intersection of Michigan Ave. and Jackson Blvd., in the heart of the city.

CHICAGO, 49.5 *m.* (598 alt., 3,376,438 pop.) (*see Chicago*).

Points of Interest: Chicago Board of Trade Building, Union Stock Yards, Field Museum of Natural History, Art Institute of Chicago, Museum of Science and Industry, Adler Planetarium, Shedd Aquarium, University of Chicago, and others.

At Chicago are junctions with State 1 (*see Tour* 1), State 42 (*see Tour* 2), US 12 (*see Tour* 9), US 14 (*see Tour* 10), US 20 (*see Tour* 11), US 330 (*see Tour* 12A), US 66 (*see Tour* 17), and the Illinois Waterway (*see Tour* 22).

Southward from the Loop US 41 follows lake shore drives past several parks and crosses the Indiana Line, 64 *m.*, at Hammond, Indiana (*see Indiana Guide*).

TOUR 4

Hard-surfaced roadbed throughout.
The route is paralleled by the Minneapolis, St. Paul & Sault Ste. Marie Ry.
between the Wisconsin Line and Des Plaines; the Illinois Central R. R. between Kankakee and Effingham; the Baltimore & Ohio R. R. between Louisville and Norris City; the Cleveland, Cincinnati, Chicago & St. Louis Ry. between Norris City and Vienna; and the Chicago, Burlington & Quincy R. R. between Vienna and Metropolis.
Usual accommodations throughout.

US 45, longest highway in Illinois, extends from lake-studded dairy lands in the north, past suburbs of Chicago, through cities and towns and interminable prairie cornfields, across the coal mining district of southern Illinois, through the wooded hills of the Ozarks, to the historic valley of the Ohio.

Section a. Wisconsin Line to Kankakee, 103 m.

BETWEEN THE Wisconsin Line and Kankakee US 45 crosses the rolling hills of the Valparaiso and associated moraines, the most vigorously glaciated part of Illinois. In the extreme north is the Chain-O'-Lakes of the Fox River system, a summer playground of Chicago; along the Des Plaines River are the forest preserves of Cook County; throughout are dairy farms producing for the urban market. In summer the green meadows and woodlands, and the ripening fields of hay, oats, corn, barley, and alfalfa are varied with the black and white of Holstein herds. In winter snow covers the scene; cows and crops are moved into the spacious red barns and tall silos that dominate the farmsteads, and the process of producing Chicago's milk goes on.

US 45 crosses the Wisconsin Line, 0 m., 14 miles S. of Union Grove, Wisconsin (see Wisconsin Guide).

MILBURN, 6 m. (744 alt., 155 pop.), a century-old village, was so named by Scottish settlers. At the principal intersection is a two-story brick store (R), built in the 1840's.

Right from the old store on a graveled road to HASTINGS LAKE, 1 m., surrounded by a 267-acre tract in which the Chicago Y.M.C.A. maintains three summer camps. Pheasant and other small game abound; the lake is stocked with fish.

201

South of Milburn the highway sweeps up and down easy grades through high rolling country.

On the shores of DRUCE LAKE (*boating and swimming*), 9 *m.*, are 300 cabins, cottages, and year-round homes; southward is the summer colony of LEWIN PARK (*cottages for rent*), 10 *m.* In the vicinity of the latter are many INDIAN MOUNDS, none of which has been excavated.

GAGES LAKE PICNIC GROUNDS (*adm. 50c per car, including use of grounds and bathhouses; camp tents $7 a week, cabins $10; restaurant*), 10.3 *m.*, is a privately owned 12-acre tract adjoining Gages Lake (L). In summer the grounds are managed by students from the University of Illinois.

At 11.7 *m.* is a junction with State 20.

Right on State 20 to GRAYS LAKE, 1.8 *m.* (799 alt., 1,120 pop.), named for the lake at its western edge (*free swimming and fishing; boats, cabins, and cottages at moderate rates*). Local industries include cement plants, planing mills, a gelatin factory, a condensery, and a corn and pea cannery.

At 16.5 *m.* is a junction with State 63.

Left on State 63 to the SERBIAN ORTHODOX ST. SAVA MONASTERY (*grounds open*), 0.8 *m.*, diocesan headquarters of the Serbian Orthodox Church in Canada and the United States. The monastery was established in 1923 by Bishop Mardary (1890-1935), a Montenegrin cleric. The CHAPEL (*open to public*), a cement stucco structure of Russian and Byzantine styles, is topped by a central dome surrounded by 12 spires, symbolic of Christ and His disciples. Behind the chapel are outdoor STATIONS OF THE CROSS. Bordering a nearby stream are grounds where the congregation picnics. Clad in peasant garb, they sing native songs and perform old-world dances to the accompaniment of odd musical instruments.

LIBERTYVILLE, 18 *m.* (698 alt., 3,791 pop.), originally known as Independence Grove, was given its present name in 1837 when the post office was established. Indians, attracted by the mineral springs that dot the area, encamped annually near the settlement. Much of the forest in which they hunted remains uncut. Among the early purchasers of land in this vicinity was Daniel Webster (1782-1852), American orator and statesman. Wealthy Chicagoans later developed many estates on the surrounding wooded hills and fertile farm lands. Except for the employment offered by several small industries, most important of which is the FOULDS SPAGHETTI PLANT on E. Church Street, Libertyville is supported by the trade of estate residents and summer vacationists. On the eastern border of the city is the BURTON R. HERRING LOG CABIN (*private*), built of cypress imported from the owner's native Sweden at a reputed cost of $100,000.

Right from Libertyville on State 176 is MUNDELEIN, 2.8 *m.* (676 alt., 1,011 pop.), formerly named Area, a word formed by the initial letters of the Sheldon School of Business Administration's motto: "Ability, Reliability, Endurance, and Action." When the school buildings were bought by the Catholic seminary, the town was renamed to honor George Cardinal Mundelein, Archbishop of Chicago. At the center of the community is the Cardinal's titular church, SANTA MARIA DEL POPULO, a small brick structure of severe Colonial lines. At the south of Mundelein is DIAMOND LAKE (*boating, $1 a day, fishing, amusement park, 5 hotels, summer cottages*), which attracts hundreds of Chicago vacationists, and rivals the town's one industry, a shoe factory, as a source of income.

On 1,200 wooded acres bordering LAKE ST. MARY in the northern quarter of the town is ST. MARY OF THE LAKE SEMINARY (*grounds and chapel open to public 8-4 daily*), one of the most elaborate and carefully planned Roman Catholic theological seminaries in the world. The average enrollment is 300. Ranged on the beautifully landscaped grounds, site of the final session of the International Eucharistic Congress in 1926, are 12 brick and stone Colonial structures, designed by Joseph McCarty of Chicago, and built between 1920-35. At the center of the group is the CHAPEL (*all services private*), its refined Colonial lines modeled after those of a frame Protestant meetinghouse at Lyme, Connecticut, that Cardinal Mundelein admired as a boy. The interior is decorated in Renaissance style. Above the altar is a picture of the Holy Family by Francisco Zurbaran (1598-1662). The chapel is the gift of the late Edward Hines, Chicago lumberman, whose son, Edward Hines, Jr., killed in the World War, is entombed in a small chapel nearby.

South of the chapel are a LOURDES GROTTO and STATIONS OF THE CROSS. Beyond, ST. AUGUSTINE's BRIDGE affords a good view of vast flower beds, one of which depicts the Cardinal's coat-of-arms. The FEEHAN MEMORIAL LIBRARY, nearby, contains valuable incunabula. Among the seminary's collection of autographs are those of several saints, and those of the signers of the Constitution and the Declaration of Independence. Other important items are a numismatic collection and a series of medals struck by the popes. Adjoining the seminary grounds on the east is the BENEDICTINE CONVENT OF PERPETUAL ADORATION (*open to public 8-5 daily; services at 4:15*), in the chapel of which nuns kneel in constant prayer.

Large tracts in the vicinity of Libertyville were owned and developed by Samuel Insull, Chicago financier, until the collapse of his utilities empire. Immediately south of Libertyville is his former estate (R), HAWTHORNE FARM (*open; apply at caretaker's lodge*). The 4,445-acre estate, representing an investment of more than $3,000,000, was developed by Mr. Insull from a few acres purchased in 1903. On the farm, always operated at a loss, he pursued his hobby of raising pure-bred Swiss cattle and blooded Suffolk-Punch draft horses. The INSULL MANSION (*closed*), with its 101 acres of landscaped ground in the northeastern section of the tract, was erected in 1921. At its rear are sunken gardens, bird sanctuaries, and an immense swimming pool; to the north are the lodge and a greenhouse large enough to serve a good-sized town; to the south are three artificial lagoons, formerly graced by goldfish and swans. Emptied now of its regal furnishings, its doors and windows boarded up, the ornate French Riviera mansion, imposing relic of a fallen dynasty, broods over its deserted gardens. Following the collapse of Insull's empire, Hawthorne Farm, with the exception of the mansion and its immediate grounds, was partitioned into smaller estates and sold.

At 21 *m.* is a junction with State 59A.

Right on State 59A to the COUNTRYSIDE DEVELOPMENT, 4.5 *m.*,
a community sponsored and promoted by Samuel Insull. On the beautifully landscaped 2,000-acre tract are the homes of former executives and high-ranking
officials of the Insull interests. On an island in artificial 495-acre COUNTRYSIDE
LAKE is the $500,000 RESIDENCE OF SAMUEL INSULL, JR. (*private*). Nearby is
the COUNTRYSIDE GOLF COURSE (18 *holes, daily fee*).

HALFDAY, 23.8 *m.* (668 alt., 221 pop.), oldest settlement in Lake
County (1836), is a quiet village with a cluster of stores and lunchrooms.

WHEELING, 28.4 *m.* (650 alt., 467 pop.), dates back to a country
store established in 1830. Formerly a relay point on the Chicago-
Milwaukee stage route, the village is now a center for metropolitan
roadhouse entertainment.

Between Wheeling and Des Plaines, US 45—here known as the
Des Plaines River Road—parallels the Des Plaines forestways (L),
a strip of woodlands maintained as six COOK COUNTY FOREST PRE-
SERVES (*marked hiking trails and bridle paths; picnic facilities at short
intervals*). In these and nearby forest lands early explorers encountered
the Potawatomi. Several Indian mounds are preserved in the woodlands along the river. It was here that Father Marquette, traveling
up the Des Plaines from the Illinois to Lake Michigan, is presumed
to have first entered what is now Cook County. In PORTAGE GROVE
PRESERVE a huge rock imbedded in the river bank is designated as the
SITE OF MARQUETTE'S LANDING.

DES PLAINES, 36 *m.* (643 alt., 8,798 pop.), founded in the
1830's, was long called Rand, in honor of Socrates Rand, the first
settler. Its present name, that of the river flowing through the community, was adopted in 1869. A commuting and industrial suburb,
Des Plaines is widely known as the site of a Methodist encampment,
held annually since 1860 (*public welcome; summer hotel and cottages
at nominal rates; reservations should be made in advance*).

Des Plaines is at the junction with US 12 (*see Tour* 9) and US 14
(*see Tour* 10). South of Des Plaines By-Pass US 12 unites with US
45 for 23.5 miles.

At 41.2 *m.* is a junction with Lawrence Avenue.

Left on this paved road to an old INDIAN CEMETERY, 1.5 *m.*, maintained by
the Forest Preserve District of Cook County. About the size of a city lot, it
contains five graves of the Robinson family, Potawatomi who befriended the
whites during the 1820's and 1830's.

South of the junction with Lawrence Avenue, US 45 traverses the
western edge of the lake plain that early settlers found to be a vast
swamp, usually submerged during the spring months. Gravel dumps,
fruit stands, market gardens, switch tracks, smokestacks, barbecue
huts, and patches of farm land flank the highway. In close succession
are boom-time subdivisions, with unused sidewalks trailing off in high

weeds, rusty water plugs, ragged tree plantings, and empty apartment houses staring across the plain.

At 46.5 *m.* is the northern junction with US 20 and By-Pass US 20 (*see Tour* 11); southward, By-Pass US 20 unites with US 45 for 13 miles. At 49 *m.* is a junction with US 330 (*see Tour* 12A), and at 52 *m.* is a junction with US 34 (*see Tour* 13).

LA GRANGE, 52.5 *m.* (645 alt., 10,103 pop.), named for Marquis de Lafayette's homestead in France, was the first suburb to be developed along the Chicago, Burlington & Quincy Railroad. Cossitt Avenue, a principal east-west thoroughfare, commemorates W. D. Cossitt, who founded the village, and, following its incorporation in 1879, became its first president. The site was first settled, however, in the 1830's. The MASONIC ORPHANS HOME (*open to public*), on an 11-acre tract at 9th and Goodman Sts., cares for children between 3 and 18 years of age. They attend public schools, but receive special training in music and manual arts at the home.

At 54 *m.* is a junction with 55th Street.

Right on this paved road to a junction with Wolf Road, 1.6 *m.*; L. on Wolf Road to Plainfield Road, 2.2 *m.*; R. on Plainfield Road to the TIMBER TRAILS GOLF COURSE (18 *holes, daily fee*), 2.5 *m.* In the yard of the caretaker's house a boulder marks the LAST CAMPING PLACE OF THE POTAWATOMI IN COOK COUNTY.

At 55 *m.* is a junction with US 66 (*see Tour* 17).

US 45 crosses the DES PLAINES RIVER VALLEY, 57 *m.*, a gorge carved by the outpouring waters of Lake Michigan when glaciers dammed its northern outlet. Later, when the glaciers receded and the lake again emptied northward, the abandoned valley was appropriated by the Des Plaines River. This natural pass between the Great Lakes and the Mississippi River was used by Indians, explorers, and fur traders. The ILLINOIS AND MICHIGAN CANAL, an important factor in the development of the State, was built through the gorge in 1848; the same route serves the SANITARY AND SHIP CANAL, which in 1900 reversed the current of the Chicago River (*see Tour* 22). In addition to these waterways and the river, the valley contains three railways, the Santa Fe, the Alton, and the Chicago & Illinois Western.

Between the Des Plaines Valley and the Sag Valley, US 45 crosses the ARGONNE FOREST PRESERVE, another Cook County conservation and recreation area.

At 59.5 *m.* are junctions with By-Pass US 12 (*see Tour* 9) and By-Pass US 20 (*see Tour* 11).

US 45 crosses the CALUMET SAG CHANNEL, 61.5 *m.*, which enters the Sanitary and Ship Canal 5 miles west, carrying treated domestic and industrial wastes of the Calumet steel district.

At 62 *m.* the highway passes through the PALOS HILLS FOREST PRESERVE (*picnic facilities*), a favorite objective of Chicago hiking clubs. Its hills and valleys, carpeted in season with wild flowers, serve

TOUR 5

Indiana Line to Wisconsin Line, 81.5 *m.*

Roadbed hard-surfaced throughout; four lanes for 58 miles in the Chicago area, two lanes northward.
Complete recreational facilities at lake resorts; accommodations otherwise limited.

IN ITS southern section, US 12 skirts Chicago; its alternate, City US 12, passes through the Loop and rejoins the main route at Des Plaines, northwest of Chicago. Northward, the highway crosses the lake country that is one of the great city's summer playgrounds. The lakes, the only natural ones in Illinois except those along the rivers, lie in pockets in the rolling moraines of Lake and McHenry Counties. The hills, still largely forested, have all the beauty of spring and summer, the riotous colors of fall, and the bright white blanket of winter. Occasionally, a herd of dairy cows reveals the farming pursuits of the region, but little else varies the recreational aspect of the land.

US 12 crosses the Indiana Line, here the Chicago city limits, 0 *m.*, from Hammond, Indiana (*see Indiana Guide*), and proceeds northwest along Indianapolis Blvd. to Ewing Ave.; R. on Ewing Ave. to 95th St.; L. on 95th St.

At the intersection of 95th St. and Stony Island Ave., 4 *m.*, is the junction with US 330 (*see Tour* 12A). Here the route divides into City US 12 and By-Pass US 12.

Left (straight ahead) on By-Pass US 12 to a junction with US 45 (*see Tour* 3), 13.5 *m.;* R. on US 45, with which By-Pass US 12 is united for 23.5 miles, to Des Plaines (*see below*), at the western junction with City US 12, 37 *m.*

City US 12 proceeds north along Stony Island Ave. to the intersection of Michigan Blvd. with Jackson Blvd., the center of Chicago. CHICAGO, 16.5 *m.* (598 alt., 3,376,438 pop.) (*see Chicago*).

Points of Interest: Chicago Board of Trade Building, Union Stock Yards, Field Museum of Natural History, Art Institute of Chicago, Museum of Science and Industry, Adler Planetarium, Shedd Aquarium, University of Chicago and others.

In Chicago are junctions with State 1 (*see Tour* 1), State 42 (*see Tour* 2), US 41 (*see Tour* 2A), US 14 (*see Tour* 10), US 20 (*see*

Tour 11), US 330 (*see Tour* 12A), US 66 (*see Tour* 17), and the Illinois Waterway (*see Tour* 22).

North on Michigan Blvd. to Lake Shore Drive; R. (straight ahead) on Lake Shore Drive to Foster Ave.; L. (straight ahead) on Foster Ave. to Northwest Hwy.; R. on Northwest Hwy. to PARK RIDGE, 33.8 *m.* (658 alt., 10,417 pop.) (*see Tour* 10), which is at a junction with US 14 (*see Tour* 10).

DES PLAINES, 38 *m.* (643 alt., 8,798 pop.) (*see Tour* 3), is at the junction with By-Pass US 12 (*see below*) and US 45 (*see Tour* 3).

Between Des Plaines and Volo US 12 is known as Rand Road, named for Socrates Rand, pioneer land-holder along the Des Plaines River, who was largely responsible for the routing of the road. The path followed an Indian trail between what is now Chicago and Janesville, Wisconsin. The highway was the principal northwestern road in 1845, and was known as the United States Mail Route.

At 54 *m.,* on the southern shore of LAKE ZURICH, is a junction with State 63.

Right on State 63 to the village of LAKE ZURICH, 1 *m.* (873 alt., 368 pop.), which has been a summer resort for a hundred years. In 1836 Seth Paine, a Chicago merchant, purchased a lake-shore tract, erected a house, hired tenant farmers, and began a real estate development. His first step was to change the name from Cedar Lake to Lake Zurich, which he hoped would suggest the beauties of the famed Swiss resort. This change seems to have been warranted, for Lake Zurich has become a popular resort center.

WAUCONDA, 60 *m.* (800 alt., 554 pop.), began with the house of Justus Bangs, built in 1836 on the shore of the lake that now bears his name. Three years later a school was opened and a young man appointed teacher. He is said to have given the village its name— that of an Indian character in a story to which he had taken a fancy. An academy opened in 1856 functioned for a decade, and then rented its building to the district for use as a public school. The mainstay of economic life is the farm trade. Supplementary incomes are gleaned from summer colonists.

At 65 *m.* is the junction with State 20.

Left on State 20 to VOLO, 0.5 *m.*, a small hamlet known since 1877 as The Forks. The community is composed of the gray and yellow frame houses common in the lake country, but achieves a certain distinction by being set atop a low hill. Sharply contrasting with the rural hamlet aspect is ST. PETER'S CHURCH (Roman Catholic), of English Gothic design, which dominates the entire countryside. The handsome yellow brick building, modeled after Salisbury Cathedral in England, has a red slate roof and a bell tower. ST. PETER'S SCHOOL, also of yellow brick, abuts the church on the east.

McHENRY, 5 *m.* (758 alt., 1,354 pop.), on the Fox River, is the western gateway to the Chain-O'-Lakes. The first settler was Dr. Christy C. Wheeler, who erected a log cabin in 1836, and became McHenry's first storekeeper and postmaster. Early prosperity came to the settlement with the erection of several hotels on the Chicago Pike, a much-used route in the early days. In 1844 the town lost the county offices to Woodstock, but a decade later gained the Chicago & North Western Railway, which brought the development of such small industries as butter and cheese and pickle manufacture. The community today is largely supported by these activities, by trade with the farmers, and by incidental revenue from vacationists.

FOX LAKE, 70.5 *m.* (745 alt., 880 pop.), to the R. of US 12, is fittingly dominated by its railroad station, for it lives on resort and tourist trade. In summer and fall, cottagers come by the hundreds and week-end excursionists by the thousands to seek relaxation on Fox, Pistakee, Grass, and numerous smaller lakes in the vicinity. On the Fourth of July the whole of Chicago seems to crowd its beaches, bathhouses, barbecue palaces, dance halls, and picnic grounds. The overflow of visitors bridges the narrow straits that connect Nippersink and Pistakee Lakes and jams the newly developed facilities of CHAIN-O'-LAKES STATE PARK (*parking lots, bathing beaches, fishing, and picnic groves free; moderate rentals for canoes, rowboats, and bathhouses*), first unit of a group of parks that the CCC is developing on reclaimed land bordering the lakes. From Fox Lake motorboats take visitors through the Chain-O'-Lakes, past the Lotus Beds (*see below*) and down the Fox River as far as Fox River Grove. (*Rates vary with length of trip; departure is from N. end of bridge.*)

Right from Fox Lake village on Grand Avenue to the junction with State 59, 1.4 *m.;* L. here on a scenic drive along the south and east shores of Fox Lake. Except for the 3,200 acres in the newly-formed State parks, not a foot of lake shore is available to the public without charge. Numerous signs advertise fishing, boating, bathing, and camping facilities for rent; rates vary widely. Competition is intense. But the view is fine, and free.

At 4.5 *m.* on State 59 is the junction with a paved road; R. on this road 3.5 *m.* to LAKE VILLA (758 alt., 487 pop.), a railroad station and resort community whose boundaries encompass a lake of the same name. On the western shore of the lake and just within the western limits of the village is the entrance (*marked*) to the ALLENDALE FARM SCHOOL (*visitors by appointment*), an experiment in practical philanthropy. Founded in 1897 as a home for neglected or homeless boys, the community has grown to embrace a quarter-section of good farm land that stretches westward from the lake. The settlement consists of a group of large red-roofed gray wooden buildings, numerous cottages, and smaller farm buildings. The farm school, a non-profit organization, cares for, employs, and educates an average of 60 boys. Fishing, boating, swimming, and other sports are part of the recreational scheme. The community is organized as a junior municipality with a mayor and city council, a court, and a police department. A monetary system has been established, and each boy is paid for his labor and charged for his board and clothes in the legal tender of the farm.

At 6.5 *m.* on State 59 is the junction with a graveled road; L. on this road 0.5 *m.* to another unit of the CHAIN-O'-LAKES STATE PARK (*boating, fishing, picnicking, no bathing*). This park preserves the wild marshland along the eastern side of Grass Lake. Directly opposite the park are the lake's EGYPTIAN LOTUS BEDS, which attract thousands each fall to witness the bloom (*4 weeks beginning in early Aug.*). The waxy, pale yellow blossoms stand from 2 to 4 feet above the water, and perfume the air for miles around.

Ahead on State 54 is ANTIOCH, 9 *m.* (770 alt., 1,101 pop.), northern gateway and principal community of the Chain-O'-Lakes country. First settled in 1836, the village early established itself as a manufacturing center of service to the surrounding farmers. Today a large flour and feed mill and several dairy products plants are major factors in the town's economic life. For two-thirds of the year these and miscellaneous services support the community on a quiet, well-ordered plane. Then the Business Association swings into full stride, merchants restock their shelves, bunting is hung, bands play, and for four months the town reaps the golden harvest poured in from Chicago by bus, railroad, auto, and trailer.

SPRING GROVE FISH HATCHERY (*open*), 75.5 *m.*, is operated by the State. Here are spawned many of the thousands of fish taken annually in the well-stocked waters of the lake country. The hatchery forwards the work of the Natural History Survey by tagging specimens of the fish released. These, when caught and reported, aid in growth and migration studies carried on by the Survey.

RICHMOND, 80.5 *m.* (819 alt., 514 pop.), was first settled in 1837. The first GRIST MILL built in the community is still in use, grinding out flour and feed by the power of Nippersink Creek. Because of its location between Wisconsin and Illinois lakes, Richmond enjoys a bit of the summer resort trade. On many a summer's night its taverns, dance halls, and tourist camps are filled to overflowing.

US 12 crosses the Wisconsin Line, 81.5 *m.*, 10 miles southeast of Lake Geneva, Wisconsin (*see Wisconsin Guide*).

TOUR 6

CHICAGO—DES PLAINES—BARRINGTON—WOODSTOCK—
HARVARD—(JANESVILLE, WIS.); US 14

Chicago to Wisconsin Line, 68 *m.*

Roadbed hard-surfaced throughout; four lanes between Chicago and Barrington, two lanes westward.

The Chicago & North Western Ry. parallels the route.

Usual accommodations throughout.

FROM THE LAKE front in northern Chicago, US 14 runs westward to the suburb of Park Ridge and then angles obliquely to the Wisconsin Line, a through-traffic highway to the Northwest. Between

Chicago and Barrington the towns are largely commuting suburbs. Westward are the wooded hills that border the lake country.

CHICAGO, 0 *m.* (598 alt., 3,376,438 pop.) (*see Chicago*).

Points of Interest: Chicago Board of Trade Building, Union Stock Yards, Field Museum of Natural History, Art Institute of Chicago, Museum of Science and Industry, Adler Planetarium, Shedd Aquarium, University of Chicago, and others.

In Chicago are junctions with State 1 (*see Tour* 1), State 42 (*see Tour* 2), US 41 (*see Tour* 2A), US 12 (*see Tour* 9), US 20 (*see Tour* 11), US 330 (*see Tour* 12A), US 66 (*see Tour* 17), and the Illinois Waterway (*see Tour* 22).

US 41 follows Bryn Mawr Ave. in Chicago from its junction with Sheridan Rd., 0 *m.,* to Ridge Rd., 0.3 *m.;* R. on Ridge Rd. to Peterson Ave., 0.8 *m.;* L. on Peterson to Caldwell Ave., 5 *m.;* R. on Caldwell to Chicago city limits, 6 *m.*

PARK RIDGE, 10 *m.* (658 alt., 10,417 pop.), adjoining the northwestern city limits of Chicago, stands on a wooded moraine that gives it its name. Here in 1853 came George Penny to verify reports of good red clay in the vicinity. He opened a brickyard and lumberyard; subsequently he produced five million bricks annually, sharply underselling Philadelphia on the Chicago market. Admiring townspeople named their new community Pennyville. When Penny protested, they yielded only so far as to rename it Brickton. Gradually the clay deposits were exhausted and with the coming of the Chicago & North Western Railway, Brickton marked its transition from an industrial town to a commuting suburb by adopting the name of Park Ridge. The PARK RIDGE MASONIC TEMPLE, 115 N. Northwest Hwy., is the original George Penny house, built in 1854 of Penny's good red brick. The two-story rectangular building remodeled in 1928, contains some of the original furnishings. The PARK RIDGE SCHOOL FOR GIRLS (*open* 10-4 *Sundays and holidays*), N. Prospect Ave., was founded in 1876 when the Women's Committee had a $500 balance at the close of the Philadelphia Centennial. Its six cottages each house from 18 to 28 girls, and the school has its own greenhouse and 40 acres of farm land and orchard.

Park Ridge is at the junction with City US 12 (*see Tour* 9).

DES PLAINES, 13.5 *m.* (643 alt., 8,798 pop.) (*see Tour* 3), is at the junctions with US 45 (*see Tour* 3) and By-Pass US 12 (*see Tour* 9).

ARLINGTON HEIGHTS, 19 *m.* (704 alt., 4,997 pop.), was settled in the 1830's when pioneers followed an old Indian trail into the region. During June and July of each year, thousands of expectant Chicagoans follow the same trail on the early afternoon specials of the Chicago & North Western, and return, frequently somewhat subdued, on the early evening trains of the same line. Their goal is the ARLINGTON PARK RACE TRACK (*grandstand* $1, *clubhouse* $2; *pari-mutuel betting*), at the western edge of town. Largest of the four major tracks in the Chicago area, Arlington, opened in 1929, has an English turf track in addition to its main one of a mile and an eighth. Here on June 30, 1932, Equipoise set a world's record by running the mile in 1 :34 2/5.

Adjoining the intersection with Dundee Road, 26.5 *m.,* is the DEER GROVE AND CAMP REINBERG FOREST PRESERVE (R). Two small lakes (*picnicking, camping, swimming*) and a herd of deer are features of this Cook County preserve.

The main street of BARRINGTON, 29.5 *m.* (824 alt., 3,213 pop.), is the dividing line of Cook and Lake counties. Founded in the 1850's, Barrington pursued an orderly development as an agricultural community until the post-World War boom. Then, attracted by the pleasant hilly country nearby, and aware of the country-squire tradition, Chicago millionaires began purchasing established farms and transforming them into country estates. Now, according to local residents, Barrington is "all shot with millionaires." The town's industrial character is inconspicuous, scarcely discernible behind landscaping and other camouflage. On the highway (R), at the northeastern edge of town, is the JEWEL TEA COMPANY PLANT (*2-hour tours conducted weekdays,* 8-4 :30), a modern building of classic lines set in extensive landscaped grounds. The tour of the plant includes the coffee, tea, research, miscellaneous products, and packaging departments. Most novel of Barrington's industrial concerns is a corporation that manufactures tableware, vases, and similar products from a metal that simulates gold and has the strength of steel. The metal's formula, developed by Carl von Malmborg, is a carefully guarded secret.

West of Barrington the country becomes more heavily wooded, with pastures and wood lots predominating.

FOX RIVER GROVE, 34.5 *m.* (771 alt., 641 pop.), a summer home and resort town, stretches along the tree-bordered Fox River. A SKI HILL, at the eastern limits of the village, is the scene of an important one-day meet held in January ($1 *adm. includes parking space*) by the Norge Ski Club. Often viewed by as many as 20,000 spectators, the meet attracts the best skiers from the Northwest and other parts of the country. The property is owned by the club, which allows the public the free use of the hill except when meets are in progress.

The FOX RIVER, 35 *m.,* is here the dividing line between Fox River Grove and CARY, 35.5 *m.* (811 alt., 731 pop.). Bordering the river (L) at the southern edge of the village is the CARY COUNTRY CLUB (18 *holes, daily fee*). Adjoining is the JOHN D. HERTZ FARM (*private*), home of a racing stable that includes Reigh Count, winner of the 1928 Kentucky Derby.

At 35 *m.* is the junction with State 31.

Left on State 31 to the junction with a graveled road, 2.3 *m.;* L. here to the junction with a second graveled road, 3.9 *m.;* R. here to CAMP ALGONQUIN (L), 4.7 *m.,* on the banks of the Fox River, maintained by United Charities and the

Chicago *Tribune* as a summer camp for mothers and children from Chicago slums. The camp consists of a group of small houses and cottages clustered about a larger building, used as a dining hall and recreation center. Wholesome food, rest, and supervised exercise make up the daily schedule; swimming and boating are featured sports. Games, reading, and other amusements are planned for the children in the evening. Camp Algonquin cares for 380 persons at a time. Eighty undernourished youngsters spend the entire summer here; the balance of the quota are given two-week vacations.

CRYSTAL LAKE, 42 *m.* (875 alt., 3,732 pop.), deploys fan-wise from a central park. Like many other communities in this vicinity, Crystal Lake was first settled shortly after the opening of the Erie Canal (1825). When the Chicago & North Western laid its tracks two miles to the northeast, the village expanded, absorbing the new depot hamlet of Nunda that threatened its existence. The well-wooded shores of CRYSTAL LAKE (*fishing, boating, swimming*) at the southwestern edge of town are dotted with numerous cottages and summer homes.

WOODSTOCK, 50 *m.* (943 alt., 5,471 pop.), was named for the Vermont town from which many of its first settlers came, in the 1830's and 1840's. Seat of McHenry County since 1844, the town is built around a square, on which are a number of Civil War monuments and a venerable spring house. The WOODSTOCK TYPEWRITER COMPANY PLANT (*apply at office*), 300 Seminary St., is that company's main plant. Largest factory in Woodstock, it manufactures typewriters that are sold extensively here and abroad. The tree-covered campus of the TODD SCHOOL FOR BOYS, 300 McHenry Ave., is surrounded by a high iron fence. The school was established by the Rev. Richard Todd, who came to the raw Middle Border in 1848 from Princeton University. Including the elementary grades and four years of advanced study, the course is based on the theory that every boy is a creator. Its dramatic branch is excellent; one alumnus is Orson Welles, a director-actor of stage and radio fame.

HARVARD, 62.5 *m.* (908 alt., 2,988 pop.), is entered from the south over the tracks of the Chicago & North Western, which brought a little boom to the town with its arrival in 1856. Harvard is now the junction point for two branches of the line. In recent years more and more Chicagoans have been taking advantage of the low rents in the nearby lake country and the rapid commuting service of the railroad, and Harvard, sixty miles out of the city, may eventually become a long-range suburb of the metropolis.

The STARLINE MODEL DAIRY FARM, at the town's northern limits, features an all-steel barn and a horizontal silo that has no post supports. The farm serves as a practical laboratory for the dairy equipment developed by the Harvard plant.

US 14 crosses the Wisconsin Line, 68 *m.*, 3 miles S. of Walworth, Wisconsin (*see Wisconsin Guide*).

TOUR 7

(HAMMOND, IND)—CHICAGO—ELGIN—ROCKFORD—
US 20

Concrete roadbed throughout; four lanes between Chicago and Elgin; two lanes between Elgin and Dubuque.
Chicago & North Western Ry. parallels US 20 between Chicago and Freeport.
Usual accommodations between Chicago and Freeport; good cabin camps between Freeport and East Dubuque.

US 20 crosses northern Illinois from Lake Michigan to the Mississippi River, traversing a region rich in historical associations closely linked with its topography. In its eastern half the highway crosses the most recently glaciated part of the State, a rolling country of fields and woodlands, low morainic ridges and frequently marshy depressions. The irregular, poorly drained land, with extensive areas suitable only for pasture or woodland, coupled with its nearness to large urban markets, makes this northeastern section the important dairy region of Illinois.

Elgin and Rockford, manufacturing centers of national consequence, lie in the broad valleys of the Fox and Rock Rivers—glacial outlet channels carved by the outpouring torrents of the Wisconsin ice sheet. Their industrial development stems from early utilization of local water power.

Section a. Indiana Line to Rockford, 105 m.

US 20 crosses the Indiana Line, here the Chicago city limits, 0 *m.*, from Hammond, Indiana (*see Indiana Guide*), and proceeds northwest along Indianapolis Blvd. to Ewing Ave.; R. on Ewing Ave. to 95th St.; L. on 95th St.

At the intersection of 95th St. and Stony Island Ave., 4 *m.*, is the junction with US 330 (*see Tour* 12A). Here the route divides into City US 20 and By-Pass US 20.

Left (straight ahead) on By-Pass US 20 to a junction with US 45 (*see Tour* 3), 13.5 *m.;* R. on US 45, with which By-Pass US 20 is united for 13 miles (*see Tour* 3), to the western junction with City US 20 (*see below*), 26.5 *m.*

City US 20 proceeds north along Stony Island Ave. to the inter-

213

section of Michigan Blvd. with Jackson Blvd., the center of Chicago.
CHICAGO, 16.5 *m.* (598 alt., 3,376,438 pop.) (*see Chicago*).

Points of Interest: Chicago Board of Trade Building, Union Stock Yards, Field Museum of Natural History, Art Institute of Chicago, Museum of Science and Industry, Adler Planetarium, Shedd Aquarium, University of Chicago, and others.

In Chicago are junctions with State 1 (*see Tour* 1), State 42 (*see Tour* 2), US 41 (*see Tour* 2A), US 12 (*see Tour* 9), US 14 (*see Tour* 10), US 330 (*see Tour* 12A), US 66 (*see Tour* 17), and the Illinois Waterway (*see Tour* 22).

North on Michigan Blvd. to Washington Blvd., 16.8 *m.;* L. on Washington Blvd. to the Chicago city limits, 25 *m.*

OAK PARK, 27 *m.* (630 alt., 63,982 pop.), is the largest community with village form of government in the United States. Appropriately named for its natural growth of oaks, Oak Park was first settled in 1833 by Joseph Kettlestrings, who came with his wife in an ox-drawn covered wagon from Baltimore, Maryland. Their descendants, and those of other early settlers, hold prominent positions in the social and civic life of the community.

Almost since its inception Oak Park has been "bone dry" and well governed. For 50 years the village fathers fought for local option so that saloons might be legally barred. This the legislature was not empowered to grant until the passage of an enabling act in 1907. By that time local option was scarcely needed, so "dry" was Oak Park in sentiment and fact. Deeds to much of the land within the corporate limits and beyond contained anti-saloon clauses inserted by the original owners. During the fight tavern after tavern had been purchased and their stock poured into the gutter.

The form of government has been simple and direct. Fathers of the village are six trustees, who direct all municipal affairs. By a tacit understanding among its citizens, the village is divided into six sections, and membership in the board is apportioned equally. All department heads (except the village clerk and village treasurer, who, with the board, are elected by the people) are appointed by the trustees. Authority is direct and responsibility is clear.

Known in the 1890's as Saints' Rest because of its many churches, now even more numerous, Oak Park traditionally centers its social life in its homes and churches, schools and charitable organizations.

Oak Park and adjacent River Forest were the early workshops of Frank Lloyd Wright (b. 1869), and today constitute a gallery of his distinguished architecture. He resided in the FRANK LLOYD WRIGHT HOUSE (*private*), Forest and Chicago Aves., the nucleus of which was built in 1891. Frame houses designed by Wright at the outset of his career stand on the south side of Chicago Avenue in the 1000 block and at 1030 Superior Ave. Though not illustrative of his mature style, these structures foreshadow his break with the closed volume mode of building.

The evolution of Wright's philosophy of open planning and harmony of site and structure is documented by a series of Oak Park houses (*all private residences*), several of which are along Forest Avenue. The N. G. MOORE HOUSE (1894), 329 Forest Ave., is a compromise between Wright's ideas and Mr. Moore's taste for half-timbered English cottages. Next door is the more typical HILLS HOUSE (1906). Others include the ARTHUR HEURTLEY HOUSE (1902), 312 Forest Ave., at the rear of which is the finest and oldest of the magnificent oaks along Forest Avenue; the GALE HOUSE (1905), 6 Elizabeth Court; and the BEACHY HOUSE (1906), 238 Forest Ave.

The THOMAS HOUSE (1904), 210 Forest Ave., is typical of Wright's prairie style and his use of plaster over wood. All rooms are above the terrace level; there is no basement. The strong horizontal lines of the structure flow into the carefully graded, landscaped setting. The Thomas House is on the site of the Protestant Episcopal Church from which the Rev. Charles P. Anderson was called to the bishopric of Chicago.

The CELEBRITY ROOM of the Blue Parrot Patio, a tea house at 1120 Westgate Ave., is furnished and decorated by student-apprentices from Wright's summer home and colony, Taliesen, at Spring Green, Wisconsin. Silhouetted in black on lemon-yellow walls are the local houses that Mr. Wright includes in his canon of notable buildings. These include the Winslow House in River Forest, and Unity Temple and the Heurtley House in Oak Park. A mammoth scrapbook designed by a Taliesen apprentice contains biographical clippings concerning other Oak Park sons and daughters who have found their way into *Who's Who:* Ernest Hemingway and Janet Lewis, novelists; Doris Humphrey, the dancer; Dr. William E. Barton, clergyman and Lincoln scholar; his son, Bruce Barton, journalist and politician; Louis Caldwell, head of the bureau of radio law in Washington, D. C.; and various artists and musicians.

UNITY TEMPLE, Universalist Church at Lake and Grove Sts., is a notable interpretation of the cubic form. Designed by Wright and built in 1905, it has been termed the first concrete monolith in the world. Molded concrete gives the appearance and strength of stone blocks and columns. Such harmony is there of color, design, and form that the lack of a steeple is seldom noticed; Wright considers the spire a false symbol—the "lifting of a finger to a terrible God."

The FIRST CONGREGATIONAL CHURCH (1918), Lake St. and Kenilworth Ave., designed by Norman S. Patton, is of unusual architectural and historic interest. The square buttressed tower on the façade resembles those of English parish churches, while the main body of the church is patterned after the Gothic chapels of Oxford and Cambridge. Of rare beauty is the stained glass in the rose windows of the nave, in the clerestory windows, and in the lancet windows of the ambulatories. Throughout the church are numerous tablets and relics of significance. In the middle of the foyer is a column from the spire of Boston's celebrated Old North Church.

A fine Biblical museum, in the basement toward the rear of the church, houses the collection of Dr. William E. Barton, pastor 1899-1924, and part of the Jerusalem Exhibit of the St. Louis Exposition of 1904. The collections include domestic and agricultural implements of the Holy Land and relics of the early Christian Church. Such treasures as a Pentateuch, said to have been copied by a Samaritan priest from the oldest Biblical manuscript extant, and an undated painting of St. John the Divine, believed to have been done by a Russian before the days of oil paint, are in the pastor's study on the second floor.

In addition to public schools of high national rating, Oak Park has three Roman Catholic institutions directed by the Dominican Order: SAINT EDMUNDS, Oak Park Ave. and Pleasant St., built in 1910 and modeled after the Palais de Justice at Rouen; the BISHOP QUARTER BOARDING SCHOOL FOR BOYS, 605 Lake St., named for the Rt. Rev. William Quarter, a native of Ireland, who in 1844 became the first bishop of the diocese of Chicago; and FENWICK HIGH SCHOOL, Washington Blvd. and East Ave., of modified Gothic design.

Three local charitable institutions are of primary social value. HEPHZIBAH HOME, 946 North Blvd., equipped with library, infirmary, doll room, dining room, kindergarten, and four dormitories, has cared for orphans of nearby communities since 1897. OAK PARK AND RIVER FOREST DAY NURSERY, a brick and stone English cottage style building at Maple Ave. and Randolph St., cares for 30 children of employed mothers. The ECONOMY SHOP, South Blvd. and Grove Ave., a clearing house for used articles, was organized in 1919 to help support Oak Park charities. The shop earned $100,000 in its first decade.

OAK PARK CONSERVATORY, 621 Garfield Blvd., is celebrated for its annual Chrysanthemum Show (*Nov. 20-Dec. 20, 8 a.m.-9 p.m.; other shows each month through May; adm. free*). Summer exhibits are held in the city parks. The best known of these is the rose collection of 204 varieties, shown at a Century of Progress Exposition in Chicago (1933-4), exhibited annually in the small park at Marion and Greenfield Sts.

RIVER FOREST, 27.5 m. (631 alt., 8,829 pop.), is one of Chicago's finest residential suburbs. Distinctly younger and more open in appearance than Oak Park, River Forest enjoys on a more moderate scale the grace and ease of living of its larger neighbor.

In 1836 came the first settlers—Ashbel Steele, his wife, two sons, and seven daughters. In a clearing on what is now Thatcher Avenue, Steele and his sons erected their house. The pioneer home became the center of neighborhood hospitality, and the small square piano, brought overland with much labor, lent a note of grace to frontier life. Ashbel

Steele and his family established the pattern that River Forest was to follow—decorous home life, quiet hospitality, and a minimization of commerce. Into this quiet pattern the intrusion of industry has been neither long nor significant. In early days, previous even to the settlement of Steele, a sawmill and gristmill were built (1833) on the east side of the river, north of what is now Lake Street. This mill, the only one for 40 miles around, finished much of the lumber that went into the building of early Chicago. Today, rigorous zoning laws limit commerce and industry to a few small businesses along Lake Street, a few blocks east of the old mill site. Not even a movie house disturbs the residential calm of River Forest.

Early communication with Chicago was by means of the old Frink & Walker stagecoach. Drawn by four horses, it carried ten passengers —nine inside and one on top with the driver. The fare was fifty cents for adults, twenty-five cents for children. Lake Street had ruts hub deep, and there were no roads running north and south between River Forest and Chicago, nothing but trails leading to the several settlements. In 1849 the Galena & Chicago Union Railroad laid a single track of strap iron along the old stage route as far west as Elmhurst. The rails were wooden riders sheathed in iron; the ties were small and widely spaced. Wood was used for fuel and stored in long sheds along the right-of-way, and the small boilers of the engines necessitated the placing of water tanks every few miles. The first station was a freight car, heated with a small wood-burning stove.

Associated with the railroad, though he arrived more than a decade later, was Daniel Cunningham Thatcher, for whom one of the streets of River Forest is named. Formerly a Chicago business man, Thatcher retired to River Forest in 1854. Two years later he purchased a section of land near the Des Plaines River and built a house. The land is now known as Thatcher's Woods, and the Thatcher house (*see below*) is the oldest building in the village. In 1859 and 1860 Frances Willard (1839-1898), the temperance leader, boarded with the Thatcher family. At that time she was teaching in the lone River Forest school. In 1929 the village named one of its new schools for her.

In 1862 Thatcher persuaded the Chicago & North Western Railway to build a station on his property. The station was called Thatcher, and River Forest was known by that name until 1872, when the present name was adopted. On October 24, 1880, the community was organized as the Village of River Forest. The village seal, bearing the motto, *Silva in Flumine* (Lat., forest on the river), attests its attractive site.

The old THATCHER HOUSE (*open daily, free*), 511 Edgewood Place, houses the Trailside Museum of Natural History, which is under the supervision of the Chicago Academy of Science. The collections, planned to show the phylogenic relationships of the several life forms, are composed of invertebrates, fish, amphibians, reptiles, birds, and mammals. A geological exhibit comprises fossils from local quarries, cross-sections of underlying formations, and studies in rock structure. Assisting the curator and his two part-time assistants is a junior staff of 15 boys and girls, 12 to 18 years of age, who receive training in biology, geology, and museum methods. Facilities include a small reference library and a microscope with prepared slides.

ROSARY COLLEGE, Forest Ave. and Division St., a fully accredited Roman Catholic liberal arts institution for women, was opened in River Forest in 1922. The board of trustees consists of five sisters of the order of St. Dominic. The Gothic buildings, of Bedford stone, designed by Ralph Adams Cram, show to the best possible advantage against the natural beauty of the forest campus. CENTRAL HALL (1925) has a cloister walk extending its entire length; it contains the chapel, library, refectory, and social hall. LEWIS MEMORIAL HALL houses a little theater, exhibition gallery, and portrait studios. Collections include paintings, tapestries, and period furniture, contributed by Mrs. Edward Hines of Evanston. The MOTHER EMILY POWER MEMORIAL HALL, the students' dormitory, contains the gymnasium and a glass-roofed swimming pool.

In 1925 Rosary College inaugurated its Foreign Study Plan, whereby students, preferably in their junior year, can spend a year in Fribourg, Switzerland, at the Institut de Haute Etudes. In 1934 the Rosary College Program of Education for Leisure, without fees, was started. Since its inception more than 1,000 adults have taken advantage of the plan to further their education.

CONCORDIA TEACHERS COLLEGE, Bonnie Brae and Division Sts., is maintained by the Missouri Synod of the Evangelical Lutheran Church to train teachers for Lutheran elementary schools. The first group of buildings was dedicated in 1913. In these, as in all later buildings, yellow brick has been used, resulting in a pleasing harmony, heightened by a studied arrangement.

There is a library of 18,000 volumes, an art collection of 3,800 mounted prints, and a natural history museum. A teaching staff of 20 gives instruction to approximately 400 students.

The DOMINICAN HOUSE OF STUDIES (*reception rooms and daily Mass open to public; Christmas Eve Mass by invitation*), Division St. and Harlem Ave., is a preparatory college fitting students for the Dominican priesthood. The single college building, of stone, sharply etched against the well-kept lawn of the treeless 40-acre campus, is cruciform in plan.

Among the Frank Lloyd Wright houses in River Forest are the WINSLOW HOUSE (1893), or Auvergne Lodge, on Auvergne Place, one of his first buildings; and the ELIZABETH ROBERTS HOUSE (1906), on Edgewood Place (*both private*). Each house reveals Wright's desire to harmonize his buildings with the terrain, to recognize and accentuate the "natural beauty of the plain, its quiet level." The RIVER FOREST TENNIS CLUB (*private*), 615 Lathrop Ave., and the RICHARD

W. Bock Studio (*private*), 7820 Chicago Ave., both built in 1906, are other examples of Wright's work.

The River Forest Women's Clubhouse (1913), 526 N. Ashland Ave., was the first women's club building in the State. Harlem House, Lake and Williams Sts., now a bottling works, is a landmark from the turnpike days of Lake Street, when it served as a combination post office, drug store, and hotel. In the 1870's it was also a tavern and grocery.

MAYWOOD, 28.8 *m.* (628 alt., 25,829 pop.), a suburban community centering in a factory district along the railroad, developed in the 1880's, when industrial growth of the west Chicago area created demands for homesites. It now has various district neighborhood patterns, all harmonious but racially different.

MELROSE PARK, 29.9 *m.* (617 alt., 10,741 pop.), is essentially a residential city. Its factory population, almost half Italian, is employed in nearby manufacturing districts.

At 31.5 *m.* is the western junction with By-Pass US 20 (*see above*) and US 45 (*see Tour* 3).

Bordering the highway (L) for three miles are the Proviso Yards of the Chicago & North Western Railway. The best view is from the entrance to the yards, reached by a half-mile concrete drive (L) marked Blind Road, 33.2 *m.* The Proviso Yards, sometimes called the "Hump" because of the incline controlling switching operations, are the largest railroad yards in the world—three miles long and one-half mile wide, 960 acres in area. By means of an electrically operated system, aided by gravity, the old method of switching by engine crews is eliminated and in a single operation freight cars are distributed and classified on 59 tracks. Through-freight is saved 12 hours in shipping time, and cars for other destinations need no longer go into Chicago, but are delivered directly to the Outer Belt Line.

The operations of the yards appear chaotic, yet extreme precision and accuracy govern each maneuver. Puffing locomotives back long trains to the crest of the hump. Brakemen uncouple the cars, releasing them for their gravity run down an incline that drops 18 feet in 300 yards. From a tower nearby an operator presses a lever regulating the electric retarders. The same operator manipulates the electric switching apparatus, sending each car to its appointed track. The cars are then picked up by locomotives for assembly into out-going trains. Each of the 59 tracks has a capacity of 70 cars; the yard can classify and handle 4,000 cars daily. It is brilliantly lighted at night, permitting 24-hour operation. Refrigerator cars are served by a modern high-speed ice plant. The engine terminal roundhouse has stalls for 58 locomotives and a system of water tanks supplied by a 2,100-foot well.

Freight cars passing through the yards are checked for dry bearings, cracked wheels, and other defects. At the warehouse great motor caravans empty their loads into tractor truck trains, which dart along the tracks delivering merchandise to designated cars. High speed and accuracy prevent shipments from accumulating.

At 33.6 *m.*, is a junction with Mount Prospect Road.

Right on Mount Prospect Road to AHLERS MILL (*open*), 1.7 *m.*, in Mount Emblem Masonic Cemetery. Oldest and most notable of three Dutch-type mills in the vicinity, it was erected in 1850 as a gristmill. A venerable landmark, the mill is most impressive at night when its great wings are lighted. The base of the five-story tower is of massive stone; the superstructure is of hand-hewn timbers. The interior has been developed as an educational exhibit. All the working parts except the millstones are of wood. Two workmen brought from the Netherlands required six months to complete the great cogwheel, 12 feet in diameter. Visitors can climb to the deck by stairs and ladders, observing at the several levels the sails, drive-shaft, control levers, grain and meal chutes, storage bins, and millstones. The parts are almost wholly in their original form.

The highway skirts (L) ELMHURST, 34.5 *m.* (681 alt., 14,055 pop.), named for the majestic double row of elms that extends for nearly a mile along Cottage Hill Avenue. Elmhurst was first known as Cottage Hill, for its first home, HILL COTTAGE (*private*), 415 S. York St. Built in 1843 by J. L. Hovey, the house was conducted as a hotel for farmers driving to the Chicago market from Fox River and Rock River communities.

WILDER PARK, west side of Cottage Hill Ave., south of the Chicago & North Western tracks, was laid out in 1868 as the estate of Seth Wadham, a settler of ample means, whose massive house in the center of the park is now the ELMHURST PUBLIC LIBRARY. The estate eventually pased into the possession of Thomas E. Wilder, who ceded it to the city for a nominal sum, with the provision that the house be used as a public library and the grounds as a public park.

Across from Wilder Park is ELMHURST COLLEGE, coeducational institution founded in 1871 as Elmhurst Seminary. Later it became a junior college, and in 1934 an accredited four-year school. OLD MAIN HALL and OLD MUSIC HALL, the original buildings, are still in use, along with newer dormitories, a library, and gymnasium.

Elmhurst has been the home of Carl Sandburg, who for some time lived in the old TORODE HOUSE, 333 S. York St. Jens Christian Bay, author and head of the John Crerar Library in Chicago, and Rosamond du Sardin, novelist, reside in Elmhurst.

ADDISON, 37.5 *m.* (689 alt., 916 pop.), a quiet old village, has been a stronghold of the German Lutheran faith since the 1840's. Named for the eighteenth-century essayist, Joseph Addison, it is of interest for its religious institutions and its century-old houses. Several of the latter, still in use, are along the highway, as is the POST OFFICE, which dates from 1852.

At the junction of Addison and Army Trail Roads with US 20 is the KINDERHEIM (*open 2-4 daily*), a two-story brick building, to which children of Lutheran parentage are admitted on recommendation of the Chicago Juvenile Court. Founded in 1902 by the Rev. Augustus Schlechte, the Kinderheim functions as an industrial and domestic training school for some 240 boys and girls.

Adjoining the Kinderheim is the 41-acre tract of the EVANGELICAL LUTHERAN HOME, an orphanage. Those of school age attend St. Paul's Parochial School. After graduation and confirmation boys are given work on farms or in greenhouses, girls in supervised homes. More than 1,250 children have been provided for and launched upon self-supporting careers since the home's inception in 1873.

At 38.3 *m.* is the junction with Mill Road.

1. Right on Mill Road to the old HEIDEMAN MILL (*private*), 0.5 *m.* Now a notable landmark, it was built as a grist-mill in 1867, and was in use until 1929. Its 75-foot sailspread, reaching to within 20 feet of the ground, is visible for some distance. The mill tower is octagonal, 30 feet wide at the base and tapering to 15 feet at the top. Its revolving arms are closely latticed to hold the canvas.

2. Left on Mill Road to the WMBI TRANSMITTER (5,000 w.), 0.5 *m.*, "the Voice of the Moody Bible Institute." Nearby is a cemetery of the 1830's. A large boulder near the roadside marks the GRAVES OF SOLDIERS OF GENERAL SCOTT'S ARMY who died during their march along this route in the Black Hawk War (1832).

West of Mill Road US 20 passes through a suburban region of golf and country clubs, farm lands and wooded marshes, local real estate developments, and the village of BLOOMINGDALE.

At 47 *m.* the highway skirts (L) the hamlet of ONTARIO-VILLE.

Left from Ontarioville, on the main graveled road running due south, to the ILLINOIS PET CEMETERY, 1.7 *m.* Here are buried canaries, dogs, cats, monkeys, and rabbits. Funerals follow a fixed routine. Birds and other small animals are buried in white plush boxes, larger animals in gray and silver-pine caskets. The hearse is a seven-passenger car, with a compartment for the dead pet. The tract of six acres, in charge of a caretaker, contains numerous granite monuments, appropriately engraved. Some have inlaid photographs of the pet. A cross marks the grave of a dog that saved its master's life.

Between Ontarioville and Elgin US 20 passes numerous dairy farms. At 50.8 *m.* the WGN TRANSMITTER (50 kw.) occupies a low Spanish-type building (R), flanked by tall towers, visible for some distance along the highway. Across the road, and slightly west, is the VILLA OLIVIA GOLF COURSE AND SWIMMING POOL (*open; greens fee 75c weekdays, $1 Saturdays, $1.50 Sundays and holidays*).

ELGIN, 54 *m.* (717 alt., 35,929 pop.) (*see Elgin*).
Points of Interest: Laura Davidson Sears Academy of Fine Arts, Elgin National Watch Factory, Elgin Watch Observatory, David C. Cook Publishing House, Northern Illinois State Hospital, and others.

Right from Elgin on State 31 to the YEOMEN CITY OF CHILDHOOD (*open*),

4 *m.*, a home and primary school for orphaned children of members of the Fraternal Order of Yeomen of America. Boys and girls between the ages of three and twelve are here admitted to a family-like environment. Later they attend high schools and trade schools in nearby communities. Three cottages accommodating 60 children comprise the main buildings. Recreational facilities on the 650-acre campus include a log cabin, swimming pool, and two artificial lakes stocked with fish.

WEST DUNDEE, 4.8 *m.* (739 alt., 1,697 pop.), was settled by Scots and English in the 1830's, and named for Dundee, Scotland. Allan Pinkerton (1819-84) immigrated to West Dundee from Glasgow in 1843, and established a cooper shop. While searching the country-side for wood to make barrel staves and hoops, Pinkerton found evidence of counterfeiting on an island in the Fox River. When transmitted to the sheriff, this information resulted in the capture of several counterfeiters. Pinkerton's talent for deduction was shortly afterwards rewarded by his appointment as deputy sheriff of Kane County. In 1850 he became Chicago's first detective.

Pinkerton's abolitionist activities in West Dundee are said to have brought about an early acquaintance with Abraham Lincoln. In 1861, as chief of the national detective agency that bears his name, Pinkerton prevented an attempt to assassinate Lincoln in Baltimore, Maryland. Lincoln subsequently commissioned Pinkerton to organize and direct the Secret Service Division of the Union Army, from which developed the U. S. Secret Service. The SITE OF PINKERTON'S COOPERAGE is at 3rd and Main Sts.

Right from West Dundee, across the Fox River, is EAST DUNDEE, 0.7 *m.* (739 alt., 1,341 pop.), a village settled largely by emigrants who left Germany because of the 1848 Revolution. Scottish and British antipathy against German neighbors prevented East and West Dundee from being organized as one community. Today, despite a homogeneous population, the two villages retain individual governments.

The HAEGER POTTERIES (*open* 8-4, *Mon.-Fri.*), 45 Maiden Lane, East Dundee, produce pottery and lamp bases. The clay is mixed by machine, shaped in plaster molds, and baked in gas and oil-fired kilns. A working unit of the Haeger Potteries was exhibited at the Century of Progress Exposition in Chicago (1933-34).

CARPENTERSVILLE, 5.5 *m.* (805 alt., 1,461 pop.), was settled in 1834 by young Angelo Carpenter of Uxbridge, Massachusetts, and his father and uncle. In the decades that followed, Carpenter all but built the settlement single-handed. He established a sawmill, a grist-mill, a woolen mill, and a grocery store. In 1851 he platted Carpentersville. One of the enterprises with which he was associated, the Illinois Iron and Bolt Company, is the economic mainstay of the community.

In his later years Carpenter gave land and houses to less affluent townsmen, and engaged in philanthropies that were continued by his widow after his death in 1880. Among these are CARPENTER PARK, on the eastern edge of Carpentersville, and CARPENTER MEMORIAL HALL, a one-story brick building on Grove Street in which the public library is housed.

West of Elgin, which marks the northeastern border of the Chicago urban area, the landscape is essentially rural. Crossroad communities serve nearby farms. The only cities of consequence are Rockford, Freeport, and Galena. Between Elgin and Rockford US 20 crosses a rolling country of poorly drained fields, pastures, and woodlands, a region of intensive dairy farming.

HENPECK, 68 *m.*, identified by a church, tavern, and service station at a curve in the highway, was once an important stop on the old

Chicago-Galena stage road. The hamlet dates from a log cabin built in 1836 by Tenas Allen. During the Galena lead rush of the late 1830's and early 1840's as many as fifty men encamped here overnight. At the time of the Civil War, Henpeck had a post office, shops, and a population of more than a hundred. The country road that turns left from Henpeck follows the route of the old Galena Trail, also known as the Grant Trail.

The dominance of dairying throughout this region is everywhere apparent in herds of fine dairy cattle, large red barns, tall silos, and uniformly well-kept farmsteads. Croplands are largely in corn, with extensive areas in hay and pasture. In contrast with agricultural practices in central Illinois, where corn and other grains are harvested as cash crops, most of the corn in this region is cut before maturity for use as silage.

TOUR 8

(DYER, IND.)—JOLIET—AURORA; US 66

Roadbed hard-surfaced throughout.
The Chicago, Burlington, & Quincy R.R. parallels US 30 between Aurora and Shabbona, the Chicago & Northwestern R.R. between Dixon and Fulton.
Usual accommodations throughout.

US 30, in its eastern section, skirts the Chicago area, avoiding the congestion of the metropolitan district. With the exception of Chicago Heights, Joliet, and Aurora, outlying industrial centers, the landscape along the route is essentially rural in character. A long-settled agricultural region, the farm lands of northeastern Illinois are rich in legend and history, peaceful and prosperous in appearance.

Between the Fox and the Rock Rivers is the highly productive dairy and beef cattle country of northern Illinois. Corn, hay, wheat, and oats roll in long swells in the cool of spring breezes, ripen to waves of green and gold in the warmth of summer sun, or impart to the haze of early autumn their rich harvest colors. Fine beef and dairy cattle attest the wealth of the region. Sheep, hogs, and occasional flocks of goats feed in barnyards or woodland pastures.

Although much of the country crossed by US 30 was termed by Washington Irving "the Grand Prairie," this northern section of Illinois is frequently forested and generally more rolling than flat. From the lake plain of the east the highway rises and falls over the hilly, forested moraines of Will and Kane Counties, then rolls gently onward across the old drift-covered upland of western Illinois, past the valley of the Rock River, on to the gorge of the Mississippi, which it enters abruptly at Fulton.

Section a. Indiana Line to Aurora, 53 m.

US 30 crosses the Indiana Line, 0 m., from Dyer, Indiana (see Indiana Guide). At 2.5 m. is a junction with US 330 (see Tour 12A).

The land locally is flat and wet, the bed of an old glacial lake. Drainage ditches are numerous, and fields are heavily tiled. Large areas are staked out for residential development; others are held for possible industrial expansion. Many acres are in truck.

CHICAGO HEIGHTS, 6.7 m. (694 alt., 22,321 pop.) (see Tour 1), is at a junction with State 1 (see Tour 1). West are more abortive suburban developments, extensive truck gardens, and wooded pasture lands.

Right of the highway at 10.5 m. is OLYMPIA FIELDS, a community developed in 1926 that consists exclusively of fine country homes adjacent to the 674-acre OLYMPIA FIELDS COUNTRY CLUB (private), distinguished for its four 18-hole golf courses. Of these, No. 4 is ranked among the five best in the United States. Here during the past eighteen years many of the championship tournaments of western and national associations have been played.

Among the million and a half dollar equipment of the club are facilities for polo, tennis, trap-shooting, and winter sports. Only life member is Charles Beach, founder of the club (1915) and promoter of Olympia Fields. His fondness for the classical Greeks explains the names of the community and of its roads, of which the principal one is Olympian Way.

The highway crosses HICKORY CREEK at 16.7 m., which roughly parallels US 30 into Joliet. All communities on or north of the highway trace their origin to the old Hickory Creek settlement, which grew up in the 1820's along the winding miles of this tributary of the Des Plaines River. Indian occupancy of the section preceded the white man's coming by at least a hundred years. The Indians favored hickory wood for making bows and arrows, and stone arrowheads are yet found along the creek. Mounds and other Indian remains exist throughout the region.

At 18.2 *m.* is a junction with US 45 (*see Tour 3*). Open cultivated farm lands and heavily wooded hills alternate as the highway enters the morainic area of Will County.

The so-called LINCOLN HOTEL (*private*), 21.8 *m.*, is a red-brown brick structure (L), built in 1846 and reputedly visited by Lincoln when traveling the old Sauk Trail. The bricks, made locally, were molded by hand from mud and grass, and set in mortar made of clay from the creek. About 200 yards east of the building are excavations said to have been used as a hiding place for runaway slaves during the days of the Underground Railway.

NEW LENOX, 24.7 *m.*, is a Hickory Creek settlement of the 1820's. Its newer development, McINTOSH SUBDIVISION, on both sides of the highway, is a community of small farms, poultry yards, and kitchen gardens. The subdivision is the product of the "back to the land" movement recently popular in congested urban areas. Jessica Nelson North, in her novel of the 1930 depression, *Arden Acres,* refers to its income homes and chicken houses, equipped with latest improvements. Lots vary in size from a fraction of an acre to five acres.

At 26.9 *m.* is a junction with a graveled road, at the east end of the 18-hole CHERRY HILL GOLF COURSE (*daily greens fee*).

Right on this road, immediately over the steep railway embankment, is GOUGARS, 0.1 *m.*, site of the first post office in Will County (1832) and "downtown" for the entire Hickory Creek settlement. Today only the farm buildings of the fourth generation of the Gougar family remain.

The GOUGAR FARMHOUSE (L), immediately across the tracks, occupies the site of the original Gougar log cabin. The house was built about 1840. Here is preserved a COLLECTION OF INDIAN AND PIONEER RELICS worthy of museum protection, among them the skull of a chief with all his gear, found in an Indian mound on the south bank of the creek, and the account books (1836-40) of William Gougar's general store, with record of sales of such commodities as flour, corn, cloth, farm tools, and whiskey. According to family tradition Chief Shabbona frequently stopped here overnight. When alone he slept on the floor, rolled in his blanket. Once when his wife accompanied him she slept on the ground outside, while he stood guard all night. The BARN (1840) built by William Gougar with the help of pioneer neighbors is still in use. It is made of boards of walnut and oak, hewn into shape with axes, and held in place by wooden pegs.

Across Hickory Creek is the GOUGARS SCHOOLHOUSE (R), 0.3 *m.* The small frame building marks the site of the Hickory Creek log schoolhouse built in 1832. Nearby, in Higinbotham Woods (R), are earthworks traditionally known as the "Old French Fort."

North of the schoolhouse, at 0.4 *m.*, the graveled road separates two units of the Joliet park system (*see Joliet*). Left is the PUBLIC GREENHOUSE (*open daily* 9-4; *Sun. and Hol.,* 9-5; *adm. free*). The greenhouse, bordered by formal flower gardens and trimly kept lawns, lies on a slight rise of ground from which trails lead westward to other units of the park system. The conservatory, which houses a variety of the more common garden flowers, is distinguished by an unusually inclusive CACTUS COLLECTION. HIGINBOTHAM WOODS (R) is a wild-land preserve of 238 acres. An earth road, opposite the greenhouse, passes a FIRETOWER (R). An inside stairway leads to a platform at the top, which affords a sweeping view of the surrounding forest area, the city of Joliet, and the farm lands for miles around.

Immediately south of the greenhouse a hard-surfaced road follows Hickory Creek westward for 2 miles through several units of the park system to a junction with US 30 (*see below*) on the outskirts of Joliet. Enroute are 75-acre BIRD HAVEN, 327-acre PILCHER PARK AND ARBORETUM, 23-acre HOBBS PARKWAY, and 60-acre HIGHLAND PARK.

At 28.7 *m.* on US 30 is the entrance (R) to the JOLIET PARK SYSTEM (*see above*), marked by Leonard Crunelle's STATUE OF ROBERT PILCHER.

JOLIET, 31 *m.* (545 alt., 42,993 pop.) (*see Joliet*).

Points of Interest: Joliet Wall Paper Mills, American Institute of Laundering Vocational Training School, Oakwood Mound, and others.

Joliet is at the junction with US 6 (*see Tour* 14) and US 66 (*see Tour* 17).

The vast form of STATEVILLE STATE PRISON (*see Tour* 17) is distinctly visible (R) at 33.5 *m.,* its light stone structure in sharp contrast with the green fields that surround it.

Between Joliet and Aurora lie the long-settled Plainfield farm lands, a prosperous agricultural region between the Des Plaines and Fox Rivers. Flat to gently rolling, the country is largely under cultivation; only occasional farm wood lots relieve the monotony of the unending cornfields.

An extensive water-filled gravel pit (R) forms small LAKE RENWICK, 38.9 *m.,* which borders the roadside for a quarter-mile. The extent of the resource, one of the most important in Illinois, may be judged 'from the activities along the railroad on the far side of the lake, where whole trainloads of gravel are frequently made up.

PLAINFIELD, 40.3 *m.* (601 alt., 1,428 pop.), named for its prairie topography, originated as an Indian village, and was first known as a trading post, founded by the Frenchman Du Pazhe about 1790, later operated by Vetel Vermette for the American Fur Trading Company. It is next recorded as a stop on the rounds of Jesse Walker, "Daniel Boone of Methodism," missionary to the Indians, who preached here in 1826. The Rev. Mr. Walker's son-in-law, Captain James Walker, built a cabin near the Indian village in 1829; the settlement that grew up around it was for some time known as Walker's Grove.

On Old Main Street, State 126, R. of the highway along the river, are several examples of the Greek Revival style of architecture popular in the 1830's, among them the HALFWAY HOUSE, built in 1834 as a station on the Chicago-Ottawa State Road. The building served as post office on the first Chicago-St. Louis mail route. At that time the Joliet postmaster was obliged to come to Plainfield for the mail. Two decades later, however, following the completion of the Illinois and Michigan Canal (1848), Joliet quite eclipsed Plainfield.

The MILES V. HARTONG COLLECTION (*apply to owner*), in Mr. Hartong's home on the south side of the square, contains Indian relics, a variety of pioneer tools and furnishings, a collection of old county and State histories, and many early photographs and drawings of places o'f interest in Will and Cook Counties. The GRAVE OF THE REVEREND JESSE WALKER, who died in Des Plaines in 1835, is in Plainfield Cemetery. Fronting the highway is a FOUNDRY AND SHOPS, where small locomotives are manufactured for use in amusement parks and for other narrow-gauge purposes.

On the western edge of Plainfield the route crosses the DU PAGE RIVER, named for Du Pazhe, the trader. The stream, bordered by a magnificent growth of oak, elm, and maple, is dammed in the vicinity of the city. Downstream (L), just off the highway, is the WOOD HOMESTEAD, girlhood home of Mrs. Thomas Alva Edison.

At 49 *m.* is a junction with US 34 (*see Tour* 13).

AURORA, 53 *m.* (740 alt., 46,589 pop.) (*see Aurora*).

Points of Interest: Aurora Historical Society, Phillip's Park Museum and Zoo, Undstad Firearm Collection, Aurora College, and others.

Aurora is at a junction with State 31, which follows the Fox River northward (*see Tour* 12A) past Mooseheart and Batavia to Geneva, 9 *m.*, at a junction with US 330 (*see Tour* 12A).

Section b. Aurora to Iowa Line, 107 m.

West of Aurora, 0 *m.*, US 30 crosses a rolling, partly wooded region of fine dairy farms. Shortly beyond the city limits are several estates of prominent Chicagoans. FITCHOME FARMS (L), 3.6 *m.*, affords an opportunity to inspect modern dairying methods. Long plate glass windows open on the "milking parlor" where twice daily a herd of Holsteins is mechanically milked.

For 30 miles the highway parallels the tracks of the Chicago, Burlington & Quincy Railroad. At SUGAR GROVE (L), 7 *m.*, the Burlington's streamlined *Zephyr* saluted the Great Northern's 78-year-old *Billy Crooks* on the morning of March 17, 1939. The historic old wood-burning engine, the first steam locomotive in the Northwest, was on its way from St. Paul, Minnesota, to the New York World's Fair. With its two ancient coaches, it made the trip by stages, stopping at night because its kerosene lamps did not allow it to travel after dark.

On the western edge of the city, on Rock Creek (L), is the old
UNIONVILLE MILL (*visitors welcome*), erected 1858. The stone walls
are 2 feet thick, and the heavy beams in walls and ceilings are of hand-
hewn oak. The cement dam is 9 feet high and 84 feet long. The mill,
still water-powered, continues in operation, grinding flour and feed
for farmers of the community.

The densely wooded wild lands upstream from the highway on
the west bank of Rock Creek are the proposed site of a State park.
The abundance of wild life, the beauty of the valley, and the wealth
of historical associations recommend the site.

West of Morrison the highway winds through wooded hills cut
by deep ravines as it approaches the Mississippi.

The ABBOTT FARM (*private*) is R. of the highway at 99.8 *m*. The
region was early associated with the activities of a notorious band of
counterfeiters, who centered their operations in the basement of the
farm-house later purchased by the Abbotts and moved across the road
to its present location. In the process of moving the building several
bundles of bogus money and the plates used in their printing were
discovered. This led to the capture of Ben Boyd, master engraver of
the gang, in his workshop in Fulton. The evidence readily convicted
him, and he was sent to Joliet prison. The gang thereupon plotted to
steal the body of President Lincoln and to use it as a basis for nego-
tiating the release of Boyd. (*See Lincoln's Tomb, Springfield.*)

At 105 *m*. is a junction with State 80 (*see Tour* 6) on the outskirts
of FULTON, 106.5 *m*. (597 alt., 2,656 pop.). The city, which commemorates the inventor of the steamboat, owes its early growth and
importance to river commerce, but is today largely a residential community, the center of a prosperous agricultural area. Local greenhouses,
conspicuous on the city's border, have more than 12 acres of rich prairie
soil under glass. Thousands of baskets of tomatoes and boxes of cu-
cumbers are shipped annually.

US 30 crosses the Iowa Line, 107 *m*., on a toll bridge (*automobile
and driver*, 20c; *passengers,* 5c; *trailers,* 10c) spanning the Mississippi
to Clinton, Iowa (*see Iowa Guide*).

TOUR 9

Roadbed hard-surfaced throughout; four lanes between Chicago and Geneva, two lanes westward.

The Chicago & North Western Ry. parallels US 330 between Chicago and Dixon. Usual accommodations throughout.

US 330, an alternate route with US 30 (*see Tour* 12), crosses the Chicago metropolitan area, penetrating the very heart of the great city. In the course of its length, the route is variously a placid country road, a bustling suburban thoroughfare, or a feverish metropolitan boulevard. North of the junction with US 30 near the Indiana Line, the highway skirts the suburbs of steel-mill Hammond, Indiana, then crosses industrial wastelands that extend south from Chicago. Twenty-six miles of the route are in the city. West of Chicago US 330 passes suburbs that have scarcely a distinguishable break in contiguity. Between the Fox and the Rock Rivers the highway follows the gentle swell of prairie farm lands and passes through sedate little cities to its western junction with US 30 at Dixon.

North of the junction with US 30 (*see Tour* 12), 0 *m.*, 2.5 miles west of the Indiana Line, the route crosses fields of corn and onions, passes through a section of the GURDON S. HUBBARD FOREST PRESERVE, and enters the sparsely populated outskirts of LANSING, 4 *m.* (618 alt., 3,378 pop.). Lansing was organized in the 1860's by Dutch and German farmers. The village has since become an adjunct of the vast industrial area concentrated at the northwestern corner of Indiana.

At 7.2 *m.* is a junction with US 6 (*see Tour* 14). North of the junction the route skirts the SHABBONA WOODS FOREST PRESERVE (L).

CALUMET CITY, 8.7 *m.* (585 alt., 12,298 pop.), R. of the highway, is a residential outgrowth of Hammond, Indiana. Much of the city was built during a real estate boom of the 1920's. Calumet is the French name for the peace-pipe of the Indians. Part of the municipality was platted in 1833.

North of Calumet City the route traverses a stark industrial plain studded with grain elevators, steel mills, oil refineries, and freight car shops.

The CHICAGO CITY LIMITS are crossed at 10.5 *m.*, near the southeastern corner of the city. The route swings L. along the eastern edge

229

of the BEAUBIEN FOREST PRESERVE, and continues N. past LAKE CALUMET to the intersection of Stony Island Ave. and 95th St., 17.5 *m.*, which is also the junction with US 12 (*see Tour* 9) and US 20 (*see Tour* 11). US 330 continues ahead (N) on Stony Island Ave. to the intersection of Michigan Blvd. with Roosevelt Road, in downtown Chicago.

CHICAGO, 29.3 *m.* (598 alt., 3,376,438 pop.) (*see Chicago*).

Points of Interest: Chicago Board of Trade Building, Union Stock Yards, Field Museum of Natural History, Art Institute of Chicago, Museum of Science and Industry, Adler Planetarium, Shedd Aquarium, University of Chicago, and others.

In Chicago are junctions with State 1 (*see Tour* 1), State 42 (*see Tour* 2), US 41 (*see Tour* 2A), US 12 (*see Tour* 9), US 14 (*see Tour* 10), US 20 (*see Tour* 11), US 66 (*see Tour* 17), and the Illinois Waterway (*see Tour* 21).

The route continues L. from Michigan Ave. on Roosevelt Road past CICERO (L), 36 *m.* (610 alt., 66,602 pop.) (*see Tour* 17), BERWYN (L), 37 *m.* (612 alt., 47,027 pop.) (*see Tour* 17), and OAK PARK (R), 37 *m.* (630 alt., 63,982 pop.) (*see Tour* 11), to the intersection of Roosevelt Road and Harlem Avenue, 38 *m.*

Immediately west of Harlem Avenue is FOREST PARK, 39.8 *m.* (620 alt., 14,555 pop.), upon the Des Plaines River, a community of the quick and the dead. In the many cemeteries that comprise nearly one-half of the town's corporate area are approximately 250,000 graves.

A block south of the castelated entrance to WALDHEIM CEMETERY, in the 900 block on S. Des Plaines Ave., R. of US 330, is a MONUMENT TO THE MEN HANGED FOR THE HAYMARKET RIOT, November 11, 1887 (*see Labor*), a symbolic bronze by A. Weinert. Memorial services for the four, Engel, Fischers, Parsons, and Spies, who are buried here, are observed each year.

FOREST HOME CEMETERY, south of Waldheim and north of the highway, is upon the site of a Potawatomi village and burial ground. INDIAN RELICS, unearthed in the course of grave-digging, are displayed in the cemetery office. South of US 330 are several congregational tracts of the JEWISH WALDHEIM CEMETERY.

SHOWMEN'S REST in WOODLAWN CEMETERY, at the southern end of the city, L. from Des Plaines Ave. on Cermak Road, is for deceased members of the Showmen's League of America. Their first plot, marked by a group of five granite elephants, was purchased to bury 63 circus performers who were killed in a train wreck at Gary, Indiana, in July 1918.

The FOREST PARK BASEBALL MUSEUM (*Mon.-Fri.,* 7-6; *Sat.,* 7-9), 7212 W. Madison St., is probably the only one of its kind in the world. Pictures from the time the game was called "Four Old Cat" through the present; uniforms and bats of such famous players as Joe Tinker; data and records since the beginning of baseball; and autographed baseballs from all leagues 'form part of the extensive collection.

West of Forest Park the road emerges from the metropolitan area and enters prairie lands that are checkerboarded by farms, sub-divisions, and country estates.

An entryway (L), 41 *m.*, leads through the 320-acre grounds of the EDWARD HINES, JR. MEMORIAL HOSPITAL (*visiting:* 2:30-4:30, *Tues., Thurs., Sun.*). The hospital established in 1920 for the care of World War veterans, commemorates the partial donor's son, killed in the War. The Federal government administers the institution.

The 29 buildings are on the site of an automobile race track, which accounts for the familiar designation of the hospital as the "Speedway." The extraordinary shape of the four-story main build-ing, 2,640 feet by 50 feet, was dictated by the dimensions of the race track grandstand, upon the foundations of which the building rests. Here are housed the tuberculosis, medical, surgical, and neuropatho-logical units, and the out-patient department. Most of the other build-ings, which are of red brick, in a Colonial style, house the 1,200 em-ployees of the institution. The cancer research unit of the hospital has issued important publications in that field.

Right of the highway, and opposite the hospital, is MAYWOOD (632 alt., 25,829 pop.) (*see Tour* 11).

BROADVIEW (L), 41.7 *m.* (625 alt., 2,334 pop.), an offshoot of Maywood, incorporated as a village in 1910, has no business dis-trict, for it is wholly residential. BROADVIEW ACADEMY, a Seventh Day Adventist coeducational school, Cermak Road just west of 19th Ave., has an average enrollment of 200 students, many of whom earn their tuition by working in the academy or on its 90-acre farm.

At 43.3 *m.* is a junction with US 45 (*see Tour* 3), By-Pass US 12 (*see Tour* 9), and By-Pass US 20 (*see Tour* 11).

Half a mile west of the junction, the road abruptly leaves the lake plain and enters the rolling moraines that spread throughout most of Du Page County. The route passes at some distance from the cen-ters of several out-lying suburbs, their church steeples, smoke-stacks, and watertanks visible to the north. From the highway these com-munities seem lost in the dense green of trees that shade their quiet streets.

At 50.4 *m.* is a junction with Main Street, a paved road.

Right on Main Street is LOMBARD, 1.6 *m.* (708 alt., 6,197 pop.), named for Joseph Lombard, a Chicagoan, who platted the town in 1868. The first white settler in the area was Winslow Churchill, who in 1834, aided by friendly In-dians, built a log cabin and established a claim to the region now the CHURCHILL FOREST PRESERVE on St. Charles Road. Sheldon Peck, journeying overland from Vermont, settled at Lombard in 1838 and built the PECK HOUSE (*private*), Grace Ave. and Parkside St., which functioned as a station on the Underground Railroad in pre-Civil War years. The neighborly aspect of con-temporary Lombard has been depicted by Katherine Reynolds in two novels, *Green Valley* and *Willow Creek*.

LILACIA PARK, W. Maple St. and S. Park Ave., a 10-acre public garden, contains more than 300 varieties of lilacs. The park is the former estate of Col. William Plum, who, in pursuit of a life-long hobby, collected lilacs from throughout the world. Plum bequeathed the estate to the city of Lombard, and upon his death in 1927 the gift was accepted and the Lombard Park District was organized. The Plum home, in accord with the bequest, houses the HELEN W. PLUM MEMORIAL LIBRARY (open), which honors the memory of Colonel Plum's wife, Helen Williams, a descendant of Roger Williams. Jens Jensen, Chicago landscape architect, planned the beautiful arrangement of the park, which has since been developed by others.

Tulips border winding paths, with lilac bushes set slightly back from them. Especially notable are the President Lincoln lilac bush north of the library and the venerable white lilac on the north side of the lily pond. On the east terrace of the library is a magnificent silver aspen. In the southeast corner of the park the brilliant coloring of a Schwedler maple brightens the scene both in spring and fall. Southwest of the library ancient apple trees border the pathway; a large gingko tree is nearby.

The Lombard Lilac League presents a pageant in May of each year when the lilacs are in full bloom. Admission to the park is free, except during Festival Week, when there is usually a small charge.

GLEN ELLYN, 52.7 m. (766 alt., 7,680 pop.), is mainly north of the highway. In naming the community, Thomas E. Hill commemorated his wife Ellyn, and the picturesque glen at the foot of Cooper Hill. The founders of Glen Ellyn once dwelt at a stagecoach stop known as Stacy's Corners, one mile north of the present business district. In 1849 the Galena & Chicago Union Railroad was constructed south of Stacy's Corners, whereupon its citizens, anxious to be on the main line, transplanted church and houses to the present site. The new town was platted in 1851. LAKE ELLYN PARK borders a small lake in the northern part of the city.

WHEATON, 55.1 m. (753 alt., 7,258 pop.), seat of Du Page County, honors in its name Warren and Jesse Wheaton, godfathers of the town and of its three great assets: the railroad, the college, and the courthouse.

In 1838 the Wheatons laid claim to the land that is now the heart of the city. A decade later Warren Wheaton contributed a right-of-way to the pioneer Galena & Chicago Union Railroad. His generosity, in complete reversal of the price-boosting tactics then common among landowners, was amply rewarded by the subsequent growth of the town.

The college came in 1853, the year the town was platted. The Wesleyan Methodists, seeking a site for an orthodox school, selected Wheaton and founded Illinois Institute, "for Christ and His Kingdom." Warren Wheaton gave the original campus. Seven years later, when the school was reorganized under the auspices of the Congregationalists, he gave every other one of his town lots to assure the financial soundness of the institution. Renamed for its benefactor, WHEATON COLLEGE, Washington St. and Seminary Ave., undenominational but fervently fundamentalist, is today the largest liberal arts college in Illinois, with 23 buildings and an enrollment of more than 1,100. BLANCHARD HALL, in the Victorian Gothic battlemented style, is named for Jonathan Blanchard (*see Galesburg, Tour* 13), early president of the college and one of the foremost abolitionists of Illinois.

Securing the courthouse was not so simple. Since the formation of Du Page County in 1839, Naperville (*see Tour* 13) had been the county seat. Wheaton as early as 1857 attempted, without success, to wrest that distinction from her neighbor on the strength of possessing a railroad and a more central location. Ten years later, however, the voters of the county determined in Wheaton's favor, and a courthouse was built. Warren Wheaton gave the land, and he and his brother each subscribed $2,000 for the construction of the building. But Naperville, intent upon remaining the seat of justice, refused to recognize the election as legal. Although the circuit court, after months of contention, upheld the vote, Naperville refused to give up the public records. Injunctions were served and counter proceedings instituted. Impatient of longer waiting, Wheaton resorted to direct action. One night in July 1868 a body of men descended upon the Naperville courthouse and made off with a wagonload of public records. Save for several that were overlooked, and which subsequently have disappeared, they are now in the safe keeping of the county clerk in the Wheaton COURTHOUSE, a large modern structure completed in 1938, which stands on the site of three earlier ones.

Although the Wheatons were the "first family" of early days, others were influential as the community developed, among them the Garys. Erastus Gary had arrived in the vicinity in 1832. His son, Elbert, the Judge Gary of steel fame, was born in Wheaton in 1846; two terms as county judge gained him the title by which he was thereafter known. The GARY MEMORIAL METHODIST EPISCOPAL CHURCH, Main St. and Seminary Ave., modern English Gothic in design, commemorates the family.

North of Wheaton on Main St. at Geneva Road is the THEOSOPHICAL SOCIETY TEMPLE (*open 9-5 weekdays*), 1.5 *m.* The modern, three-story building, of Cloister brick with Bedford stone trim, set in the midst of extensive landscaped grounds, was designed by Irving K. Pond, Chicago architect. MURALS by Richard B. Farley in the reception room depict the evolutionary process as interpreted by Theosophy. The LIBRARY of more than 15,000 volumes, primarily on occult subjects, is one of the largest of its kind in the country. Various speakers from many nations have addressed the open meetings held at four o'clock on the fourth Sunday of each month. Addresses are followed by a tea and musicale to which visitors are invited. Classes in theosophy (*Wed.,* 8 *p.m.*) are open to the public without charge.

At 57.3 *m.* is a junction with a graveled road.

Left on this road is the CHICAGO TRIBUNE EXPERIMENTAL FARM, 1 *m.* (*open in summer; free guide service*). A similar farm, under the direction of the

Tribune, is near Yorkville, (*see Tour* 13). The farms, established in 1934, are owned and operated by the Chicago *Tribune* in the interests of Mid-West agriculture. In co-operation with Federal and State agencies many improvements have been made in crops and livestock. Resistance to insects, drought, and frost has been developed in many strains of field corn. Many varieties or strains of rare and unusual crops are grown from seeds obtained from distant parts of the world. An annual event of the farm season is the horse and mule pulling contest held each summer at the Wheaton farms.

GENEVA, 66 *m.* (720 alt., 4,607 pop.), is on both sides of the Fox River. The antithesis of all that is martial, the peaceful riverside community indirectly owes its existence to the Black Hawk War. Soldiers returning from the frontier in 1832 extolled the Fox River country to footloose Easterners, some of whom ventured to the area within the following year. Following its founding, Geneva became an hospitable "jumping-off" place for pioneers bent on traveling farther west.

The elm-shaded sidestreets of Geneva contain frequent examples of mid-nineteenth century dwellings; notable among them is a GREEK REVIVAL HOUSE, 220 S. 3rd St. MILL RACE INN, southeast corner at the highway bridge, housed the first blacksmith shop in Geneva. Opposite, is an OLD MILL, still operated by water power, and using the original burrs to grind some of its products. The STATE TRAINING SCHOOL FOR GIRLS (*open* 9-4, *Mon.-Fri.*), S. Batavia St. on the east side of the river, provides academic, commercial, and vocational instruction for girls committed by juvenile courts.

1. Right (north) from Geneva on State 31 is ST. CHARLES, 2 *m.* (802 alt., 5,377 pop.), a century-old residential, industrial, and commuting center on the Fox River. The elaborate $600,000 HOTEL BAKER, which occupies the site of the old mill around which the pioneer community developed, is suggestive of the wealth that is concentrated in St. Charles' homes and nearby country estates. POTTAWATOMIE PARK, on the river at the north end of the city, preserves a fraction of the wildland beauty which has attracted many wealthy Chicagoans to the Fox River Valley.

2. Left from Geneva State 31 follows the Fox River 9 miles southward to a junction with US 30 (*see Tour* 12) at Aurora (*see Aurora*).

The RIVERBANK LABORATORIES (R), 1.3 *m.*, in a building of ultra-modern design, were established in 1919 by Colonel George Fabyn (1867-1936) for research in acoustics and to manufacture tuning forks, sound meters and other acoustical equipment. Colonel Fabyn's ability to solve codes and ciphers proved of great value to the Federal government during the World War. The vast FABYN ESTATE borders the river (L).

Right from State 31 at this point, 0.6 *m.* on a graveled road, to the PECK MERINO SHEEP FARM, where prize-winning American Merino sheep have been bred since 1860.

The two-and-a-half-story ultra-modern CAMPANA PLANT (*tours*, 9-4, *Mon.-Fri.*, 9-11 *Sat., on the hour*), 1.7 *m.*, is separated from the highway by a spacious lawn (R). The exterior of the building consists solely of glass blocks and pale green tiles in long horizontal rows.

BATAVIA, 3 *m.* (719 alt., 5,045 pop.), was named by early settlers for their home in New York. The business and residential sections are about equally divided by the river into an East Side and a West Side. As in Aurora, the post office, city hall, and other municipal service buildings are centrally located on an island. Factories that line both banks of the river manufacture windmills.

Among the earliest sites chosen for settlement following the Black Hawk War (1832), Batavia, because of its triple advantage of water power, fertile soil, and surface limestone, began its industrial career in 1837 with a flour mill. By 1850 it had developed an extensive commerce in limestone, which gave it the nickname of "Quarry City." Several fine old houses built of this local stone still stand along the highway. Among these are LOCKWOOD HALL (R), and the SNOW HOUSE (L), at the southern edge of town, both in the Greek Revival style. Right on Union Avenue is BELLEVUE REST HOME, built in 1856 for the Batavia Institute, a private academy soon superseded by public schools and taken over in 1867 by Dr. R. J. Patterson, a specialist in mental and nervous disorders. Mary Todd Lincoln was a patient here in 1875. The room she occupied retains the ornate dark walnut furniture fashionable in her time.

MOOSEHEART (R), 5 m., is a community founded by James J. Davis, the United States senator from Pennsylvania, and supported by the Loyal Order of Moose. The institution provides home, educational training through high school, and technical training in several trades for 1,000 children of deceased members of the order. The grounds are open from sunup to sundown daily (*guides available for each unit; cafeteria open to visitors at noon weekdays*).

Known to radio listeners as the City of Childhood, Mooseheart answers the description in almost a story-book sense. Here is a scientifically directed minia-ture society whose affairs are conducted by the child citizens themselves, aided by adult advisers. The children live in small groups in cottages, each headed by a housemother. Living conditions approximate home life as nearly as possible, and although all children, because of admission limitations, are fatherless, Moose-heart provides jobs for many mothers, thus saving a further break in the family.

Boys have a choice of training in one or more of eleven trades or profes-sions; girls, in six. Each boy or girl receives full apprentice experience. When a new unit is to be built, the drafting class draws the plans and makes the blue prints, the concrete class produces structural materials, and the sheet metal class provides roofing and drain pipes. Other groups stand ready to paint, paper, or varnish; and the tin shop makes such utensils as dish pans and dust pans.

Apprentices in beauty culture and barbering gain experience with an aver-age of 450 haircuts per week. Students in the power machine sewing class see the suits and dresses they make actually worn by the members of the community. Girls manage the cafeteria, under a trained supervisor. Student typists and bookkeepers assist in the business office. Journalism classes co-operate with the print shop in producing local reading matter. Children with musical or artistic gifts are trained to earn an income in orchestra, band, or designing studios. About 15 per cent out of each graduating class go to college. At the age of eight each child is taught to do his own shopping and to keep a check book. From junior high school his work is paid for in actual money, and he must budget his accounts so that by graduation he will have saved at least $50.

Near the landscaped entranceway, which is marked by a monumental shaft, is the CLOCK TOWER, commanding an inclusive view of the 1,200-acre grounds. East is the rolling, wooded valley of Fox River; north, 20-acre Moose Lake; and south, the school buildings, athletic field, and playgrounds. West are the city's 125 buildings. Outstanding are the RECEPTION COTTAGE, where children undergo preliminary observation; the PHILADELPHIA MEMORIAL HOSPITAL, with state-house cupola; the OHIO PLAZA RESEARCH LABORATORY, also with cupola; and the one-story units of the PENNSYLVANIA BABY VILLAGE. The ROOSEVELT MEMORIAL BUILDING contains an auditorium seating 1,000, which is used as church, theater, or dance or banquet hall; the school bank and the community department store are also here. More than 3,000 children have been admitted to Mooseheart.

West of the city is the 800-acre farm, its grain-fields, gardens, greenhouses, and dairy barns operated on the most modern of agricultural methods. Vegetables, meat, milk, and eggs are produced for the community. In the clock tower are the CAFETERIA and the DISPLAY ROOMS where pottery, cakes, and other products of the specific training given older children are exhibited.

West of Geneva US 330 winds through undulating farm lands, at intervals entering brief tunnels formed by parallel rows of overarching elms.

The STATE SCHOOL FOR BOYS (R), 70.7 m., the companion institution of the State school in Geneva, cares for an average of 650 boys between the ages of ten and seventeen. In a village that consists of 6 farmhouses and 14 red brick, tile-roofed cottages arranged around a square, the boys are given academic and vocational training. The school is not a penal institution; "sentences" are worked out in terms of work units and scholastic credits.

At 75 m. is a junction with State 47.

Left on State 47 is ELBURN, 0.8 m. (848 alt., 548 pop.), a farming center that dates from 1854, when it was platted along the Galena & Chicago Union Railroad. Public sentiment in the vicinity, as in all of Kane County in the 1850's, was definitely abolitionist. Tradition has it that Lincoln, while visiting a cousin in Elburn in 1858, was greeted by a local organization calling itself the "Lincoln True Hearts," which pledged him its active support in the senatorial contest. Northern Illinois was as strongly pro-Lincoln as southern Illinois was pro-Douglas.

At 2 m. on State 47 is a junction with a graveled road.

Left on this road to JOHNSONS MOUND (picnic facilities), 4.9 m., in a unit of the Kane County Forest Preserve. The mound, which rises noticeably above the low, rolling farm lands, is attractively developed as a county park. From the keeper's cottage at the entrance a road (closed to automobiles) circles the mound to its summit. Right of this road, a few hundred yards into the woods, is SHABBONA ELM, standing in solitary grandeur in an opening of the forest. The tree has been identified by experts as approximately 325 years old. Portia Gilpin, in Memoirs of a Giant Tree, tells the stories this lofty water-elm might tell, could it speak. A bronze tablet in front of the tree, placed by the Fox River Valley Woodcraft Council, states that the tree was named "in honor of the Pottawatomi chieftain of this region . . . on the 12th Sun of the Wild Rose Moon, 1922."

DE KALB, 91 m. (886 alt., 8,545 pop.), named for Baron Johann De Kalb, major general in the American Revolutionary Army, was known until 1938, when the industry was transferred elsewhere, as the "barbed wire capital of the world." In 1874 Joseph E. Glidden patented an improved barbed wire. About the same time Jacob Haish patented a barbed wire manufacturing process. The patents clashed, and the longest drawn-out litigation recorded in patent infringement jurisprudence resulted. GLIDDEN HOSPITAL, 1719 S. 1st St., is a memorial to Joseph Glidden. HAISH MEMORIAL LIBRARY, Oak and N. 3rd Sts., commemorates its donor, Jacob Haish. The building, designed by White & Weber of Chicago, is of Indiana limestone in soft shades of buff and brown. It is considered one of the most beautiful modern buildings in Illinois. Fred M. Torrey, of Chicago, carved the four interior panels depicting art, history, fiction, and science, and the two exterior ones depicting the author and the reader.

NORTHERN ILLINOIS STATE TEACHERS COLLEGE, founded 1895, occupies 67 acres of natural woodland on the Kishwaukee River. The five buildings of the college, R. of the highway at the western end of town, accommodate an average enrollment of 950 students quarterly.

HOPKINS PARK, on the northern edge of De Kalb, provides, in addition to picnic and camping facilities, a modern swimming pool and bath house (*nominal fee*), and an open-air auditorium.

Right from De Kalb on 1st St. is COLTONVILLE, 3.2 *m.*, identified by a rural schoolhouse at a junction with a graveled road. On the R. side of the road, immediately opposite the schoolhouse, is a monument that marks the SITE OF THE FIRST COURT HELD IN DE KALB COUNTY. Nearby, slightly to the north, was an old Potawatomi Indian village. A depression on the Adee farm, which now occupies the site, reveals the place where the exhumed body of Capas, chief of the Potawatomi, lay.

ROCHELLE, 108.5 *m.* (793 alt., 3,785 pop.) (*see Tour* 4), is at a junction with US 51 (*see Tour* 4). West of Rochelle extensive fields of asparagus line the highway for two miles. The 1,500 acres of intensively cultivated land are owned by the Rochelle Asparagus Company, which operates a local cannery.

ASHTON, 118 *m.* (817 alt., 868 pop.), a thrifty German-American village, centers upon the MILLS AND PETRIE MEMORIAL, a community building named for the partial donors. The modern structure of stone and yellow brick, erected in 1936, houses a library, a stage, and a gymnasium that may be converted into an assembly hall, play room, or roller skating rink.

DIXON, 135 *m.* (659 alt., 9,908 pop.) (*see Tour* 12), is at a junction with State 2 (*see Tour* 4A), US 30 (*see Tour* 12), and US 52 (*see Tour* 15).

TOUR 10

CHICAGO—JOLIET

Four-lane concrete roadbed between Chicago and Joliet, two-lane hard-surfaced southwest; heavy traffic, sharp corners, and narrow pavement necessitate cautious driving.

The Atchison, Topeka & Santa Fe Ry. parallels US 66 between Chicago and Joliet; the Alton R. R. between Joliet and Springfield; Illinois Central System between Springfield and Mount Olive; Litchfield & Madison Ry. between Mount Olive and Edwardsville.

Accommodations at short intervals.

US 66, the most heavily traveled major highway in the State, cuts diagonally across Illinois between the great population centers of Chicago and St. Louis. Along its course are the State Capital and half a dozen State institutions. Industrial cities and county seats in which Lincoln practiced law alternate with farm villages and mining towns that will be long remembered in the labor history of the State and Nation.

Section a. Chicago to Joliet, 40 m.

CHICAGO, 0 *m.* (598 alt., 3,376,438 pop.) (*see Chicago*).

Points of Interest: Chicago Board of Trade Building, Union Stock Yards, Field Museum of Natural History, Art Institute of Chicago, Museum of Science and Industry, Adler Planetarium, Shedd Aquarium, University of Chicago, and others.

Chicago is at the junction with State 1 (*see Tour* 1), State 42 (*see Tour* 2), US 41 (*see Tour* 2A), US 12 (*see Tour* 9), US 14 (*see Tour* 10), US 20 (*see Tour* 11), US 330 (*see Tour* 12A) and the Illinois Waterway (*See Tour* 22).

Angling southwestward from Chicago, US 66 crosses the southern portion of CICERO, 7 *m.* (610 alt. 66,602 pop.), largest of Chicago's suburbs. Although its northern and eastern limits touch Chicago, Cicero is economically independent of its huge neighbor; its Western Electric plant alone employs, at peak periods, more than the suburb's total working population.

In the middle of the last century only 10 families lived on the swampy lowlands where Cicero now stands. At the first township

238

election in 1857, 9 of the 14 persons who voted were elected to office. The township grew slowly until Civil War days when its farmlands, enhanced in value by the needs of the embattled North, began to attract scores of homesteaders from the East. Cicero was incorporated as a town in 1867 and continued to progress. The dank lowlands were drained by some 50 miles of ditches; offshoots of the main community were bound together by a system of permanent roads; and in 1869 Cicero received a city charter.

Foresighted land speculators perceived that Chicago would advance irresistibly westward, and in the last quarter of the 19th century boulevards, delineated along cornfield furrows, were elegantly named. Hetty Green, the eccentric millionaire, and Portus Weare, shrewd wheat speculator, were prominent among the early dealers in Cicero real estate. With a flair for promotion, Weare built a 20-room frame house, designated "Ranch 47," which stood at the northeast corner of 52nd Avenue and 25th Street. Surrounding "Ranch 47" were rows of cabins copied from those in the Klondike. In the following decades Cicero was weakened by territorial losses and strengthened by industrial gains. Two sections of Cicero were annexed to Chicago in 1892, and in 1901 the contiguous communities of Berwyn and Oak Park seceded to establish separate municipalities.

Stimulated by the growth of Chicago and its own development as an industrial area, Cicero more than tripled its population between 1910 and 1920. Among those attracted to Cicero in the booming twenties was Al Capone, "Public Enemy Number One," who established headquarters in a hotel near the Western Electric Company plant and organized a chain of speak-easies, honkytonks, and gambling houses along the streets on the north and west sides of the plant. Attended by some 200 henchmen, Capone here directed the affairs of his brewing and related enterprises until his indictment by a Federal grand jury at Chicago in 1931. The inhabitants of Cicero, pained by the notoriety that Capone's operations had brought their city, immediately purged their government and made intensive efforts to efface evidence of his activities.

The city has slightly more than a hundred industrial plants. Saws, stoves, castings, forgings, building materials, and telephone equipment are the main products. Generally neat and closely knit, the residential sections consist in large part of compact blocks of detached, two-family brick houses, with double porches and miniature lawns.

The J. STERLING MORTON HIGH SCHOOL, 25th and Austin Sts., is known among educators for its curriculum and advanced methods of instruction. The broadcasting station WHFC (1420 kc.) is at 6138 Cermak Road.

The huge WESTERN ELECTRIC COMPANY PLANT (*closed to visitors*), Cermak Rd. and Cicero Ave., was established here in 1902. Prior to 1929 the company employed 40,000 workers in manufacturing telephone equipment, audiphones, broadcasting systems, and other electrical appliances.

Left from Ogden Ave. on Cicero Ave. 1.5 *m.* to SPORTSMAN'S PARK (*half-mile track*) and the HAWTHORNE RACE TRACK (*one-mile track*), which straddle the line between Cicero and Stickney. The two race tracks, of local importance only, conduct one-month meets during September and October on a non-conflicting schedule.

Cicero merges imperceptibly with BERWYN, 9.2 *m.* (612 alt., 47,027 pop.), named for a town in Pennsylvania. Berwyn, unlike the usual Illinois municipality that grew from a Black Hawk War village to a Civil War town and then to a World War city, was ready-made in 1890 by Charles E. Piper and Wilbur J. Andrews, two realtors who provided their subdivision with essential facilities and relied on the future growth of Chicago to supply a populace. Berwyn was incorporated as a village in 1891, and chartered as a city in 1908.

During the first two decades of the present century, Berwyn was a typical suburb in which harried commuters relaxed of an evening, weeded gardens, set hens, and mowed their lawns. Indicative of this period are the many flat-roofed one-story houses, sold on the supposition that the buyer would in time save sufficient money to add a second story and transform the structure into a two-family flat, which seldom happened. A large part of the commuting population then worked in the Western Electric Company plant at Cicero, by reason of which the city was plunged into mourning on July 24, 1915, when the *Eastland,* chartered for a company excursion, rolled over in the Chicago River and drowned 812 persons. The majority were from Berwyn.

The metropolitan population continued to expand until it reached the bursting point. World War prosperity released the pressure, and in 1921 Berwyn experienced a frenzied building boom. Blocks of bungalows, each the counterpart of the other, rose on the prairie as fast as hands could lay brick, spread mortar, and attach roofs. A bare rectangle of land frequently became an inhabited city section within three months. Municipal building codes were rigidly enforced throughout the boom, accounting for the trim substantial dwellings of present Berwyn.

Berwyn is wholly residential; its economy lags or races with the quantity of production in Cicero or Chicago plants. The inhabitants are predominantly Bohemian by birth or descent.

GAGE FARM, Harlem Ave. between Cermak Rd. and Riverside Dr., has been the subject of frequent litigation since 1881. In that year Chicago obtained judgment against David A. Gage for losses totaling $507,700 which had occurred in his term as city treasurer (1869-73), and acquired his 225-acre farm as part payment. By the expansion of the metropolitan area the value of the farm gradually increased until it exceeded by $1,000,000 the amount of the judgment. Mrs. Clara

Gage Clark, David Gage's daughter, brought suit to obtain the differ-
ence between the judgment and the enhanced value of the farm. A
Federal District Court ruled that Chicago had a clear title to the property, and in 1934 the United States Court of Appeals upheld this
decision. Until converted into a nursery, its present use, the idle property cost Chicago $99,500 in taxes paid to Berwyn.

At 10.3 *m.* is the junction with US 34 (*see Tour* 13).

On the left the highway borders STICKNEY, 10.8 *m.* (605 alt.,
2,005 pop.). The town, although its limits touch Chicago, is incompletely developed, and offers few accommodations other than a considerable stretch of taverns. In the southwest corner of MOUNT
AUBURN MEMORIAL PARK, 41st St. at Oak Park Ave., is a Chinese
burial ground, where the traditional Chinese rites are observed. Mourn-
ers in the cortege are each given wrapped nickels; punk sticks are
lighted; a bottle of rice whisky is passed around. Three portions of
food—pork, rice, and chicken—are left at the grave, with three sets of
chop sticks. Most of the graves are temporary; the remains are
exhumed at intervals and shipped to China in small steel boxes.

LYONS, 11.1 *m.* (615 alt., 4,787 pop.), stands at the edge of one
of the earliest known sites in the State—the portage between the Chicago and Des Plaines Rivers, used by Marquette and Jolliet and by the
Indians before them. Today Lyons is largely residential, its working
population finding employment in nearby manufacturing towns and in
Chicago.

At 12.5 *m.* is a junction with State 213.

Left on State 213 to SUMMIT, 1.1 *m.* (602 alt., 6,548 pop.), situated at
the imperceptible crest of the watershed between the Great Lakes and the
Mississippi drainage systems. Rain falling on the east side of town drains into
the Atlantic Ocean; that falling on the west side into the Gulf of Mexico. The
gargantuan CORN PRODUCTS COMPANY PLANT (*visitors welcome*), in the southern part of the city, is the largest corn refinery in the world. It is highly
mechanized; employs 1,700 persons when working at capacity; and grinds as
much as 80,000 bushels of corn a day. Corn is here processed into syrup, starch,
cooking oil, and scores of by-products used in the manufacture of candy, chewing tobacco, beer, mucilage, fireworks, ink, and stationery.

Bordering the highway (L) is a tremendous LIMESTONE QUARRY,
14 *m.* From a distance the narrow-guage trains seem like children's toys
scooting about the quarry floor or crawling up the long incline of the
crusher.

At 15.5 *m.* is a junction with US 45 (*see Tour* 3).

The LYONSVILLE CHURCH (L), 17.3 *m.*, at the crossing of Wolf
Road, is reputedly one of the oldest Congregational Churches in northern Illinois. It served as a recruiting station during the Civil War. Back
of the church is the MAPLE CREST GOLF CLUB (18 *holes, daily fee*);
across Wolf Road is the INDIAN HEAD GOLF CLUB (18 *holes, daily
fee*).

Lyonsville marks the eastern limit of the flat lake plain of ancient Lake Chicago, the forerunner of Lake Michigan. Westward lies the faintly rolling, wooded Valparaiso Moraine, one of the long crescent ridges of debris left by the glaciers.

STATEVILLE (L), 36 *m.*, is Illinois' new modern prison for men (*visiting limited to friends and relatives of prisoners*). The prison, largest of the State's penal institutions, raises its light brick walls in the center of a 60-acre enclosure, near the middle of the 2,200-acre State Penitentiary Farm. Care of the 4,100 prisoners, all first offenders more than 26 years old, is as modern as the building.

JOLIET, 40 *m.* (545 alt., 42,993 pop.) (*see Joliet*).

Points of Interest: Joliet Wall Paper Mills, American Institute of Laundering Vocational Training School, Oakwood Mound, and others.

Joliet is at the junction with US 30 (*see Tour* 12), and US 6 (*see Tour* 14).

Section b. Joliet to Bloomington and Normal, 93.5 m.

South of Joliet, 0 *m.*, US 66 leaves the valley of the Des Plaines and cuts diagonally cross-country, bridging the Kankakee and the head waters of the Mazon, Vermilion, and Mackinaw Rivers.

ELWOOD, 10 *m.* (646 alt., 257 pop.), serves a countryside that has witnessed a notable experiment in farm rehabilitation. In 1924 Arthur States, manager of the Roger Wharton estate, introduced improved agricultural practices that enabled ten of the twelve tenants of the estate to purchase land of their own with their share of farm income.

WILMINGTON, 17.7 *m.* (549 alt., 1,741 pop.), manufactures roofing and serves as a shopping center for Kankakee River resorts. A century ago, Thomas Fox laid out the town of Winchester on this site. In 1854, when another town proved prior rights to the name, settlers incorporated the village as Wilmington. Fox improved his investment in land by building a grist, saw, and carding mill, around which the community developed. Coal diverted attention from agriculture for a short time during the 1860's, but the town has always been essentially a trading center.

ISLAND PARK, a 35-acre wooded island in the Kankakee River, is one of the popular picnicking spots of the vicinity (*restaurants, cabins for rent, facilities for picnicking, boating*).

BRAIDWOOD, 22 *m.* (585 alt., 1,161 pop.), is surrounded by heaps of eroded, vari-colored earth, thrown up in the process of strip mining. In 1865 settler William Henneberry, in sinking a well, struck a rich 3-foot vein of coal 70 feet down. The new field attracted many mining syndicates, some from as far as Boston. By 1873 the community had grown to 3,000 and was incorporated as a city; in 1880 the population numbered 9,000, and as many as six long coal trains pulled out of

Braidwood daily. Miners lined up for three blocks at the pay window on pay day; 117 saloons, a large race track, and a music hall flourished. In the following decade more pits were closed than opened; as new fields were discovered in the vicinity, residents jacked up their houses and wheeled them to the new bonanzas. Mining was resumed in 1928 with modern strip methods, but intense mechanization precluded a revival of the roaring days of old Braidwood.

During its boom days, with an influx of thousands of transient miners of every nationality, Braidwood served as a laboratory both for labor organization and for the establishment of safety practices in mining. Impetus was given the movement by such tragic disasters as the flooding of the Diamond Mine (*see Tour* 15), which in 1883 took the lives of 74 men. Racial strife complicated the problems of labor, especially in 1877, when Negroes were imported by the operators to break a 9-month strike. Out of the Braidwood field have come such figures as John Mitchell, national labor leader; W. D. Ryan, Illinois arbitrator of mining disputes; Dan McGlaughlin, union leader and mining executive; and John H. Walker, State representative. Anton J. Cermak, Bohemian youth who later became mayor of Chicago and was killed (1933) in an assassin's attempt on the life of President Franklin D. Roosevelt, worked in the mines here until he was seventeen.

Braidwood is at the junction with US 52 (*see Tour* 15).

GODLEY, 24.5 *m.*, now merely a highway stop with one school, a few taverns, and a score of scattered houses, was once a booming coal town peopled by a thousand Scotch, Irish, and Welsh, the overflow of Braidwood's mining population. During the 1880's, 21 mines were in operation within a mile and a half of Godley; by 1906 all were closed. Bohemians have since settled in the village. Their pursuits are largely agricultural, and Godley's boom mining era is recalled only in the great "gob-heaps" that almost encircle the town.

BRACEVILLE, 26.5 *m.* (583 alt., 219 pop.), repeats the story of Godley—the census of 1890 reported a population ten times today's. Slag heaps in the vicinity are monuments of past activity; sad little piles represent the sporadic efforts of unemployed miners to salvage a few tons of coal from the closed mines.

GARDNER, 29.5 *m.* (590 alt., 869 pop.), is surrounded by slag piles, but beyond lie the farmlands that support the town as the center of a grain and stock-raising region.

DWIGHT, 39 *m.* (641 alt., 2,534 pop.), is known to thousands as the home of the KEELEY INSTITUTE (*visitors welcome*), an institution for the treatment of alcoholism and drug addiction. Dr. Leslie Keeley, a Civil War surgeon, came to Dwight after the war and continued the study of alcoholics that he had begun among Union soldiers. In 1879, when he made his famous pronouncement, "Drunkenness is a disease and I can cure it," he was sharply challenged by Joseph Medill, editor of the Chicago *Tribune*. Medill selected six of the worst alcoholics he could find in Chicago and sent them to Dwight for Keeley's treatment. When they returned, Medill capitulated and admitted, "The change for the better was so great that I scarcely recognized them. They went away sots—and returned gentlemen." The Keeley Institute has treated more than 400,000 patients, including 17,000 physicians and many hundred women, and has branches in California, Arkansas, and North and South Carolina. The average cure takes four weeks, and is based on Dr. Keeley's original assumption that chronic drunkenness is a disease of the nerve cells, and must be treated as such.

Occupying the old buildings of the Keeley Institute and the Livingston Hotel is the DWIGHT VETERANS HOSPITAL (3-4:45 *Mon., Fri., Sun. and holidays*), W. Main St. and Mazon Ave. A unit of the Veterans' Administration Facility, the hospital accommodates 225 patients.

Right from Dwight on State 17 is the STATE REFORMATORY FOR WOMEN (*arrange for group tours in advance*), 2 *m.* Completed in 1930, it is a small community in itself, occupying 160 acres, a third of which are wooded. Eight limestone buildings of the Normandy cottage type are arranged informally around a burr oak grove. Other structures include the Medium Security Building, where sick inmates are treated; a recreation center named in honor of Jane Addams; administration offices; and a receiving cottage. The reformatory resulted from the concerted action of State clubwomen to secure an advanced penal institution for women in Illinois. The prison aims to rehabilitate as well as confine.

Between Dwight and Pontiac the highway proceeds through a region of rich cornfields; the grain fields and the small trim farmsteads are text-book illustrations of the Illinois farm.

TOUR 11

CHICAGO—JOLIET—STARVED ROCK STATE PARK

Draught on Sanitary and Ship Canal, 20 ft.; on Des Plaines and Illinois Rivers, at least 9 ft. Minimum vertical clearance on the waterway, 16.5 ft. (over Sanitary and Ship Canal). Channel markings: (L) black and white (nun) buoys; (R) red can buoys. Where unmarked, the channel is in the middle of the river. In other than the channel, and particularly in lakes and sloughs, the water is commonly shallow, and sand bars and other obstructions to navigation are numerous. Only craft of very light draught should leave the main channel.

Strip maps and two Government publications pertaining in part to the Illinois Waterway are available, without charge, to pilots of pleasure craft: *Pilot Rules for the Rivers Whose Waters Flow into the Gulf of Mexico*, and *Regulations to Govern the Use, Administration, and Navigation of the Ohio River, the Mississippi River above Cairo, and their Tributaries* (apply U. S. Engineer's Office, 433 W. Van Buren St., Chicago). The raising of the waterway bridges and the locking of boats over the dams are services rendered all craft without charge; there are, however, certain restrictions, which are set forth in the above mentioned publications.

Mooring, fueling, and repair facilities and overnight accommodations are available at the larger cities. Camping and lodge facilities are offered at Starved Rock and Pere Marquette State Parks; for rates and reservations address Concessionaires.

THE ILLINOIS WATERWAY, although essentially a commercial highway, is growing increasingly popular as an avenue of pleasure travel. Its historical associations are the richest of any of the traveled routes in the State. In beauty and variety its scenery rivals that of any part of Illinois; the opportunities it affords for hunting and fishing are exceeded only by the Mississippi in the southern part of the State. Along its course are some of the wildest and least populated sections of Illinois. The waterway has been, perhaps, the most significant single factor in the history of Illinois, and upon that factor emphasis is here laid. For this reason the larger cities and State parks along the route are treated briefly and only insofar as they pertain to the story of the river; their full descriptions are cross-referenced to other parts of the book.

245

CHICAGO (598 alt., 3,376,438 pop.) (*see Chicago*).

Points of Interest: Chicago Board of Trade Building, Union Stock Yards, Field Museum of Natural History, Art Institute of Chicago, Museum of Science and Industry, Adler Planetarium, Shedd Aquarium, University of Chicago, and others.

Chicago is at the northern end of the Illinois Waterway. The CONTROL LOCKS, 0 *m.*, at the entrance to the harbor, mark the beginning of the Chicago River, which formerly emptied into Lake Michigan approximately a mile to the southwest. During the hundred years of engineering since the Illinois and Michigan Canal was begun, the flow has been reversed—the river has been made to drain out of the lake, rather than into it. The locks, opened in 1938, prevent the pollution of lake water, which sometimes resulted during storm periods when the river backed up into the lake.

Right of the locks is NAVY PIER, built by the City of Chicago in 1916, used for amusements, expositions, and the docking of lake steamers. Here are the offices of the harbor master, sales and storage rooms for small boats, and service facilities for pleasure craft. West is NORTH PIER TERMINAL, on Ogden Slip, where lake freighters and an occasional European tramp tie up at the great warehouses.

Left of the locks is the U. S. COAST GUARD STATION, and in the southwest corner of the harbor, the ILLINOIS NAVAL RESERVE ARMORY. South of the breakwater is a YACHT BASIN, jammed in summer with every variety of pleasure craft, from saucy cat-boats to long sleek yachts. Farther south ADLER PLANETARIUM dominates the tip of Northerly Island, its red granite walls and bronze dome in sharp contrast with the Grecian white of SHEDD AQUARIUM and the classic mass of FIELD MUSEUM, a short distance west. Ahead and L. the imposing façade of the Loop rises along the west side of Michigan Ave.

The OUTER DRIVE BRIDGE, 0.4 *m.*, opened October 5, 1937 by President Roosevelt, links the north and south lake shore drives. When the full sweep of this lake boulevard is completed, motorists will be able to travel a continuous parkway the entire length of the city, from the Indiana Line to Evanston.

The MICHIGAN AVENUE BRIDGE, 0.8 *m.*, marks the point at which the Chicago River formerly turned sharply to the south, to enter the lake at what is now the foot of Madison St. It was established in its present course in the 1830's. Left at the bridge is the SITE OF FORT DEARBORN, the military post established in 1803 around which developed embryonic Chicago. Right is the white tiled WRIGLEY BUILDING and, opposite, the graceful Gothic lines of the TRIBUNE TOWER.

The MERCHANDISE MART, 1.4 *m.*, wherein hundreds of American manufacturers maintain offices and showrooms, rears its great mass on the R. Twenty-five thousand people spend a third of their lives in this building, which has a total floor space two-thirds the area of the Loop.

At a sharp southerly bend of the river, 1.6 *m.*, the NORTH BRANCH OF THE CHICAGO RIVER enters the main stream. Below this point the route follows the South Branch; the reversal of flow, accomplished when the South Branch was linked with the Des Plaines River by canal has made it the main stream.

At 1.9 *m.* the river passes two of Chicago's finest office buildings: the CIVIC OPERA BUILDING (L), built by Samuel Insull in 1929, and the DAILY NEWS BUILDING (R), fronted by an extensive plaza along the waterway.

Along the river, for the greater part of its length, sometimes clearly in view, again hidden beneath tall buildings, is the network of rails over which moves the volume of freight that makes this city the busiest rail center in the world. Right, at 2.1 *m.*, is Chicago's UNION STATION, into which many of the rails are diverted. The NEW POST OFFICE BUILDING, 2.3 *m.* (R), is the largest structure in the world devoted to the handling of mail.

Downstream, the river flows between parallel networks of rails, bordered by warehouses and manufacturing plants. For a mile or so it follows a course that was straightened in the 1920's to facilitate the extension of streets south of the Loop. It then curves slowly westward, and for nearly two miles is bordered (R) by a dozen slips along which are the docks where lake freighters and Mississippi River barges load and unload. On 21 acres of State-owned land at this point, the State proposes to build a modern river-and-rail terminal.

At the SOUTH FORK (L), 5.5 *m.*, is the junction with the abandoned ILLINOIS AND MICHIGAN CANAL, which the modern waterway parallels to La Salle. Opened in 1848, the canal was for 30 years a vital influence in the development of the State, and by linking Chicago with the Mississippi River enabled the lake port to outstrip St. Louis as the dominant commercial center of the Midwest. Railroad competition in the latter half of the century reduced its traffic, but the canal continued to operate into the early 1900's. Today its hundred-mile right-of-way is being developed by the State for recreational purposes, and the old towpaths are being converted into pleasure drives.

At 6.1 *m.* the waterway leaves the river and enters the SANITARY AND SHIP CANAL, which it follows for 30 miles to Lockport.

The canal, opened in 1900 as the Chicago Drainage Canal, serves the dual purpose implied in its new name: to remove the treated industrial and domestic waste of Chicago and some of its suburbs, and to replace the outmoded Illinois and Michigan Canal as a highway of commerce. Principal users of the canal are a few large independent companies and the Federal Barge Line, a Government owned and operated fleet of barges and towboats that carries freight between Chicago, Minneapolis, St. Louis, Kansas City, and New Orleans.

The channel, 20 feet deep and 160 to 300 feet wide, is cut through solid rock in its first seven miles. On calm days this stretch is easily navigated, but in stormy weather the passage is difficult, for a heavy wind can wreck a small boat upon the rocks. However, such winds are rarely experienced, since the canal lies in a deep valley and on either side is a high spoils bank, formed of the excavated rock through which the channel is cut. These high embankments screen the adjoining lands, which are utilized by railroads and varied manufacturing plants.

At 13.2 *m.* is the OLD CHICAGO PORTAGE FOREST PRESERVE (R), a section of the once heavily traveled portage between the Chicago and Des Plaines Rivers; the route of Indians, explorers, missionaries, traders, trappers, and soldiers; the crossing between the waters that flowed eastward past Quebec and Montreal and those that found their way southward to New Orleans and the Gulf.

Jolliet crossed this low divide in 1673 and envisioned a canal that would link these two waterways. La Salle followed him, and a decade later, in reporting the geography of the region, noted the possibility of a canal through the portage. His enthusiasm for the project, however, was tempered by his experiences in traversing the portage. At times of high water, he noted, the floods of the Des Plaines so completely inundated the region that a canoe could pass from one river to another in water at least two feet deep. But during the low water stage the Des Plaines was often completely dry, and the Kankakee, with which it joined to form the Illinois, carried so small a volume of water that a canoe could not be floated above Starved Rock. In short, La Salle pointed out, a canal that would effectively link the Chicago and Illinois Rivers would have to be, not half a league in length, as Jolliet had optimistically reported, but the maximum length of the portage, nearly 100 miles. The Illinois and Michigan Canal, opened 165 years later, measured 96 miles, from Chicago to La Salle. The length of the modern Sanitary and Ship Canal, less than a third of this, is made possible only by the diversion of a considerably greater volume of water from Lake Michigan, and by the use of modern engineering in damming and dredging the channels of the Des Plaines and Illinois Rivers.

Immediately west of the portage the DES PLAINES RIVER enters the valley (R), and parallels the waterway for 23 miles to Lockport. Left is the old Illinois and Michigan Canal. On either side of the mile-wide valley the wooded bluffs rise sharply to the rolling upland. Between approximately 18 *m.* and 23 *m.* the ARGONNE FOREST PRESERVE (L) borders the valley—an extensive Cook County recreational area largely in its original wildland state. West of the preserve is the mouth of the CALUMET SAG CHANNEL (L), 23.5 *m.*, a tributary of the Sanitary and Ship Canal. This channel, which leads southeast to Calumet and Indiana Harbor on Lake Michigan, is being improved to accommodate barge traffic.

LEMONT (L), 26.9 *m.* (605 alt., 2,582 pop.), an old towpath town, raises its hill-crowned head among the trees. Downstream is the village of ROMEOVILLE (L), 31.3 *m.* (590 alt., 133 pop.), which developed along the Illinois and Michigan Canal. The industrial plant visible from the waterway is a GLOBE OIL REFINERY. Petroleum and petroleum products are among the principal goods transported on the waterway; they are second only to coal in tonnage.

A BUTTERFLY DAM occupies the center of the channel at 34 *m.* Its function is to serve as an emergency dam should the one at Lockport fail to function. Inasmuch as it remains open at all other times, it is not equipped with locks.

At LOCKPORT (L) 34.5 *m.* (582 alt., 3,383 pop.), once an important shipping and transfer point on the Illinois and Michigan Canal, is the lock that controls the volume of water withdrawn from Lake Michigan. Here were the offices of the canal company, among whose records are preserved many documents pertaining to the days of the canal's construction and operation. These include maps, field notebooks, correspondence, newspapers of a century ago in which bids for canal contracts are advertised, and such miscellaneous records of the disbursing office as the pork and flour contracts for 1838-39. Among the items is a prospectus of the Illinois Central Company offering for sale, in 1855, 2,400,000 acres of "selected proven farm and woodlands in tracts of any size to suit purchasers, on long credit at low rates of interest, situated on each side of the railroad, extending all the way from the extreme North to the South of the State of Illinois."

Right, at 35.5 *m.*, are the buff limestone buildings of STATEVILLE STATE PRISON (*see Tour 17*), set squarely among the varied greens and yellows of cultivated fields.

LOCKPORT LOCK AND DAM, 36.1 *m.*, marks the end of the Sanitary and Ship Canal. The lock chamber is 110 feet wide, 600 feet long, has a lift of 41 feet, and can be filled or emptied in 12 minutes. The upper gates are of the vertical lift type, each 20 feet high and weighing 190 tons. The lower gates are 60 feet high, are of the mitering type, and weigh 315 tons apiece. Two emergency dams, of 50 and 75 tons, are part of the lock's equipment. They are for use in the event of damage to the lock gates. A feature of the Lockport development is a small chamber for locking pleasure craft. None of the other locks on the waterway is so equipped.

Adjoining the locks is the HYDROELECTRIC POWER PLANT (R) of the Chicago Sanitary District, the only property retained by that authority when it surrendered title to the Chicago Drainage Canal, as the Sanitary and Ship Canal was known before it was acquired and improved by the Federal government. By measuring the amount of water passed through the turbines, and by computing the volume used for lockage purposes, Army engineers in charge of the waterway control the total amount of water diverted from Lake Michigan. This diversion, as established by the United States Supreme Court in 1930, averaged 5,000 cubic feet per second until December 31, 1938. At that time it was reduced to a maximum of 1,500 cubic feet per second, a volume of water that some shippers and canal authorities believe to be inadequate to maintain sufficient flow for sanitary purposes and adequate channel depths for navigation.

Downstream from the Lockport Dam the waterway follows the improved channel of the Des Plaines River for 18 miles to its junction with the Kankakee. JOLIET, 38.5 *m.* (545 alt., 42,993 pop.) (*see Joliet*), long an important shipping point on the river and waterway, is bisected by the canalized stream, which flows at street level in the northern part of town, but near the southern border of the city is actually at a higher elevation than the valley floor, so that boats sail along above the general level of the city. Only the residential districts on the wooded bluffs are high above the canal.

BRANDON ROAD LOCK AND DAM, 41.2 *m.*, is the second of the series on the Illinois Waterway. The lock, 110 by 600 feet, has a lift of 31 feet. The dam, which has a retaining wall 2,000 feet in length, not only maintains the upstream level, but also confines the waters of BRANDON ROAD POOL, a turning basin considerably above the level of the valley bottom. Headgate structures for a possible power house have been built into the dam, but no power development has as yet been undertaken.

At the southwest corner of the pool is one of the locks of the Illinois and Michigan Canal, now permanently closed and used as part of the retaining wall. Downstream, the old canal (R) parallels the modern waterway, and seems by comparison a tiny ditch, with its trickle of water that seeps through the lock gates. Gone is the pageant of barge and packet, the holiday crowds on canal excursions, the drivers and horses along the towpaths. In its place is the modern waterway, sleek and efficient in its long graceful dams, its electrically operated locks, navy-trim in their bright coat of aluminum paint. Its modern steel barges, four, six, eight, ten at a time, locked in tow, pushed up or down the waterway by twin-screw, Diesel-powered boats, move in one tow more freight than the entire fleet operating on the old canal could have carried in a week. The old canal was done to death by the railroads; the new waterway competes with them on an equal footing.

Index

Other WPA reprints by Chicago Historical Bookworks

Catalogue of the WPA Writers' Program Publications: September, 1941. By the WPA Writers' Program (1941). $7.50

Bibliography of Illinois, Chicago and Environs. By the WPA Writers' Program (1937). $15.

Check List of Chicago Ante-Fire Imprints: 1851-1871. By the WPA Writers' Program (1938). $35

Bibliography of Illinois Poets Since 1900 (to 1942). By the WPA Writers' Program (1942). $14.95